IN PIECES

IN PIECES

an anthology of fragmentary writing

EDITED BY

OLIVIA DRESHER

IMPASSIO
PRESS

Permissions Acknowledgments appear on page 395.

Cover Art: *Lovers* by Si Lewen
(The image is composed of bits and pieces
of Lewen's former works.)
Photographed by Gary Hillstead
Design: Phil Kovacevich/Kovacevich Design

This book is printed on recycled, acid-free paper.

Impassio Press is an independent literary press devoted
to publishing a variety of fragmentary writings,
with a focus on journals, diaries and notebooks.

Library of Congress Control Number: 2005935121

ISBN-13: 978-0-9711583-5-1
ISBN-10: 0-9711583-5-5

IMPASSIO PRESS
P.O. Box 31905
Seattle, WA 98103
www.impassio.com

I believe that today more than ever a book should be sought after even if it has only one great page in it: we must search for fragments, splinters, toenails, anything that has ore in it, anything that is capable of resuscitating the body and soul.

—HENRY MILLER (1891–1980)

Truth doesn't reveal herself completely to anyone; everyone sees her in pieces.

—CHRISTOPH MARTIN WIELAND (1733–1813)

We are all made up of fragments.

—MONTAIGNE (1533–1592)

CONTENTS

INTRODUCTION

by Olivia Dresher

This collection presents a wide variety of contemporary fragmentary writing. Its purpose is to honor the fragment as a literary genre in its own right.

Though fragmentation is a characteristic of our current times and is also reflected in modern literature, published fragments are not entirely new. The ancient writings of Sappho and Heraclitus, for example, have become classics…as well as such 18th and 19th century writings as Lichtenberg's aphorisms and Joseph Joubert's notebooks. More recently, the 20th century fragments of Fernando Pessoa, in his *The Book of Disquiet,* are fine examples of fragmentary writing. But Pessoa's fragments are more than that: they are fragmentations that he actually lived.

In 1798, Friedrich Schlegel wrote: "Many works of the ancients have become fragments. Many works of the moderns are already fragments at the time of their origin." Though I value fragments whether they were intentionally written or exist only as scraps of larger works written hundreds of years ago, the focus of *In Pieces* is *intentional* fragments written since the early 1950s.

· · ·

One quality of fragmentary writing is the lack of a traditional beginning or end. Instead, the two are merged into a brief and concentrated middle. A fragment is a "slice of life," a short expression or description of a thought, memory, insight, mood, perception, image, or experience. When reading a fragment, one can jump into a paragraph or even a few lines and feel an immediate involvement. Fragments can stand alone, separate from one another; they are written (and can be read) in quick, illuminating bursts and can feel complete just as they are. There's an energy within a fragment that gives the writer and reader a sense of freedom, leaving much to the imagination.

· · ·

Several years ago I co-edited an anthology of contemporary journals, diaries, and notebooks titled *Darkness and Light: Private Writing as Art*. The collection included journal excerpts as well as two essays on the subject of the journal as literary art. (A few of the authors published in *Darkness and Light* also appear in this anthology.) But whereas *Darkness and Light* focused exclusively on one form of fragmentary writing and included the works of only 14 contributors, *In Pieces* focuses on some of the many shapes that fragmentary writing can take and includes pieces by 37 different contributors. Besides selections from diaries and notebooks, *In Pieces* also includes aphorisms, vignettes, selections from letters (including letters written in haiku form), and an essay (written fragmentarily) on the postcard as fragmentary writing.

Journals, diaries, and notebooks are inherently fragmentary, hence they are well represented in this collection. The dates written in a diary break the writing into pieces, and the entries—whether long or short—are written spontaneously, in spurts. One who writes in a notebook isn't concerned with plot or an overriding structure, so the writing can take whatever shape and direction the author wishes.

· · ·

Most of the contributions in this anthology consist of a series of separated fragments, the length of each fragment ranging from one line to several pages. The actual contributions range from 2 to 28 pages. I've also included several short works that involve story-telling—writings that have a fragmentary feel in some way or consist of fragmented paragraphs rather than a series of separated, unrelated fragments.

The majority of the pieces are non-fiction and personal, written in the first person. A few are fictional. Stylistically, they range from semi-formal to experimental and cover a variety of subjects. Some of the writings are psychological, others are philosophical, poetic, spiritual, or political...or a mix of these. Some are inspired by abstract thought, others by nature, travel, or the tangible aspects of the moment. A few simply play with words. Many are serious in tone, some are light, while others contain humor or irony. The pieces in the book are arranged according to length, mood, style, and subject so they contrast with one another. Written by both well-known and lesser known writers, many of the contributions are published here for the first time.

Authors of various ages are represented, ranging from late teens to over 70. The number of women and men are about evenly divided. Most of the contributors live in the United States, though a few live elsewhere, including Australia, the United Kingdom, and Italy. All but two are still living.

Some of the contributions were submitted to me specifically for this book project. Others consist of selections I made from some of the book-length submissions I received as editor of Impassio Press. I've noted "selections" underneath the titles of those pieces that consist of fragments I selected from full-length manuscripts. (The titles given to these selections are the same titles that appear on the unpublished manuscripts.) In a few cases, "selections" also indicates fragments chosen from a published book now out-of-print or selections from writing published on-line.

. . .

One of the more fragmentary contributions in the book is Guy Gauthier's piece, *Journal Fragments*. I've corresponded with him on the topic of fragmentary writing and we've exchanged many thoughts.

Gauthier writes, "Some fragments were intended to be fragments, and some are 'unintentional,' i.e., they were meant to be a completed work, or maybe a completed paragraph, but the writer wasn't able to finish them. But even when there is the intention to write fragments, we must let them happen naturally, we must let them break off, so to speak, at a point of their own choosing. The fragments should happen by themselves."

He also writes, "I doubt if any writers start their careers with the idea of writing fragments or unfinished works. It's something you come to realize about yourself. You learn by experience that you are incapable of larger construction, i.e., something like *War and Peace*, because you can't control or direct the flow of your creative energy. You realize that you are better suited to fragmentary writing—or in my case, a journal."

. . .

Many of the writers in this anthology have also published works in other genres (poetry, plays, novels, etc.); a few of them only write fragments. Whether or not the fragmentary form is a contributor's main form, the writings included in this collection have been gathered together as a tribute to the diversity of fragmentary writing.

I have yet to discover a precise definition of the fragment, though my own evolving definition—as this anthology illustrates—tends to be wide. It is my feeling that the fragmentary form, more than any other form, gives writers the opportunity to travel as far away from the boundaries of traditional genres as they feel they must in order to express their truths.

IN PIECES

FELICIA WAYNESBORO

Pulled from the Fire

(selections)

01/31/93

My mind is on fire and any thoughts not pulled out of the flames and laid to resuscitate on paper, incinerate.

04/28/93 – Old Technology

Those things that look like hairs that get trapped on a strip of old film—the kind of film that is shown on a pull-up projection screen—are they actually hairs? Why are they always there?

Those long hairs that get caught on a strip of film—there's always only one hair at a time. One mesmerizing, magnified, larger-than-life hair that wriggles and undulates submissively for a while on the side of the film, then pauses while the film crackles around it. Pauses while the "action" lays backdrop in another world where the hair is not supposed to exist. The hair does not exist / and yet is there, in fact.

You cannot take your eyes away from each rare hair as long as it lingers, no matter what else is going on on the screen. A fish out of water. The dance of the unseen.

How does it get trapped there? Bobbing, writhing. The projectionist must know but turns a blind side to the solo dancer. Then suddenly it flicks away—a cinematic sleight-of-hand—and in a single frame, is gone. It is anticipated but it is vanished.

It is missed.

05/26/93

Sitting nearby while someone reads something you have written is like having blood taken—it's alright as long as you look away.

??/??/94 – In the Laundromat

The bedspread is too large to fit our washer at home so we find ourselves in a laundromat today. Its low technology has a comforting, mid-century appeal. Its dreariness should be depressing but the day is warm and my husband and I are together, being caressed by a noisy, mechanical breeze, so all is right with the world.

The back door is open and through it I can see a small peopleless townscape with wooden houses and what appears to be a very old but pert, still functioning gasoline pump. I say to Bruce that it looks like an Edward Hopper painting. He looks at me—indulgently entertained—and tells me I am a romantic.

09/30/94 – Living with Things We Don't Understand

There are people in our society who understand how mysterious things actually work—things like FAX machines, interactive video games, remote controls and microwave ovens. But these people are so few in number that they have little impact on our inadvertent awe of the common things we live with that we do not understand. Have people always lived with things they do not understand? Of course, there was nature and there were gods, tales and myths fancied to explain various natural phenomena. But how long have we lived with human-made things which we do not comprehend?

Wheels and gears are clear in analog watches or on carriages; we marvel at their cleverness but we fathom them. But no matter how often "bits and bytes" may be explained to us, society never really grasps how it is that personal computers are able to respond to our bidding.

Fire hurts immediately, but what happens to the body pierced by invisible energy passing through it on its way from a remote control to a DVD player?

06/21/95 – The Man at the Movies

The man in the row in front of me laughs at the same things that I do. He is a stranger in the dark; nearly everyone here is a stranger to one another, congregated in the dark to see a movie at the local "art house." The film is a serious one and the audience is accepting it quite soberly. But the man in the row in front of me sees the intentional humor in the drama. We are not afraid to laugh, he and I, though no one else is laughing.

I can see the back of his head and his profile illuminated by the light from the screen. I can see that his skin is the color of coffee with cream—another thing we share though I doubt that he knows this because he cannot see me—and that his face seems kind. A faint, unacknowledged current flows between us because of the shared sensibility.

Then a moment happens on the screen and the man laughs but I do not. I see the humor but the moment is multi-layered and swiftly reaches depths beneath its jocularity. My loyalties are to the film; the man has laughed alone. I feel I have abandoned him—as if I were in a relationship that, sadly, I outgrew.

04/08/97

There is no guarantee that things that seem as if they ought to be actually ought to be.

07/28/97 – Sleep

People who are awakened after falling asleep prematurely—while merely resting or watching television, perhaps—usually deny that they were asleep. (Men, especially, leap to the denial.) Why? Is it that we perceive the relinquishing of alertness as a weakness or vulnerability? Is it that we fear we will be challenged over some tangible or intellectual territorial privileges if we do not remain vigilant? Or is it more that it is, in fact, difficult to perceive just when we are awake and when we are not—just how deeply slumber must submerge us before we are officially asleep?

There is that wonderful, scary moment when you are in bed and intending to go to sleep when you notice that a thought has broken up, has fragmented into cerebration without cohesion; the point at which reflection begins to become dream, and sleep—if not impeded—will follow. It is, at once, peaceful and unsettling.

Perhaps it is the sense of surrender that we find shameful.

08/25/97

My husband is white and was raised Mormon. He says that every-thing he was taught about persecution, which the Mormons suffered mightily, was meant to teach him to have faith. I am black and I say that everything I was taught about persecution was meant to teach me to have rage. Yet it is he who has developed the greater portion of rage and I who have developed—not faith but—the greater portion of tolerance and empathy. We have each been taught poorly.

01/10/98 – Sides

My side of the bedroom is a nest. My side of the bed is not far from the wall and the greatest access from my side of the room is to the inner mind. Many of my favorite books are piled up against that wall; there are photos and reproductions of artworks that inspire me. There is a deck of cards and there are other games that one can play solo. There are a couple of mirrors. The only access to the outside world is a window, two stories up—tower-like.

His side of the bedroom has the only true access to the outside world. The telephone and the clock are over there—also the televi-sion. Because the house is built into a hill, the window on his side is actually at a first floor level from the ground. The door to the hall-way is on his side of the room.

These conditions are reflections of who we are. I am most serene when I intellectually cosset myself, while his serenity comes from having avenues of warning and action.

01/22/98

What if an artist plays music while she is working and she loves it and it helps her work but the model hates it? Does it affect the outcome of the work?

01/29/98 – Dust

Eight-eight years on earth—the shank of the 88 years spent tending a home—my neighbor said to me, "You fight dust all your life," then, playing with the irony, she added, "and in the end you become it." So it wins after all.

In reality, we are becoming *it* the whole time. Our dandruff is it. The top layer of our skin is constantly shedding and settling somewhere as it. Everything is it. We are part of what we are fighting.

02/22/98 – Seeing My Child from a Distance for the First Time

Standing on a high hill in the park, looking down into the playground, I see my daughter—aged one year—my beautiful, sweet gem with a hired babysitter for the first time.

I have never before seen you from a distance. You have always been in my arms, or in your father's arms, or your grandmother's, or a friend's across the room. Or you were toddling toward a toy or sitting in your high chair with us at the table. You were always near me. And now I have come to this hill deliberately to see what it is like to see you from a distance. My heart is floating outside my body.

03/15/98 – Museumgoers

There is a graceful dynamic to visiting a crowded art museum that borders on courtly dance. The people are reverent—giving even what they do not understand a chance to make itself clear. They glide. They peer at the works yet keep a radar-like sensitivity to the sphere around them, aware not to trespass into anyone else's energy.

03/19/98 – Scandal on the Bus

Seal, my ex-domestic friend on the Wilkes-Barre bus, told me today that eight drivers in recent years have left their wives for women they met on the bus.

05/21/98 – Mr. Rogers

The impish babysitter had gotten the children to admit that, whereas they loved Mr. Rogers dearly, they didn't like his curtains—that his curtains were, in fact, ugly. They admitted it with downcast eyes, not certain whether this admission was their first betrayal.

06/13/98 – Reading

I like to enter the minds of others; to slip inside as you do when you borrow the raincoat of a friend, glide your arms through the sleeves, slide the shoulders over your shoulders and go out into the rain protected by an unfamiliar layer between your body and the raindrops. Sometimes you run your hands into the pockets to keep them dry and your fingers discover hidden holes within the folds—holes in the pockets of your perfectly presentable friend's presentable raincoat. This unexpected intimacy stirs you.

Sometimes the damp brings out the smells of other rains your friend has walked through; other rains that have dried within the fibers and are now released into your notice as you walk. That is what it is like to read a really good book. That is why I like to read a novel so good that the story does not get in the way. It's like walking around in that borrowed raincoat and feeling rain as your friend feels rain.

04/02/99

It would be a lot more painful to sympathize with the complexities that my mother must feel—that she has no words for—than it is to resent her for the shallowness of her responses.

04/18/99

I have just seen the legendary French film *Breathless* and observed nihilism and joie de vivre playing tag.

09/10/99

Why is it that programs designed to support and encourage women always make me feel worse?

01/07/00

We are all bubbles—we exist and then we burst into an invisible essence.

02/04/00 – What?

You'll be riding alone in the car with her when she suddenly reads a sign out loud. She'll read something like, "The freshest air in town." Aloud. And you'll expect her to make some observation about it, some comment, some musing. But she won't make any observation; there's just silence.

08/05/00

My former lover admitted that he kept me entrapped by belittling me into feeling that I would be helpless without him. My husband, whether he realizes it or not, accomplishes much the same thing by excessively pampering me.

09/18/00 – Seen from the Highway

An old wooden house, a red house, abandoned with the front and back doors completely open so that I can see through to the overgrown, sunny field beyond. The red paint—the color of cheer, passion and terror—as faded as the cheers, passions and terrors that must once have abided there. Who, what, why, when? How soon did the neglect begin to show?

09/28/00 – An Extremely Personal Pleasure

When reading a good, substantial paperback, one tends to bend the pages already read backward, curling them under like the wave of a scroll with the fingers of the left hand.

Then comes that satisfying point when one finds oneself folding back the latter half of the book instead with the right hand; when one has passed the halfway point and the bulk of the pages read— the thoughts, images and meanings absorbed—is thicker than those yet to come.

06/21/01

Many people substitute cleanliness for taste. People with no taste— I do not mean people with bad taste; I just mean people with no taste at all—are frequently neat and clean.

09/11/01

I was piecing together bits of information—overheard here, reported there—and as I ascended the stairs from Boscov Department Store's basement to go back onto the sunny street, I heard a man from the Customer Pick-up department on the store's phone. He seemed to be talking to a family member or, at least, to someone he cared about. "I don't know," he said. "We're under attack by terrorists."

He had said "WE" are under attack. There was none of this town's usual I-wouldn't-live-in-New-York-City-for-anything attitude in his words. Just bonding under stunning fire.

07/17/02

I love the patience of a percussionist waiting for his moments. He does not have to be patient tonight though; tonight they are playing Ravel's "Bolero" in which the percussionist is the hero and waits for nothing.

07/18/02

It is like conducting an orchestra that doesn't need you.

08/25/02

The car in the fast lane passed us, breezing down the highway with several family members moving about inside. I could see a magazine on the ledge of the rear window with the pages leafing open in the air stream and I could feel summer all over us all.

GILES GOODLAND

Thought Experiments

(selections)

there is a sound for each feeling, and these sounds are not words

· · ·

to sigh is to sing in snake language, to sniff is to whistle in dog-talk, to snicker is to sob among mice

· · ·

all of the facts have come to light and light has burnt them away

· · ·

anything can happen but nothing happens twice because daylight loosens bones and we are sick of miracles

· · ·

the snow sleeps under the door and the dirty cupboards have all been cleaned

· · ·

what remains of silence dissolves into earth and clouds are the thoughts of hills

. . .

we slide through time as if on ice and thus see it as we do the slipping of stars into the mouth of the horizon

. . .

what we say solidifies, and you feel time's heat on the back of the hand

. . .

the soul releases its weight in the laugh that had for years secretly been implying it all

. . .

rust is fire in slow motion

. . .

plates shine like teeth when you open the cupboard

. . .

cars are fast sculptures

. . .

the emptiness of playgrounds during and just after rain

. . .

the quality of silence an alarm clock has the moment before it rings

. . .

all of the things that connect the body with thought before words

. . .

a sentence that has never been spoken

. . .

the sound a word makes when left alone

. . .

the exhaust of the absolute and the trail left by the invisible

. . .

the salt in the sea the soap in the bath the sugar in the tea

. . .

the freedom created by the fall

. . .

the last time you saw a truly wild animal

. . .

the way what you really saw gets mixed with what you saw on TV

. . .

the color of your laugh as it dissolves in air

. . .

a child still waving minutes after the car left

. . .

the skidmarks that time joyrides over your forehead

. . .

the spermy quality of the mist on a March morning

. . .

the way a willow swings in counterpoint to the wind

. . .

the cancer under your warm skin

. . .

a jet unzipping a seamless sky

. . .

the sun has been exploding for so long now it's beginning to look normal

. . .

the best philosopher does not think things through because to know
is to destroy and to learn is to lose

. . .

death is where questions become unanswerable & we forget how to
move our limbs

. . .

scraping the door open we understand the slow shape of hills

. . .

each thought should contradict the next because night contradicts
day and sleep contradicts self

. . .

the sky's reply to earth is moderated by the earth's knowledge of the
ocean

. . .

silence is as long as creation but there is adequacy in the numbering
of stars

. . .

all perception is relative to the fact that ice is melting on mountains
and at great oceanic depth stone congeals

. . .

the sun radiates only sunlight while the moon is a pool of reflection

. . .

the sun admits nothing whereas we all know what the moon contains

. . .

you distort the answer by posing the question and there is a hole in the floor of every sentence

. . .

if we could understand the language of birds it would no longer be song

. . .

dogs may be stupid but are never wrong and dreams require no proof

. . .

time is woven into your clothes but you cannot trace it to where it meets your skin

. . .

what a person contains operates as a universe and the space between thoughts is infinite

. . .

slow noises break no windows but the speed of thought outpaces
planets

. . .

to say a thing makes it true because the steel of language cracks
through the wood of thought

. . .

you can only commit good acts unconsciously and evil acts consciously so the more aware we are the worse

. . .

what cannot be repeated must be true and everyone is momentarily
aware of the one secret task

. . .

the spaces between lies and the patterns they make are as close as we
get to truth

. . .

we are connected as two dreams on consecutive nights in all possible
shades of rain

. . .

a flashlight with no batteries provides enough light to see the unconscious

. . .

after my thoughts have made love to each other sometimes there will be a poem

. . .

you live entire lives each night and in opening your eyes forget almost everything

MARY AZRAEL

High Alert:
Fragments from 2003 Journals

1/29/03

Woke up to the radio news—Bush's State of the Union speech. Have to force myself to keep writing. A word is a commitment, a choice: this, not that. About the coming—coming? I hope not—war: of course I don't want the killing. I don't want the smashing of buildings, the burning. I don't want the hatred and grief, the "winners" and "losers." I don't want the gloating or the humiliation. So why do I hesitate to put my name on a list of people who don't want war? Finicky separateness. If I sign a petition, I'm part of a group and I don't easily become part of a group. Feel a contrarian impulse in groups. Afraid of losing control to the mass. Wariness. Who are these people? What do they want, besides "no war"? If I were standing in front of my grandchildren and they asked me "war or no war?" I wouldn't hesitate. "No war!" So why not add my name to a petition on the web.

2/7/03

Heavy snow. All down the slope, rumpled white, the hawk's cry like a stone knife. When I turn my palm over, the skin of my forearm twists and creases—a worn-thin sleeve over straight bones, like Granny's arm when she was old.

2/16/03 – New York

Strange convergence of a blizzard, its quieting white-out, and Code Orange, high alert. Yesterday, before the snow, several hundred thousand anti-war demonstrators made their stand downtown. Overheard some young people telling stories of police on horseback scaring them. Tonight in the subway stations, soldiers in "camouflage" (dappled green/gray/brown is hardly camouflage in a city!) carrying big black guns—AK47s. Made my stomach knot and burn with fear. What if one of them got spooked and started shooting? Can't imagine what kind of terrorist attack would be made less deadly by young men (boys!) with big guns in a crowded place like a subway station. People say their presence is a deterrent. But it seems just as likely that their presence—potential violence—invites violence.

2/26/03

Distracted, always distracted now. Newspapers and magazines piling up, so much information, 24/7 TV news, split screens, crawl lines, radio talk shows, government officials on C-Span, so many opinions. Friends and relatives email and phone. Talk talk talk and the war machine rolls on.

On the radio this morning I heard a woman in a Mexican marketplace—"I wish George Bush and Saddam Hussein would just beat each other up until they were exhausted and their anger would go away." That *is* what they'll do, but they'll do it by proxy—beat each other up until we're exhausted and broken and anger goes away. Then after a long time numbness may go away and grief come through. Then the next generation will set out looking for glory in war again. Our human nature? Suppose we have a built-in war need as fixed as the laws of gravity. I don't want to believe it.

3/9/03

Our latest resolution proposed to the UN gives a deadline for Saddam to disarm: March 17. Next week. Everyone knows he won't do it. So we're telling the world, expect war on March 17. Constant talk of troop movements, battle groups, weapons of mass destruction, allies, terrorist threats, explosions, dead and wounded. Has there ever been peace in the world? Maybe it's always like this somewhere.

3/13/03

For the first time in a month, the snow is melting fast. Rivulets flow from everywhere into the shallow glaze sliding down Rolandvue Road—broad slick scales of water overlapping. After the still, quiet heaviness of snow, all this shining movement feels light and free. Peace here at this moment, whatever the newspapers say. Can't focus on politics. My mind goes blank. Can't keep the adversaries straight. Which group is which—they all have flattering names made up of abstractions, they all sound alike—and who are they fighting against? It's a blur, monotonous to flatline.

3/18/03

Missed the war speech last night. Heard the last sentence on the car radio, sitting in the parking lot after the grandkids' Purim carnival. Can't remember Bush's words—just his voice, which was *soooo* soft, like someone trying to lull a child to sleep. Drove home through billows of low fog, the sky perfectly clear and bright with the full moon, the road ahead almost invisible.

3/20/03

Alone all day. Turned on the TV twice. Want to know what's happening in Iraq and then I'm disgusted with myself for being a spectator. But what I see doesn't connect with reality—talking reporters, a map of Iraq and Kuwait, headlines that creep along the bottom of the screen, and images from the field telephones—abstract-looking, shifting mosaics of light and dark green, interpreted by reporters as "tanks on the way north from Kuwait to Baghdad." Most of the time people are traveling, waiting to fight. Intense boredom and exhaustion. That's what I feel. And shame. To be party to this monstrous violence, with all the self-righteous religiosity and sentimentality it's wrapped in, and not to be able to make an effective move against it.

3/23/03

The clock is slow—a slow column of mechanical ants marching. Tired, rattled.

4/1/03

Can't get it out of my mind—the newspaper photo of a big awkward-looking American soldier sitting cross-legged on the ground with a four-year-old Iraqi girl in his lap. Her mother had just been killed. The child appeared calm. The solder was staring at nothing. He looked stricken, like his life was ruined.

4/2/03

Our Commander-in-Chief says to The Enemy, "We will hunt you down. We will find you." He doesn't watch the war news. He doesn't attend funerals of soldiers or visit their grieving families.

4/7/03 – Phoenix

Driving south to Phoenix, saw the silhouettes of the saguaro cacti. They stood up, sharply black along the tops of the black hills, against the western sky bright silver after sunset—stark shapes like weird crosses or skeleton-people saluting the passing cars. We were caught in a convoy of huge high cattle trucks trimmed all around with little lights like Christmas decorations. The mudguards had red, white and blue maps of Texas on them, and across the back doors the words Cattle Driver Rocking H—the new cowboys driving the herds to be butchered. Through the holes in the trailers we could see the eye or the muzzle of a cow.

4/8/03 – Phoenix

At the museum an exhibition about the Indian boarding schools— the well-intentioned, terribly misguided policy of the U.S. government taking Indian kids from their families and sending them far away to school to be "Americanized." Everyone who sees the exhibit finds it shocking. But we're at it again, this time in Iraq—imposing our ways, convinced they're best for all, never imagining we could learn something of value from the Iraqis. Why isn't this shocking?

Nothing soft to look at here. Dry air, intense light. Severe blue sky. Then, at the desert botanical garden, a hummingbird building her nest—miniature basket of spider webs and fine plant fibers. Just the right size for two eggs, it will expand to hold the babies as they grow.

4/16/03

Suddenly the woods say *Spring*. Tiny leaves open enough to show their leaf shapes. Sprays of purple and pink wild hyacinth spill down the slope along with daffodils transplanted from the garden by squirrels. This is my favorite time in the woods, before the high canopy thickens and solid green shuts out the sky.

6/9/03 – Alaska

Sunset lasts for hours, then a bright twilight—I can see birds long past midnight. But it does get dark for a little while. And just before the last light goes, there's a time when the cold feels deadly serious and sleep feels dangerous. Children know to resist it—ask for another story, another drink of water, another warm body to lie beside.

6/12/03 – Alaska

Fear, for me, is the big spoiler. In the train climbing 3000 feet above Skagway, couldn't look down. Couldn't look at the milky rushing river far below—"class 6 rapids no-one has ever gotten through." Couldn't look at the boulders that had rolled to the edge of the track, or the ones that *might* roll. Kept my eyes focused on the wildflowers and lichens growing close by on the uphill side of the train. Small details. Solid rock. Only when I allowed myself to feel how small and nothing I am could I let go of fear and look down into the valley.

6/22/03

Can't hold a thought from beginning to end. Feel like a late fall spider whose web has gone crazy, lost its purposeful pattern, its beauty, and grows in a corner like a torn net full of gaping, irregular holes. When I see those disorganized webs, I imagine the cold has slowed the spiders down, made them too drowsy to sustain the form, the useful form they need in order to live.

8/12/03

Allie, home from Costa Rica, showed us her album—pictures of herself and the other teenagers digging footings, mixing cement, making jewelry, swimming, dancing, clowning, posing with their new Costa Rican friends. But the two photos I'll remember—she was wrapped in towels, one a sarong and one a high turban after a shower, with a tropic-green wild bird perched on her finger. It had flown in the open window. Her friend snapped the first photo the instant it landed, and caught Allie's amazement, her gasp, the shock that must've gone through her. The second one showed them, beautiful Allie and the bird transfixed, gazing at each other—pure spirits, for all their flighty energy, holding each other still.

8/20/03

Irritable. Looking for a fight. Suicide bombings in Baghdad at the UN headquarters. And Jerusalem. Can't feel sorry enough for all the victims, people I don't know. Can't protect my children from what might happen some place where they might be. Can't escape the generalized, amorphous "threat" everywhere. Adrenalin pumping: fight or flight. Flight is impossible, and I don't know how to fight something this big. So I watch for an adversary to fit my need, something I can handle. Feel touchy, defensive, sad.

Yesterday morning so clear and sparkling blue, I felt uneasy. My first thought was "September 11 was like this." That in itself is sad—that a beautiful morning feels menacing.

9/11/03

Nobody mentions the date. The radio stations have regular programming. A yellow linden leaf fell by the front door, the center black with a jagged hole, dry and brittle like burned paper.

9/12/03

I decided to go with Helen and the Women in Black to stand along Charles Street, to be part of The Peace Path. Clusters of people gathered in front of churches and schools, a crowd at the Friends Meeting House, and a solitary woman or man here and there. Most held signs. Helen hung hers around her neck—a big placard she made and stapled to a yardstick: *MOURNING VIOLENCE.* Standing facing the traffic, with her solid, calm conviction, she seemed larger than herself. The unanswered question for both of us: is it possible for human beings to live without war? But even if it isn't, she wants to stand, visibly mourning violence, to remind people not to be callous and indifferent.

Many honked their horns, smiled, nodded, waved, or made the "peace" sign (ironic that the two-finger V used to mean military victory). Each time, I felt goose bumps break out on my arms, my back, my neck—all over my body. I was startled by the feeling, a much more intense connection than speech or touch. I'm leery of the uplifting sensation of solidarity. I never want to give in to it. Ever since I saw newsreels of the German masses shouting "Heil Hitler" I've been afraid of political groups swept away by powerful emotion.

The other surprise was the hostility of a few men—some, not many, yelled "Fuck you" or "Why don't you move to Canada" or flipped us the finger. I didn't feel threatened, just curious. Why did we provoke such anger—three gray-haired women dressed in black standing on the sidewalk with our sign. What did our being there mean to them?

9/24/03

The hawk swoops in low. Trim silhouette, skylight breast, granite-dark back, like a fish designed to confuse the eye of a predator. The songbirds stop singing. At 4 o'clock the white light is thin, the hawk on a branch holds still except for its turning head, yellow eyes alert for movement in the sharp, bowed grass.

9/30/03

Fall suddenly cool, my 60th birthday approaching, I realize I can't protect any of us. So what have I been doing? Cleaning! Not just cleaning but re-thinking the use of space and eliminating everything broken or ugly. Trying to make the whole house more like a healthy body—free of a thousand little obstacles and pains. I get lost in the activity, find it as satisfying and interesting as writing. Seems like I should make fun of myself for this, but the truth is, if somebody gave me the gift of a month with no obligations except house cleaning, I'd be excited and happy. Getting ready for a new life where everything matters. Now. Not "later."

10/8/03

Chilly by the window at 6:15, the white gold sun almost down. Friday night between Rosh Hashanah and Yom Kippur, too sleepy to be alone with a blank page. I keep nodding. My eyes close and thoughts are fast and slippery, interesting, and when I pull my head up and open my eyes, I can't remember them. Is this how it feels to be old, like Cousin Esther who only wants to sleep? Whatever I write, unless it's connected with another person, I say "so what!" My little thoughts. So what! But the act of shaping the flow of ink, the smooth curliques and dots and lines, gives me pleasure, like whistling—filling a blank surface or a quiet place with something human and beautiful and light, ephemeral.

10/13/03

Have to remind myself of what I told my student. Her poems are like nobody else's—what her particular brain takes delight in, what she does with the serendipitous convergences of her dreams and waking life. She has a deep serious, humorous twinkle and she doesn't explain the strange vivid images and odd leaps. Not many people get what she's up to. She wondered, is that ok?

Did I tell her to clear things up, try to write somebody else's idea of a poem? No! Throw yourself into it, write hundreds more. Teach people to hear what you hear and love it. If you back off, lose your nerve, your way of being in poems will be lost to us.

10/22/03

Sitting on the edge of the bed, near midnight, between Anna's 35th birthday and Zachary's 7th—my two bright spirits. This morning I went through all I remembered of their births. I can see how old people end up telling the same pared-down versions of the same memories over and over. I'm doing it in my mind already—repeating a few vivid details that never lead beyond themselves, never hook up with new words or new thoughts. Suppose I took one of those memories and wrote a poem. "The poem refreshes the world," Wallace Stevens wrote. The poem refreshes the love in my heart.

10/25/03 – Rhinecliff

Walked across the field in the dark. Far from cities, so many bright stars, the Milky Way like a long *shuuuuush*, a long whisper in the sky. If I stand alone and look too long, I start to panic. Feel I'll be lost. Feel the threat of some force that could break through the fragile screen and show me something overwhelming—something that would kill me or drive me crazy. I made myself breathe slowly and hold still. Felt the dark inside. Stood in the same field this morning and looked up—a bright blue sunny sky, the ground white with heavy frost—and tried to understand that the stars were still there.

KIM STAFFORD

The Blue Corn Way

Some dreams give words, fragments, maybe a sentence. No image at all, just a spoken phrase, a set of words suspended like the credits following a film. When I wake, the words are all I have. From many such records in my pocket notebooks, I glean these few...

+ + +

Dream: a package of hummingbird food called "The Untold Glory."

Dream: an Oregon state cop tells me, "In the summer we have a lot of stray women."

Dream sentence: "Marriage best protects the unmarried self."

Dream: an old person has discovered the meaning of life: "Gather/Scatter."

Dream sentence: "My last recollection is all I am."

Dream image: When I lie on my back and my feet fall open, they are a book where I can read the story of every road I have traveled.

Dream sentence after love with my wife: "Complete, complete grace, long duel."

Dream sentence: "The cost of the human chain." [what it takes to bring people together]

Dream: a play called "Bureau of Missing Persons" (a company provides the ultimately frightening service of bringing back a lamented person from one's life—reconstructing a character from a dream-tap: this returning character challenges everything).

Dream sentence: "Eventually, a thief will steal from his own."

Three word-dreams on the first day back at work after summer:

1. I tell my father, "We're riding on the exhaust" (i.e. straddling the exhaust pipe to travel…and exhausting ourselves…addicted to exhaustion as denial of the true life);

2. "yearnity" (i.e. the life of good longing in the present, the infinite possibility of the present);

3. "endurance doers" (endless doing—without true accomplishment).

Dream: I am writing with a felt-tip pen on the white sweater/left shoulder of a woman: "Notes & Signs" (she won't mind, I tell her, because I am writing something she has taught me—i.e., she is my muse): book title for notebook gleanings...or for a class in writing rich fragments: Notes & Signs.

Dream account: "The Blue Corn Way" is a kind of life that consists of one essential habit: "Say what is."

THOMAS R. HEISLER

Insider Artist

(selections)

the dust turned to gold in my little fingers
My first day of school I didn't go.
How could I leave my mom? Answer, I couldn't.
After I didn't get on the bus, we sat in the dining room. I sat on one side of the table and my mom sat on the other. The way I remember it, the room was dusty as all hell. If it were as dusty as I remember it, we both would have died from the dust. So it couldn't have been *that* dusty. Early fall, I guess it would have been, light came through the blinds and turned the dust gold. My mom sat across the room from me and wept. It was the saddest I'd ever seen her. It was the saddest I'd ever seen anything. All that dust.

. . .

I sometimes yell at the top of my lungs everything that's fucked up with this world and the price we're going to pay like one of those guys you see with leaflets or between sandwich boards on crowded street corners.
Except I do it in the shower, and really just because I like the way my voice sounds in there.

. . .

"Books are my life," I said to anyone who would listen. Nobody did, but I guess I should have expected that since I was alone in my apartment at three o'clock in the morning with my blinds closed. "Well," I said, "at least I've got you, Gertrude Stein." She didn't respond. She's a snob. Apparently I'm not *intellectual* enough, or so she says, although I suspect her refusal has nothing to do with that whatsoever.

I suspect our problems go much, much deeper.

. . .

When someone says "how's it going" or "what's going on," I get the answers mixed up and say "not much" to the first and "pretty good" to the second.

By the law of probability, you'd say, if I were simply picking responses at random, I would get them right about fifty percent of the time. In my case, this is not so. I am at about a ninety percent failure rate. What gives? you ask.

(Here's the secret don't tell anyone shhhh:

I'm getting them wrong on purpose. Because the more wrong answers you give, well, when you finally do get one right, that sure is *something*. All I'm trying to do here is create a little something from all this nothing.)

. . .

I try to agree with everything the person I'm conversing with says. After that person has said *everything* and I've agreed with everything, that's when things get *really* uninteresting.

. . .

I used to flatter my enemies to the point where I forgot they were my enemies. In other words, I began to *believe* my own flattery and they became my great friends.
Once they were my friends, however, *then* I drove them to despair.
I couldn't stand having friends.
I was so afraid of losing them.

. . .

When there isn't anything more to say, *that's* when you should do most of your talking.

. . .

Maybe pretty soon I'll run out of things to say completely. Maybe I already have and I'm in denial. Maybe I'm like a water storage tank of words and eventually I'll be empty.
Maybe we're all water storage tanks of words and we'll all soon be empty. If so, and everyone lived long enough to be empty, and no new babies were born into the world, we'd have a completely silent earth.
What would *that* sound like?

. . .

working and reworking my resume i'm like james joyce eight words a day for seventeen years
On my resume, under "hobbies," I put "cultivating my inner life," because my dad said potential employers want to be able to account for all of your time. They don't like it, he said, when they get a guy who does a lot of sitting around doing nothing.
I got an interview, and the interviewer seemed a little perplexed. It said, next to hobbies, first "water-skiing," then "cultivating my inner life."

"Cultivating your inner life," he said. What exactly does *that* mean?" Rather than explain it, I told him to look at me for a minute or two, because supposedly when you have a rich inner life, every little action, even just sitting there, expresses itself on your face.

"I'm not sure," he said, "what to be looking for."

Which, I thought, is the problem with these corporate people: they don't understand anything unless it's presented with overhead projectors and all that business. So I charted out my inner life on transparencies, and in the second interview, I asked to have the lights dimmed and made my presentation with the projector. I used green marker for suffering, red for enlightenment, and so on.

I got asked back for a third interview, but in the end they were looking for somebody with more experience.

• • •

When my dad and I talk, he's talking to an idealized son, and I'm talking to an idealized dad.

So there are really four of us in the room.

That's why things get so confusing.

• • •

We speak in complex code, as all fathers and sons do. If we're in the car going somewhere that takes more than a few minutes and I say that I have to go to the bathroom, his question, "Do you *really* have to go?" goes, of course, far beyond bodily function. In that one question, he asks me all questions all fathers have asked all sons throughout all time.

• • •

*i turn the light off in the closet and close the door and that's when i'm
most me*
I like to have a lot of different shoes because they all make different
sounds and with each pair it's like a new conversation.
When you spend as much time alone as I do, shoes are pretty much
all you got.
I develop these intimate relationships with my shoes as a result, and
so if I see a pair in the back of my closet I haven't worn in a while, I
might go ahead and wear them even if they don't go with my outfit.
That's why sometimes I'm accused of being unstylish.
But to others, I'm a trend-*setter.*
Of course when my closet gets too full, I have to clean out some of
them, and dump them at the Salvation Army. I guess I feel a little
bit better knowing the money goes to feed poor people.
But not that much better.

. . .

It's so hard to know when to laugh anymore now that everybody's
always funny.

. . .

he wore white loafers i thought philosophers have no affectations
"One of the symptoms of an approaching nervous breakdown is the
belief that one's work is terribly important," Bertrand Russell said.
"But Bertrand," I said, "If we don't believe in our work, if we don't
believe in the importance of our work, then what else *is* there?"
"Nothing," he said.
"Oh, Bertrand," I said, "you can't possibly believe that!"
"Oh, no?"
"No, Bertrand, no. There's got to be *something!*"
"Says who?"
"But if there's nothing, then…" At that moment, I broke off and

went straight to my apartment and got canned goods for another eight years.

He, I guess feeling badly, tried telling me he was just *saying* that. That he didn't actually *mean* it.

It was of course too late.

. . .

i always get the cart with the busted wheel somehow
My dead best friend hates grocery stores, too: the horrific fluorescent light and no hiding places anywhere and having to place your order clearly and succinctly with the deli guy and that awkwardness when there are several carts in an aisle and you have to negotiate with other shoppers to get past. That's why he never goes.

Or maybe he doesn't go because I never invite him.

I guess I don't want *anyone* to see me in that kind of shape.

. . .

"You're so quiet tonight," my professional girlfriend said.
I couldn't think of one single thing to say to that.

. . .

I said to Nobody:
Anyone who writes books wants to die and wake up in a different epoch.

. . .

she stopped by after work and brought me little gifts like i was two although i felt a hundred two
"You always see the dark storm cloud where a lot of other people see the silver lining," said my professional girlfriend trying to help me

out of my so-called funk so we could get back to going out to dinner and having sex and stuff.

"Ummph." I responded.

Later on, after she left me alone in my apartment looking out the
window, I watched a cloud come in off the horizon. It looked a
little dark or silvery, depending on whatever word you'd choose.

This, I thought, would show me if she were right or not.

When the cloud finally got to my apartment, it dropped a little
drizzle and she'd brought me a small plant I'd put out on my porch
which had needed water and I'd been too lazy or depressed to water
it myself so maybe *that* was the silver lining.

That got me out of bed and into some new clothes and out the door
to walk over to her apartment.

On the way over, I got absolutely pissed on.

My dead best friend explained:

The cloud *behind* the cloud with the silver lining is the one to watch.

• • •

come to me with a maudlin frown and bubbling eyes

When people say, "I've got some real bad news," I get so excited I
can hardly contain myself. Because I've heard all the good news there
is to tell and though it sometimes sounds nice to hear, when it's all
said and done, the good news never really changes anything.

But if it's the right bad news, which means, if it's bad enough bad
news, maybe it'll change *everything.*

I said to my dead best friend:

As long as there's bad news, we still got hope.

He nodded, but I could tell he wasn't so sure.

• • •

I really *like* trouble. Big trouble. Because then when I'm with people I can say, "We're going to get through this thing," and "If we all stick together, we can beat it. Together, we can move mountains."

I like it any time I can be that boring and unoriginal and still people will nod as though I've just said something wonderful.

If we were to do the human race over again, I'd suggest developing language only to the extent that it would include a handful of expressions along these lines, adaptable to a wide range of human experience. All you would have to do is learn maybe a hundred expressions, and you'd be all set.

Admittedly, people would be pretty boring, but not nearly as boring as they are now with all their originality.

• • •

the last supper that wasn't a thing like the last supper
At our last dinner together before I moved for the last time in their lives, we had our last meatloaf that I ate most of and our last bottle of red wine that I drank the least of and our last discussion of world politics that I hardly contributed to because of my ignorance of world politics and our last conversation on how on earth I was going to be a success that I hardly contributed to because of my ignorance of how on earth I was going to be a success. And after dinner, the last time, the three of us, mom, dad, and I, would wash the dishes, the last time I would dry by hand the oversized dishes, the ones that don't fit in the dishwasher, and the last time my dad would tell me, before I got on the elevator down to the lobby, how proud he was of me, and the last time I would not believe him, and the last time my mom would tell me she loved me and the last time I would not say it in return, and the last time my dad would say something sort of funny that to me was sort of sad trying so fucking hard to make me smile again and just having no fucking idea how, and the last time my mom would hug and try to feed me, literally feed me, the good

warm stuff out of her body that she knew I so desperately needed, and the last time standing there waiting for the elevator to come and not having any idea what to say but wanting to say something to make them think that I was all right and they were all right and everything was going to be all right, although certainly not sure of *any* of these things myself, but that didn't matter as long as they thought I thought that, and getting on the elevator for the last time and as the doorman closed the gate, thinking all of these things and wanting to say all of these things, and saying at last only
bye.

• • •

i feel like a convict going to the chair but i get to keep walking
I'm closing the door behind me and leaving everything old in there and when the next tenants walk in they can open the windows and the porch door and let out the old air and they can vacuum up the million year old dustballs and put their furniture in completely new places and the old carpet imprints left by my furniture will
slowly
slowly
slowly
disappear.

• • •

I stop for coffee before getting on the highway and still every single person looks at me because there is something wrong with me.
But there's nothing *seriously* wrong with me and people lose interest when there's nothing seriously wrong.
So they look back down at their newspaper for their dose of seriously wrong.
Then lick a finger and turn the page.

EBERLE UMBACH

Weiser River Valley Pillow Book
(selections)

For a year I kept a journal inspired by reading Sei Shonagon's "Pillow Book." The vision of life in 11th century Japan that came through in her work in the form of lists and short prose was fascinating to me, and I thought that the particular way of life in the isolation of Adams County, Idaho, would adapt itself well to the form.

+ + +

SQUALID THINGS

The smell of an empty school corridor lined with lockers above which are student drawings of ways to save the environment.

A trowel that has rusted with dirt still on it.

Chicory that has flowered close to the ground after being mowed.

An unmatched sock.

THINGS THAT GIVE THE SENSATION OF FALLING

Standing in a supermarket aisle surrounded by varieties of canned tomatoes that seem to have proliferated since the last time you were there. Varieties of breakfast cereal also create this sensation; varieties of tea, however, do not.

Thinking about a phone number you have lost.

Being about to fall asleep and waking suddenly.

PAIRS THAT GIVE PLEASURE

When the leaves of the cottonwood trees by the side of the highway are the exact same shade of yellow as the double line.

When the line of a jet trail in the eastern sky is the same color as the clouds around the setting sun.

How sometimes I hear the traffic on the highway above my house and it sounds just like a river.

Eating pears and grapes together.

THINGS THAT MARK THE TURN OF THE MILLENNIUM

When the new millennium began I could feel nothing that marked it, and I decided that it was not real in any sense that mattered. But later I started noticing things.

The phrases "space-age technology" and "the Atomic Age" were suddenly dated.

The thought that appeared, unbidden: all reality is virtual.

During a downtown revitalization meeting, a prototype for a building based on local historical architecture was displayed; the date plaque on the false front read "2000" and I felt a chill run down my arms.

For the first time, seeing computer parts at the dump.

THINGS THAT MESMERIZE

A design of squares on a linoleum floor.

The grain and knots of pine paneling.

Water stains on a plaster ceiling.

Lines of print when you are very tired.

THINGS THAT ARE PRIVATE

Love.

Grief.

Writing.

ON THE WAY TO THE POLLS

At the corner, a line of cow skulls, very neat and clean, on a fence-post. On the way back, a herd of cattle coming at us, turning into the old homestead I call Shangri La. It has the most falling-down buildings and equipment. Even an old schoolhouse and two small silos. No one lives at the house, where there are curtains in the windows but no glass.

THINGS THAT WINTER CHANGES

The bottle of soy sauce in my cupboard seems wildly improbable— so exotic, sitting there, as the snow piles up and the temperature outside could kill.

My cleaning frenzies are happier, less panic-struck, and have more to do with spaces than surfaces. More like a squirrel burrowing into cupboards and closets.

The pumice stone becomes a place you travel to, a narrow blue bay in Greece lined by white pumice cliffs and white bits of rock floating on the water.

The flowers on the Christmas cactus seem in motion—salmon leaping or bright birds in flight.

Seeing a wasp or even a Chargas beetle—instead of an impulse to destroy them, there is a sense of kinship, of being survivors together.

FRAMES IN THE LANDSCAPE

Gateways.

Fence lines.

Partially ruined buildings.

THINGS THAT DISTANCE DOES NOT CHANGE

A miniature white carriage from Chinatown looked as exotic in San Francisco as it does on my bookshelf.

Doritos, Pepsi, Milky Ways—the food items that have infiltrated the highway system and look the same everywhere.

ALL I HAVE IN MY HEAD TODAY

All I have in my head today is music. The writing I'm working on could not be farther from my mind. Everything in my head organizes itself into rhythmic units of 2's and 3's, building into 8's, into 12's. The leaves on the ground where they appear between patches of snow are doing it, the straw bales, the clumps of bushes against a white hill, everything is doing it—as if an audible pulse in my mind is going through my eyes and becoming visual.

STRANGE HOW THE WORLD SEEMS BRITTLE

Strange how the world seems brittle when a layer of fog closes in just behind the line of the closest hills. There is an illusion that things have gone two-dimensional and, if struck, would be shot through with tiny cracks.

WHEN YOU HAVE NOT SEEN THE SUN FOR DAYS

When you have not seen the sun for days, that delightful sense of a blank white page diminishes—instead of being a space in which things look magical, it becomes a space in which it is impossible to imagine anything at all. Now we are walking on thin ice, now we must be very careful with going through the day. The furniture, even, seems closer together—the space inside compressing while the space outside is becoming infinite.

EIGHT DOLLARS IN DECEMBER

3 cucumbers
2 green peppers
1 bunch spring onions
1 bunch spinach
1 head cabbage

THIS LAND HAS MANY NAMES

The Central Highlands
The Heartland
The Weiser River Valley
The Payette National Forest
Gateway to the Seven Devils

THINGS WITH LANDSCAPES IN THEM

Easter eggs of sugar that you can look into through one end and see a rabbit, a baby chicken, a flower.

Houses.

The dark wood railings on my grandfather's desk, those tiny balconies, and pigeonholes making a suggestion of wings, the tiny chambers behind them from which at any moment people might rush out in bright colored robes and start waving.

THINGS THAT MAKE THE SKIN CLAMMY

Being about to teach a class.

Shoveling snow in forty degree weather.

Approaching a city on a highway.

Intense anger, unexpressed.

Getting ideas for songs.

ELEGANT THINGS

Pine cones on the bough.

Kokanee salmon in streams before they spawn.

The Snake River seen from Kinney Point.

Finger cymbals.

A field of winter wheat, just sprouted.

IT IS RARE FOR A THING TO BE BOTH POIGNANT AND AMUSING

You go down to the lakeshore to skate, and on a snowy dock extending out into the ice you see several pairs of brightly colored boots, pointing outward. There is no one in sight all the way across the frozen lake.

FINE LINES

Between gentleness and danger when handling a parrot.

Between faith in yourself and overweening pride.

Between a love of beauty and affectation.

Between intense joy and a loss of center.

Between neighborliness and falsity.

Between splendid decay and discomfort.

THINGS HARD TO UNDO

Words spoken in anger.

Backing the car into a snowdrift.

Debt.

An improvised harness for a large drum.

Leaving an ingredient out of a recipe.

Bitterness and families.

MARCH REVELATIONS

At home, red rhubarb uncurling, and yellow crocuses. On the edge
of the highway, the fawn-colored carcass of a deer, flattened into the

ground by snowmelt, and a fragment of blown-out tire emerging as glossy and black-purple as a crow.

On the window, a tiny ant crawling, and by the wild plum tree, the ant hill swarming again.

FULL CROW MOON

It's the only time of year that there are crows in abundance here, though the next town to the north has them all spring and summer.

They appear at the same time that the willows suddenly glow their pale moon yellow.

Crows, like magpies, catch the attention as individuals. They can trick you. They don't get hit by cars.

THINGS NEAR AND FAR

Stop light: 30 miles
Rice vinegar: 30 miles
Fast food: 75 miles
Hell's Canyon: 75 miles
Mall: 100 miles
Airport: 100 miles
Rodeo: 15 miles
Lettuce: 15 miles
Gun club: 2 miles
Church: 2 miles

THINGS THAT GLEAM

Lighted windows at night, seen from the highway across dark fields.

A small brass faucet, in moonlight.

A broken piece of china, half-buried in the spring that runs through the draw.

SPRING IS NOT

Spring is not compassionate—it's every bud for itself and there is no time for sadness, no sense in generalizing from the superabundance of specifics, the undifferentiated inundation of detail. The sorting mechanism is slowly dismembered under the tiny, relentless tendrils of vines.

THERE ARE TIMES

There are times when it feels like you have to make up the world every day—when there is no carry-over at all from the day before. Somehow, during the night, it was all washed away—the bulwarks against doubt and shame, the levers that adjust the delicate balance of anger, compassion, and independence. These and all the other triangulations simply fall apart, and there you are again, unprotected, with the howling voices of your mutilated culture coming at you, and you try again for one more act of wizardry that will deflect them, turn them into gargoyles so you can walk away from the castle, find out how the rivers have changed course again, in the dark time.

TOWELS ON THE BATHROOM SHELF

The faded pink one, with holes—for orphan days.

The thick black one that sheds slightly—when the illusion of opulence reveals its flaws.

The deep-blue one—perfect, a reward reserved for harmonious days.

Striped ones—always go on the hand towel rack, for unexplained reasons.

The peach one—somewhere between the pink one and the blue one.

Turquoise—you have to be feeling a bit brash for this one.

The ones my companion brought with him to live here—still look exotic and exciting.

My grandmother's, with rose appliqués—are fading, poignantly— death again.

STRANGE SIGHTS

In the pond, in slow motion, a bullfrog which has its mouth almost entirely around another's head.

A baby porcupine in the garden, without quills, defenseless.

A wasp wrapped up like a mummy in a black widow's web.

THINGS ABOUT THE CATALPA TREE

Its heart-shaped leaves seen through the kitchen-sink window and a section of spiral staircase.

Its late-leafing and rather coarse abandon—and then the perfection of its blossoms, the speckled funnel and whorled lips.

The strange, sweet-astringent smell you can smell from the pump-house. Then the tree goes invisible until the dangling pods turn brown and catch your eye.

INCURABLE

It doesn't matter what the words are, when your beloved is tested, diagnosed. The cottonwood with their terrible beauty went spinning out of reach, untouchable. As the hours passed, the presence of death made poetry everywhere—absolute perfection of line and form—it was appalling. How did I live through those two days? He said, please don't cry any more, he said it very gently. I went to sit in the draw where the spring comes out of the earth and runs down. When I came out, I had stopped crying. I took his hand, loving him so much. And now we have begun.

INCURABLE, REVISTED

Incurable hope.

Infectious laughter.

Untreatable irreverence.

THE ROAD THROUGH EASTERN OREGON

Onions from the onion trucks lying on the roadside.

In one field, piles of different colored onions, reminiscent of crop circles, sand paintings, and other ancient mysteries.

A house in the shape of a lighthouse on the edge of a dry field rippling dust.

ABOUT MY BELOVED

When he moved in, he brought a colander with his kitchen things, so that we had two in the household. This upset me at first, giving me the sense of panic I get when there is too much stuff. How he persuaded me, gently, that it was all right to possess two colanders. Then the first night, making supper together, that we used both of them: one for salad, one for pasta, and I laughed at how useful, in fact, abundance could be.

AT FIRST

At first I thought that living with the shadow of death would somehow invalidate everything. But the opposite is more true: it is that shadow which completes things, which creates the thin bearable edge of unbearable beauty—which returns that beauty to the everyday, the immediate, the inalienable. I always forget this, and, always, remembering it again seems insurmountably difficult—at first.

THE WEIGHTIEST DECISIONS

Deciding never to have another job where stockings would ever have to be worn.

Deciding to write every morning.

Buying land.

Deciding to love my beloved.

SUMMERY THINGS

A bullfrog's bright green head resting on duckweed in matching green.

The smell of apples fallen into the spring from the wild apple tree in the draw.

Filling the swamp cooler at night by starlight, and the thick swathe of the Milky Way.

THINGS THAT MAKE YOU REALIZE THAT LIFE IS PERFECT

Light falling on the open doorway to the music room.

Rain falling on the tin roof of the garden shed.

A wind so gentle it would be unnoticeable except for the rattling it makes among the dry cornstalks.

BALLET OF CHICKS IN THEIR SHELLS

Twenty years ago I choreographed a dance to this piece. Yesterday I saw, for the first time, an actual chick pecking its way out of its eggshell.

How strange to have images that are abstractions, that miss the point so completely. The struggle of the chick to peck its way out is way more horrifying than playful, its peeping from within, a sound that is desperate with exhaustion.

Typically, the eggshell is the dominant image, in the abstract—the hard shape cracking cleanly. What's left out is the elastic membrane, flexible as the shell falls away, the opening slits in it that swell and widen as the being within moves.

SPENDING THE WHOLE DAY WRITING MUSIC

When it's easy, it seems that the sounds are already there, all I have to do is listen. All it is, is suspending fear, listening past panic and sense.

Rapture is simple, but not comfortable.

That night, sleeplessness: the sound of rain dripping onto the straw bales unbearably loud, the moths crashing into the screen window.

SAVING GRACES

On the lawn, among the browning leaves, the occasional underside of a cottonwood leaf bright and silvery as a coin winking up at you.

The internal voice, that laughs at itself. A friend, who echoes it.

Coming home on a cloudy night, past Mesa Hill, the scattered lights of houses around the post office and the store down in the valley.

ANDREW T. McCARTER

Entries and Exits: A Notebook

(selections)

You first began following her, you thought, because you were a man and she a woman; because she was beautiful and blind to her beauty, being blind; because she clutched in her left hand the taut leash of her harnessed guide-dog, which she followed with prudent stride, her posture locked like a Roman charioteer's; because, together, she and her shepherd appeared to be the six-legged mythical animal that would lead you to the exit of your private labyrinth.

. . .

Dance performance. I always focus on a dancer's eyes. Same with my dentist. Intimacy of this sort.

. . .

Does he feel as distant from his fellow men as men do the stars?

. . .

The claustrophobic one who couldn't leave his apartment; so claustrophobic, he couldn't wear clothes.

The man so frightened of heights, not only could he not stand upright, he could not sit up in bed.

. . .

The ambulance silenced by eyelashes.

. . .

He has learned that as he holds his mother's hand he can walk with eyes closed, and so does, but for only so long as he can stand it, until they open of their own accord, suddenly, and randomly lock his vision on the first person he sees. And he watches that first person, without even a blink, until the stranger has vanished into a little shop, has turned a corner, or has simply disappeared into the distance behind him, leaving him, the little boy, neck-craned and looking back....

. . .

My voyeuristic conception of the afterlife. I wish for a heaven only as high as the maple tree canopy outside beautiful Danielle's bedroom window across the street.

. . .

The same at 11 as at 87, the feeling of falling in love seems to be.

That one should fall in love on one's deathbed.... "After all, young and old leave life on the same terms. None leaves it in any way but as if he had just entered it," writes Montaigne.

. . .

One of our oldest questions: the question of our own mortality: our quest for immortality. I used to think that it was a question of the voice asking the question that is its answer. I now suspect that the most profound treatise on the subject can only be expressed with a voice abstracted to laughter desperate for escape....

• • •

1, 2, 3: my self will be annihilated; my body, outlasting my self, will decompose; my notebook, outlasting my self and body, will be consumed by silverfish.

When one is in love, the desire for immortality multiplies maddeningly; we want to preserve our lover, body and soul, and preserve ourselves to experience her.

The mating-call of immortality is the sound of laughter.

Why, in the end, is a mere century or less on earth a prerequisite for eternal life?

• • •

Her beautiful laugh: A long and drawn out wheeze followed by a loud and singular "HA!" (as though she blows up a balloon until it pops!).

• • •

Hearing that she is beautiful, she covers her face: two equally beautiful hands.

She shakes her hair to untangle the sunlight. Diamonds shake similar light in their tin cups.

. . .

My attraction to older women...

My reaching for them with the desire to pull them back through the years as from the edge of an abyss?

My attraction to the abyss itself, my desire to acquaint myself with death before my time?

Or is it a combination of both—two desires flaming up in conflict?

. . .

Mature women with an irresistible, charming disregard for mortality, who give you a glimpse of the little girl they once were.

. . .

Day off. Night off. How to describe my Fall. Afternoon. I have already stepped off the sidewalk carpeted with leaves, over the leaf-clogged gutter, and am walking slowly in my heavy and highly polished patent leather shoes down the smooth black asphalt of the right lane of a quiet city side-street. It is mildly liberating to be walking with such slow care along a strip of asphalt reserved for the travel of cars. Observation: the number of fallen leaves dwindles toward the broken yellow line. I take care to step between the few tawny brittle leaves in my path; their edges curling up from the asphalt, they seem to float like little boats on black water; the tips of their serrated edges raised, as if aspiring back toward their branch, accentuating the grim solidity of the asphalt below....

. . .

I stand at a window locked shut but shattered open.

. . .

Karen is reading, stilled with concentration, still as a photograph which has stopped time, trapped chance. The urge to look at photos of her taken from a time before I knew her....

. . .

She coaxes him into eating a red petal already plucked and in repose in the palm of her hand, soft as the palm of her hand.

. . .

X. concludes with a lowering of her head, her hair closing like a luxuriously weighty stage curtain over the scenery of her face.

. . .

She is the woman with the penmanship ideal for writing the word "alas."

. . .

Caress a cat a woman holds to her shoulder, and it is as though you are caressing her.

. . .

At 20 years, thrilled with the prospect of finding meaning; at 30, giddy with the suspicion that there is none to be found.

. . .

A sky like the side of a cliff coining the fossil of an old moment's sun.

. . .

The past feels more beneath than behind. Not so for the moving man, who feels the flow of air on his face, who inhales the future. But the man standing still, the only flow he feels is that of gravity.

. . .

Very much what I imagine the feeling of immortality to be: the feeling of those days I skipped school to go to a public library, and either sit and read before an enormous window overlooking the rainy street, or check out a book to read on a sunny park bench.

. . .

An obsolete phone number of an old friend. With what clarity you remember dashing it off onto a scrap at your desk while it is dictated to you over the phone. And now, seven years later, it appears in your hand, delivered from the gritty bottom of an old box.

. . .

I return to my old university, to the library where I spent an infinity of hours, to one of the books I read with such passion, to its cover, pages and typeface with which I became so intimate, and I wonder how many other hands it has passed through these ten years.

. . .

Linear time like a train, and to each boxcar its generation. Yet not only to be able to think back to a place, but to be able to return physically to the place to stimulate the memory.

• • •

I can remember things once only; from then, I remember memories.

• • •

I desire a personal library absent of all fluff, essential, however large. When I weed through my library, pulling books to be sold or donated, it is less like weeding a garden, less like pruning a shrub, less like the patient work of bonsai, than it is like the whim of a malicious prison warden who, sauntering before a row of prisoners standing upright as the spines of books, fingers two or three for elimination.

• • •

An old friend who had studied handwriting analysis in Sweden had only this to say about mine: It is so full of contradictions, it leaves the page essentially blank.

• • •

Must not spend my life reading with the voraciousness of one cramming for an exam: Must not make my life the night before a test.

• • •

Hesse, *Beneath the Wheel*, the first book to affect me, my first book, read again after seventeen years.... It's like following the streets of a town that was one's home long ago. Phrases become familiar, images recognized, causing one to pause, linger contemplatively as in those corner hideaways one used to frequent, conjuring feelings, memories of the life one lived there, in that town, on those pages.

. . .

Among the curses of being human is being able to read only one book at a time.

. . .

Better to be a butterfly failure than a chrysalis success.

. . .

Because I refuse to reduce my ideas about the world to convictions simple enough to fit on a bumper-sticker, those who do, perceive me as not having done enough thinking about certain issues in order to be able to do so, when quite the contrary is the case…. It suddenly strikes me that those bumper-sticker convictions serve precisely the same purpose as the vehicle bumper itself.

. . .

Boston fire, 1872: The city in ruins, the men in coats and bowler hats become architecture among the rubble.

. . .

Life is short, art is long. But life is getting longer and art shorter.

. . .

Electricity crawling over stone.

. . .

Young girl, yellow hair, blue eyes, blowing a growing, quivering, thinning pink bubble.

. . .

in the sky
a lone cloud
look at it

. . .

Biography of the left hand written by the right...

. . .

A snake devouring a mouse; a crocodile, a monkey; a shark, a human being. Perversity of watching lower life forms feed on higher.

. . .

The thing about women is, they're so damned womanly!

. . .

This desire, more correctly, this *impulse* (sexual and suicidal) to empty my bank account (every penny) and mail it (anonymously, as a devotion) to a woman I have never met (whose name and address I choose at random from a telephone book?) and will never meet.

. . .

Profound resemblance between TV's "canned laughter" and the sound of a toilet's flushing.

. . .

A stretch of black railroad track fifty yards from the little wooden church which is holding a funeral service. An approaching whistle whisks away the words of the priest; a loose pew vibrates like the devil; and, for one brief moment, we all look through our tears, to the stained glass windows, to see what we can of the train, its cargo of God-knows-what.

. . .

Holy water hot-tubbing.

. . .

I often listen to recorded birdcalls while driving. So piercingly clear, so solitary and soothing, they make me feel motionless, focused, no matter how fast I drive, no matter how much a blur I make the roadside trees. This sense of stillness while traveling allows me to experience a rebirth when I arrive at my destination, when I crack open my car door like a fragment of shell.

. . .

Sliding on my back down a snowy slope of Observation Hill, craning my neck back to look upside down uphill at her sliding about 25 feet behind me—the soles of her boots, puffy coat, raised mittens, the peak of the hill rising behind the pom-pom of her hat.

And this is a contorted metaphor for what aspect of our relationship? There need not be one, metaphor or relationship; it is enough that I'm perhaps the only one to have seen her from this perspective.

. . .

She engages in responsible action, whereas I indulge in irresponsible thought; the honeymoon would be disastrous.

. . .

Considering the feelings involved with loss, the loss of a love relationship in particular, what an immense sadness must accompany death, the loss of the entire world around you, including you.

. . .

Alone is the biggest word I know, even bigger than the word God.

. . .

The boy sleeps in the fetal position, his ear pressed to the pillow. For years he hears the monstrous, monotonous footfalls of something horrible approaching. One night he will realize that it is his own pulse, his own heart, he is hearing. Tonight the boy sleeps in the fetal position, in the shape of an enormous ear.

. . .

I remember the ghost-town road of my grandmother's dusty mantel, where the framed photographs of dead relatives (relatives I never knew) stood propped up like stage-set storefronts for the shooting of some spaghetti western.

. . .

With an enthusiasm similar to the one which compels parents to record and date their child's first giggle, their child's first word, and perhaps even their child's first profanity, this child, in adulthood, should take it upon himself to record his first formulation of the absurd, the first time he senses his own mortality, and the date of his first maniacal cackle, which will inevitably follow.

. . .

Hands snug in the pockets of your oldest coat, you trudge through the park, across the virgin, ankle-deep snow, in the bitter cold, becoming more and more conscious of your own core of warmth. You pant, see that you are alive by the sight of your own breath; you stumble more often in the soft snow with each new step...but without any fear of falling.

. . .

Noontime a man walks along the street; his shadow, well-defined, is the size of a child.

. . .

Insomnia. Instead of counting sheep, synthesize disciplines—art, literature, philosophy, politics, science—century by century, in reverse order—20th, 19th, 18th, 17th, 16th, etc.—all the way back, to when disciplines were already synthesized, back beyond the Greeks, to the Mesopotamians of approximately 9,000 BC, perhaps even beyond...until one loses, quite rightly, consciousness.

. . .

From the window of his dark apartment, he looks out on the universe of streetlights, as from within an extinguished sun.

· · ·

A conception of death: One sits in a pitch dark room, writing by feel with a pen one suspects probably contains black ink, on a black sheet of paper one imagines to be white.

· · ·

Our attraction to the abyss. Death is the one we mistake, years later, for our first love—Birth. We mistake the casket for the cradle, the moist grave for the womb.

· · ·

I have the philosophy of a man who, having twisted and turned in the spider web of ideas, begins a very satisfying laugh at the hopelessness of his situation.

· · ·

This notebook would be unnecessary if I could write laughter, that ultimate articulation.

AUDREY BORENSTEIN

Shards

Summer Into Autumn, 2000

June 29. Life lived intensely, fully. The sun summerbright, the air
summerhot, the traffic appallingly heavy. At our lunch stop at a
picnic table on which we perched the cooler with our sandwiches
and fruit, I felt for a long, long moment that my heart was failing.
A magnetic pull, a pull of the gravitons in another world…. He
spoke in a voice studded with stones and bits of glass and gems of
anguish and awe and suffering. I have never heard him so deeply
moved by anything I've written. It stirred his soul…. I want there to
be perfection. It cannot be, yet that is what I desire…. There are
echoes, strains from Elsewheres, otherlives.

· · ·

August 1. I told W that my belief is that God is a tragic Figure, that
God is not omnipotent, and that I feel great compassion for God,
which I also feel God requites. Long ago, I said to B that Judaism
may have a tragic sense of life and paganism a comic sense of life.
And B replied that he thinks it's just the opposite.

· · ·

August 26. That is what keeps me keeping on, old compañero:
a sense of bearing witness for a time to come (or an Elsewhere

dimension), a sense of this mission that is a burden and a grief so deeply incised on my soul that I lie awake filled with existential angst and sorrow, reaching for some connection with God, for a language in which to speak to God, to rise above this dense, dark forest.

. . .

September 11. In letters he wrote perhaps 175 years ago, the artist John Vanderlyn lamented the materialism, the puritanism, the anti-intellectualism of people in this country. He wrote of a society without regard for the arts and for the life of the mind as a wasteland. You would think these words were spoken by a companion walking at your side today. How they resonate.

. . .

September 18. The sea of suffering that is this world, this life.

. . .

September 24. "Selichot" means "pardons," "forgiveness." I read aloud a poem by Amichai who had died on Friday: God watching over the children in kindergarten. B commented on the many mentions of the word "shadow" in Hebrew poetry. I said that Jung sees the shadow as the unrealized portion of the psyche. Deer-swift, B commented that's a European view: in the desert, in Israel, one doesn't often see a shadow. He said it's thought in our tradition that it's a sign of God's protecting Presence. After a moment I asked if perhaps this isn't so different from Jung's thought—we seldom realize the Divine Presence protecting our lives.

. . .

September 25. Musical chairs. That is what we are playing when we dream, perhaps. Changing worlds, changing lives; and when the music stops we hurry to the nearest dimension. And if those playing with us are quicker? Well, there is death and there is Death. Perhaps.

. . .

October 2. Shanah Tovah, old compañero, a good and sweet 5761 to you. Moodshifts of the atmosphere: grey and overcast and heavy, damp air and then after a while, yellowbright sun, swiftly yielding to cloudy mist. Like life, like life.

Winter Into Spring, 2001

January 1. Yesterday evening, just before dusk, the sky seen through the meshes of bare branches: a sea of violet suffused with streams of amber light above still waters of pure azure changing, changing, glowing ever more amber, then the violet deepening, darkening …and a porpoise rose out of the whitening soft blue, lone swimmer in that changeling sea, mauve God's-eye, giant gold-rimmed dolphin suspended there…vanishing in the dark increase.

If you stay there, presently your eye will discern shapes, you will remember that the darkness too is dappled.

. . .

February 22. If the universe could, it would laugh at all human endeavor.

. . .

May 10. This cool day of emerald firebursts in the trees, I am thinking of the shape-shifting going on in the scrolls of you, old compañero, of how that challenges the shaping of the life told in autobiography and in its distant cousin, biography.

. . .

June 1. I was "here" in form only, "here" as in a sketch the architect makes: the spaces throb with emptinesses to be or not to be filled. Just now I am thinking of the ghosts crowding about our lives, parents dead, siblings long absent quarrelling with us still inside the vestibule.

. . .

June 2. Half the morning we talked, making a clearing in thoughts that were mired in sadness yesterday.... One of the best thoughts we arrived at together is the injustice done by seeing a person only in the one context.... I said to him that in the odd moment—while doing housecleaning, for example, or falling asleep—I imagine him in some milieu in which I do not figure at all (in the Navy, for example, or chairing a Department meeting as he used to do) so that I might see him more whole. "Just the other day," I said, "I imagined you as a little boy in a corner somewhere, playing quietly, having your own thoughts. And I loved you as that little boy."

. . .

June 6. A good wake-up call for the writer, this call for manuscripts to be saved for the year 3000. One asks oneself what could possibly endure for a millennium that would be of interest to readers then. This, I think: that, dwelling in Possibility, I will be writing to the spark of my soul returned to this "darkling plain"—and perhaps I will be contemplating this from another universe.

Summer to Summer's End, 2001

June 22. I want ardently to shed light on their paths, but only God can do this. A test of spirituality: how to pray with one's whole heart to God Who so often—so often!—seems too far away to hear, seems dangerously like a mirage to the wanderer in this desert.

The desire to impart may be a reminder that one is made in the image of God. But God does not live our lives for us. When those close to one do not come to one seeking light, one grieves. So God must grieve when we forget God's presence in our lives.

The impossible dream: to make of this a work of art.

· · ·

July 1. When one who imparts can't cure what no human being can cure, there is a deep change between the one who would give and the one who would receive, because of the disappointment *on both sides.* Love or affection or desire may be born anew—or lost forever.

We want to be deceived when we project. And we love the feeling of imparting. But unless we accept our limits, our human-ness, it will come to grief.

· · ·

July 4. The curse, the gift of insight impels one to play God. This is what is meant by the odd phrase that one "knows too much." It means one knows more than may be humanly bearable, because one also knows one is not God.... But even God is not God, because God chooses not to be omnipotent; God gives us free will.... If God did exert Godly power, we would be no more than puppets.... The gods and goddesses are representations of attributes of one God, a

God who created human beings perhaps out of loneliness, perhaps out of the cosmic longing to connect with creation in a way that would reveal the nature of God *as perceived by the created*. Perhaps this was God's way of developing consciousness, awareness of Godself—by creating beings who reflect in their deeds the nature of the One Who created them in all its complexity. By setting us free, setting us *in motion* on this journey of self/Self-discovery. By entering into a covenant with us, granting us freedom that we might partner God in this journey of revelation.

We are mortal; we live in Time; therefore, to us the revelation is ongoing, a "continuous" revelation. The seal of this covenant is love.

· · ·

July 8. There is no "tabula rasa." Each of us has a soul carrying some heritage from forces that have been contending through previous generations.

· · ·

July 10. How do you wear your Hebrew name? As a cloak you don for certain occasions? As armor against "the slings and arrows of outrageous fortunes"? As a beam of light, a laser, like the rays emanating from the face of Moses after his direct encounter with God, a ray of light in the center of your mind, a third eye you train on appearances (apparitions) to see what lies beyond them, underneath them? Or as a lucky piece, an amulet? Or a scarred second skin you shed, misfortune by misfortune, your whole life long? What's in a name, a Hebrew name? History, the story of a spiritual ancestor woven into the tapestry of our civilization, that tells you how to find the threads of your own story, so that you recognize what you are weaving with your deeds? (Fortune-telling, because your Past is also your Future.)

. . .

July 18. "The future is the growing edge of the present," Heilbroner wrote. What to do in the face of a grave moral wrong in which the wronged is an accomplice?.... I am a watcher in this night.

. . .

August 1. The truth he spoke: "Everything you treasure has no meaning for her." It has been so from the beginning. The awareness of this glistened in the sun; I lingered in the shade of a longing that had outlived Possibility.

. . .

August 6. Last night's dream of an elsewhere place where the threads of fates are spun in other patterns.

. . .

August 13. Thunder rumbling, the air sodden, prayers lifting their wings, moving outward toward near-universes connected to this one.... She spoke of God as "intelligent energy." I said she must feel more attuned to the vocabulary of Physics than of Metaphysics.

. . .

September 7. Our common ground: students of life, witnesses ceaselessly calling to one another in point counterpoint of the two traditions, the spoken and written word. (Your pages, old compañero, are strewn with phrases of this strange music-making.)

. . .

Saturday, September 8. The reality of the photograph of one with whom you have communicated only by letter or telephone can never resemble the imagined person, not even remotely. It is bound to disappoint, even to seem to betray your trust in the honesty and integrity and good intentions of a being who, by face-to-face meeting or in the first photograph before your eyes, proves to be someone other than the face and figure possessing that voice in whom you have confided.... You feel almost despair, almost that you have to begin all over again to develop a relationship to this stranger.

That is the infinite wisdom of the God of Israel and of Islam, never ever to make the Godself visible.

Old compañero, you too are in this way made "in the image" of God.

$$\cdot\ \cdot\ \cdot$$

September 13. "In a moment, it was no more." Words of Senator Mansfield mourning the assassination of President Kennedy echo in my soul. And then I hear FDR's words marking "a day of infamy." On the golden September morning just two days ago, we drove to our daughter's home, having no knowledge of the horror....

A body blow—massive—leaves you numb, struggling to absorb the shock. And the grief, the black flower of it, unfolds hour upon hour on that day that became night before mid-morning.

Who can comprehend the scale of such a disaster? Who can know what lies on the other side of this turning point in the life of this country and in the life of the world?

RICHARD GOODMAN

Virginia Beach, Virginia
(Summer, 1954)

We had gardenia bushes in our front yard. In the summer, the smell of gardenias went straight into my body like morphine. I was almost naked, in my bathing trunks all day, a ten-year-old boy. I ran through the entire Virginia summer day like this. The scents and smells of the hot day, the heated grass, and the ocean-infused air enthralled me. Every sensation stroked my body—the scent of figs, the ebb and flow of ocean smells, and the scent of gardenias. I breathed summer.

My body was slim and small. I was smaller than the gardenia bush. I leaned my head toward it. The white soft flowers were here and there. I found one I could reach. I lowered my face to it. The sweet fumes coursed through me. The sun beat on my bare back. I was thrilled. I was being taught by nature, my more forthright mother, the intricacies of sensuality.

The gardenia petals were like un-ironed cotton. If I touched a petal, a brown corruption appeared where I had placed my finger. I watched with guilt as the tobacco-hued stain moved slowly across the snowy surface. The movement was as slow and sure as lava. It could not be undone. After a day, the blossom was dead. I had marred something perfect, a lesson too deep for me to fathom.

In the evening, my mother would sometimes clip three or four gardenias from a bush. The smells of summer quietly settled down to their evening lives. My mother would put the gardenias in a boat-shaped silver bowl full of cool water. I watched the water bead and slide on the side of the bowl. She placed the bowl in the center of the dinner table. The gardenias floated on the cool water's surface. As we ate our supper, I would from time to time look at the floating gardenias. Nothing in the world was as white. White floating gardenias.

STACY CARLSON

Digging It Up: Notebook for a Novel
(selections)

Stacy Carlson kept a notebook while she worked on her first novel, "Crescent." The story of a writer emerging by way of a novel, her notebook—which became a work in itself—chronicles the creative process as well as daily life, travel, memory and dream…

+ + +

I'm going to bring this pen down off its high horse. Weep a river, pen, because I'm coming for you. I can hear Marquez's townspeople in their moldering coffins, hair growing, scratching the damp wood with fingernails curled like serpents. I can hear poor Vardamon crying in the barn. I hear Ed Abbey, old Griz in his desert. I cradle his leathery face because we know some of the same things. Yes, I gather you up.

But here comes Joe Campbell and I must melt down into the earth to understand the origins he talks about. I look up and there's Wm. Blake inside my own heart. Behind him Swedenborg, the crazy loon! Your angels hang every which way, some facing the sun with high-powered sunblock and shades, others nearer to the sloping creatures below, with baseball caps protecting their bald spots. There's John Updike watching it all from a shingled porch on Martha's Vineyard.

Two well-bred women swim naked in front of him and they've got names like Diana and Helen, because he knew his stuff just like all the other Johns in the neighborhood: Casey, Barth, Cheever, and I did learn something in college, didn't I?

But I found Persephone when I got out, and I trail after her, of course. She walks downward into the earth. She feels clay under her fingernails and drips of ancient groundwater hit her. Her dress is caked with dirt and she walks toward a man who would pluck her from her girlhood and lay her down under the ground. All flowers and architecture and sky disappear but she walks on her own, touching the hard backs of sow bugs and the slippery ends of worms in a place that reminds her of a beginning so far away she cranes her head just to remember the shape of a shadow on the wall, the outline of a story as it was sung to her as an infant. She runs deeper. Of course she runs and runs to find it. The pen is my tool, after all.

· · ·

Coffee shop bustle. This warm bakery atmosphere makes me tired. I'm searching for my story. Grover said *don't write about it, just write it.* I'm searching for the story like the grizzlies wave their heads back and forth underwater in the Alaskan streams looking for salmon. I was surprised they could see underwater until I realized I could see underwater too, even in saltwater. It's just a matter of opening my eyes. I figure if I write this town of Crescent and just keep writing, something will emerge. Just keep moving the pen across the page and be brave. I sound like the leader of an infantry squadron: Keep your head up and your boots moving. Just slog through the mud. Writing is like a relationship with water: you strive to go deep, to see the mystery, to be closer to orbiting ancient creatures and the root of humanity, but more often you stay peering down from the surface, afraid to let the water become three-dimensional. I need to plunge and struggle down against my nature.

Charles Dickens said *The whole difference between Construction and Creation is exactly this: that a thing constructed can only be loved after it is constructed; but a thing created is loved before it exists.*

• • •

Da Vinci. Occupied and preoccupied by a persistent problem: how do you drain a swamp? How do art and science (land and water) coexist—not even coexist but exist within each other, entwined? I smiled in the crowded museum today, reading the explanatory blurbs above indecipherable pages of the codex. They said: *Here again, Da Vinci explains his method to drain a swamp.* Crazy loon. He strove to upset the water table, to upset the nature of things, to upset the way we look at art or science. Was water interfering with the land? Was science interfering with art? The idea of draining a swamp is inconceivable to me. Like separating art and science, in his eyes. He explained the reason for both a dried-up swamp and artistic science. It's right here, under glass in a display case: 500 years ago, written backwards in Italian. Right here, plain as day.

• • •

Rain coming down tonight, watering my restless spirit. My lover sleeps in my bed with the sound of Russian monks chanting and I sit for a while. Warm inside my own moment, why wouldn't I write it here, safe in the page. After a week of sadness I found home again, in restlessness itself. Again, watch those black threads move, weave across the page some pattern. I lose track of what writing means and move one thought into another. Monks chanting in solitude, a train of thought vocalized and brought into the air. I remember that night in Notre Dame, the river passing slowly, the sculptures leaning, almost suicidal, off their roof. In my mind the cathedral looms like a ghost ship, white in the blue night. Inside, the weary traveler awakens to the sound of voices in a minor key. Newly arrived in Paris, nowhere to go until late at night, sleeping on two cathedral chairs, feet against a pillar, she awakens to the rhythm of rain falling and behind the rain the monks who sing somewhere far back and out of sight. Those voices now heat up the vaulted air and the tones shine amber and orange and conjure the colors of the rose window. She doesn't reach out but moves farther into the song and shuts her eyes again. Without vision, the symbolic structure of the church crumbles and she hears the song anew: it is blood flowing through a vein. The music is life itself and a struggle for understanding. A song begins inside her, the words always the same question: Who am I?

. . .

Dig down, now, beneath the surface into layers and layers of loam. I accept the use of metaphor as my shovel. The words are the tool, the hole deepening as I work. The extension of words from my hand and my head lowers me down. No more prologue. I'm scared. I face the same old hyena in my mind, old wolf-shadow: *you're weak, empty, delusional, small in heart.* I feel more acutely than ever I'm not dedicating my life fully to art. To these scrawls. To this deepening chasm. All my people, the people of Crescent, are hanging in suspended animation, arm in arm and cheek to cheek, frozen in their dance.

. . .

Remembering that day in the Alcazar, I leaned over the railing of a green fishpond and a Koi kissed the end of my finger. That night, drinking apple wine with Kate, Antonio the innkeeper spoke to us and I translated. I was proud, sitting there, translating for the other girls, so they could hear his words about us all being children of the earth, and how he was the angel (no matter how heavy and drunk and how patched his shoes) who hung suspended outside our windows and wished us goodnight.

. . .

I must go to the cemetery and flood myself with names.

. . .

I have a vision of all the former inhabitants of a house sitting on the porch just before sunrise. They are ghosts in a foggy morning drinking lemonade out of elegant glasses. They disappear as dawn lightens. They are sad to go, they miss life. They share the history of the house.

. . .

Cling to the filament of possibility. Let the characters wander off in my brainstorm. Try to dream about it, or speculate on the dream that might be: Isaac drives the truck straight out of town for eight hours straight. He gets way up into British Columbia, in the forest, on the coast. He sits and drinks the strongest coffee ever and contemplates his life. He eventually decides to come home again. When he walks in the door he looks at his wife and sees her for the first time.

. . .

I know about the world from reading and hanging around in junk stores.

. . .

I visited grandma on Saturday. She's convinced she's a millionaire and owns the whole nursing home. "It's so strange how your life turns out," she told me, shaking her head. "You start out a poor little girl on a wheat farm, and you end up a millionaire." She was confused by all the other tottering folks around. "Who in the world is *that*?" There is a curious sisterhood there—many more women than men, many of them carrying their purses around uselessly.

. . .

Golden October roses and water like mercury under the Ballard Bridge as I drove home from work. Once again the inexplicable excitement of autumn brushes against me. Burrowing in sweaters and soft scarves. I want heavy rain and hot coffee to cut the bite in the air.

. . .

I need a kick start, jump start, roll start, some spark. I feel like I'm walking on tundra: the ground cover is interesting and intricate, but it's not the ground. I can't feel the story under my feet. But such legends of my homeland I'm reading: albino spirit-bulls diving soundlessly into lakes and stories of unearthly children clinging to the barnacled back of an unnameable monster. Ghoul John the grave robber, snatching up the lids of burial canoes and snaking off with the skulls. The tales are short and choppy and I grow restless. An elk running off with a maiden, a murdered woman turned to soap at the bottom of a glacier-cold lake. Drowning, drowning.

. . .

Standing with my father in the open-air passage between train cars, our train slowed and another train, going the opposite direction,

passed. Our conductor leaned out his window to give the other conductor today's newspaper. A Dutch man sharing our window tells
me I have many fathers on this trip and we laugh, my own dad next
to me, laughing on a train in Mexico.

. . .

Crescent is a book about the fragmented ways our inheritance
reaches us.
The way patterns of family silence keep us in tension.
How half-heard stories give us refuge.

. . .

The fernery: gigantic fiddleheads, the tightly coiled journey. Fruit
bats hang above like heavy black droplets, Job's tears indeed. Already
I feel a certain androgyny in solitude. I caught my reflection today
in a dark artwork in the museum, and gasped that I'm a woman.
Veils of isolation are welcome, really. The monologue in my brain
has no gender to me, so seeing my image is like seeing a stranger. I'll
let ambiguity have its way with me for now.

. . .

Will my journal take a turn for the visual if I don't replace the
camera I just broke?

. . .

Yesterday, the cowboy asked me "what do you do?" Since I'm out of
a real job, and I'm in Australia, I said "I'm a writer." He said "Are
you any good?" I said something like, "well, I'm always learning. I'm
a lot better than I used to be." He leaned down to me, in his hat and

boots and good jeans, and said "When people ask you that, you know what you have to say?"

"What?"

"Say, Shit yeah I'm good."

He's right, of course.

. . .

When Captain Cook came to Australia in 1770, he passed by the Galapagos. His botanist, a guy named Banks, picked up two tortoise eggs. He managed to incubate them on board, all the way back to England where he hatched them. One survived. Two hundred and thirty-one years later, that tortoise is still living and I saw it today, here in Queensland near the Glass House Mountains. I was standing there in front of the cage with my mouth hanging open, staring at that tortoise for half an hour. Other people came and went. One boy asked if I was praying, that's how weird I must have looked. I said yes. It was a highlight of my life to look that creature in the eye.

. . .

Tonight I sat on the edge of a burning cane field and watched the sun go down.

. . .

This story is a dove in my hand. I've made it up to the rooftop, flung open the rickety old door and walked into the wind, into the vast horizon and the unobscured skyscape. But I'm holding the dove too tightly. Have I broken its wings before I have the chance to let it go? Or will it fly when it's ready.

JASON ANTHONY

Albedo: Fragments of Antarctic Time
(Summer Notebooks, 1994–2002)
(selections)

Aug. 10, 1994: I've begun final preparations for a voyage to the ice, my first Antarctic logistics. All travel requires the triage of departure, the lists of what-to-bring and what-to-leave-behind, but now I plan for a supposedly comfortable expedition to the world's most alien environment. Do I pack for work, for war, for vacation? Yes.

· · ·

How to be a witness to an ice age: stand back, scratch your insulated head, fill a notebook with incomplete thoughts. Sketch the gap you hear.

· · ·

Antarctica is the meditative white gate to all the darkness we cannot know. We don't understand this local quietus, much less the black universe beyond it, but here we go.

· · ·

The past, the charismatic past, has been wiped clean by this bright absence. The world is white. This albedo that makes it impossible to name what it is I've arrived at has also made pale the places I've left behind. Snow-dressed ice extends to every horizon. Oblivion, I realize, is a great bright place. It is as shy of meaning as it is devoid of content.

. . .

"And how could one, here, speak of arrival or departure? Everywhere: oblivion, the unmade bed of absence, the wandering kingdom of dust." —Edward Jabes, *The Book of Questions*

Here the snow is dust, small and hard. It shifts like sand. It makes a bed that constantly unmakes itself, a floor without wall or dimension. This snow is the white teeth of the wind, and the wind is the voice of this silent kingdom.

. . .

August: a brief truce while light speaks with time.

. . .

No birdsong, no horsefly buzz, no burp of frog, chatter of squirrel, no life talking at all. This place sings, though my ears have too much vocabulary to hear.

. . .

What We Import: Everything... Nothing was here before us, and nothing is here for us. We do not have the luxury of importing our own Nothing to this place. The United States, like the imperial powers that provisioned journeys to the afterworld at Giza and Xian, has intensely furnished a voyage down into this other world. We fill our ships and planes with Something, we make mock-ups of towns and domestic interiors out of every stitch, inch and ounce of it.

We are simultaneously Potemkin, the Potemkin villagers, and the royalty willfully ignorant of the façade. We have great work to do.

. . .

Winter: no difference between night and day. Summer: no difference between day and night.

. . .

Sept., 1994: Waking To A Window: In these first Antarctic days, my thoughts tumble over each other as if in empathy with the storms outside my dorm window. I'm suddenly the sheltered confidant of an elemental world, witness to the vast wind furious with snow writing itself across the sea ice. Each surge of the gales is matched by the growing incandescence of the sun. Like the lit blossom of a dandelion, it emanates from the froth. Around it, night is luminous with the radiant tones of iris and forget-me-not.

I'm in Dorm 204, on the end closest to Winter Quarters Bay, and on the side that faces McMurdo Sound. The dorms are more or less lined up side by side, giving nearly every room a vista onto another bland brown dorm, but I'm one of a lucky few that have a clear view of how ice has given its quietus to both ocean and mountain. I've swiped a chair from the lounge and wedged it between the foot of my bed and the north wall, right in front of the window. I sit and watch spindrift seethe across the sea ice like spit across a red hot stove.

The weather right now is sometimes atrocious, often miserable, and always stunningly beautiful. During evenings spent alone (I'll have no roommate until October) in the shell of my room, I watch it all in happy disbelief. My dreamlife too is whirling out of control, with images of the world I left behind trying to find anchor in this frozen harbor. Each morning when I wake to my window, the brushstrokes of supernatural light paint me even farther out of the corner of my old expectations.

After work on the worst days I sit and stare through the window for hours. The intense realness of what is happening here faces off against the equally real challenges to perception. The Transantarctic peaks seem 10 miles away, though it's more like 70. There are no smells here but those we bring. Our summer day will be four months long. Snow piles up under clear skies and sets like light cement.

The alien aesthetics dislodge me from what I thought I knew about life on Earth. Here is my Antarctic window, and it contains nothing of the immensity on the other side. I am contained by it, instead, just as much as I am held warm by these walls. Yet through this window I lose myself to this somehow intimate cold chaos.

• • •

Thinking myself into oblivion, happily. And taking notes.

• • •

Imagining The Plateau: Wind fills the white spaces with literal white noise. I imagine, then, that the Ice I cannot see is a monument of wind built upon those sounds whose wavelengths are so great and so cold-shattered that we on the coast are awash in the fall of harsh fragments only.

. . .

No elbows of dark branches against this gossamer sky, no leaves to flutter slightly each time the wind unnerves them. No roots or grass to thread these thin clouds to this ice.

No solace to exchange.

. . .

September is the month for strange skies: nacreous clouds and noctilucent clouds bring weird light to our indigo evenings. Both are at home only in the polar regions, and both only in the long twilight between winter and summer. Noctilucent clouds are over 50 miles high, so high that they're still lit by the sun long after it has set for us. They are bright well into an Antarctic twilight that has already altered our notion of what happens after darkness falls. Little else is known about them.

Nacreous clouds are iridescent and dense, silky and colored like mother-of-pearl: the hues are a muted neon, like oil-on-water but brilliantly backlit. Ten to fifteen miles high, they act as flamboyant catalysts for the atmospheric chemistry that depletes the southern ozone layer.

Our eyes, stunned by the Antarctic world of ice, become useful again, rewarded with these rare and ephemeral sparks that speak to life, however distant.

. . .

Wind: Wind is the journey Antarctica makes into us. For us, working into it, wind is the Antarctic reality, the Antarctic curse. It cuts through layers of our insulation like a practiced knife. There are absurd moments when I try to fight back, trying to be a wind to the wind, trying to numb the numbness, or deny the freezing of flesh.

But to be a force without rest, without existence that senses, tries to know/intuit/guess, is not endurable. To be a force, yes, that's our goal, but recognize the frame: ours, perception, carved by wind. A wind-carved stone is called a ventifact. To work outside in Antarctica is to become a ventifact.

. . .

Antarctica, as the seismically quietest continent, rarely experiences earthquakes. The ice either suppresses actual motion or deadens the perception of it, or both. Knowing that the ice somehow binds the continent so tightly emphasizes my sense of Antarctica as a great simple place, the simplest on Earth.

. . .

Art And Antarctica: Language grows cold. Here we find only unrooted grammar, mere fragments of speech, nothing much to be said. August and September give rise to lyrical syllables, before the declarative phrase of summer utters itself in earnest.

The Ice influences the structure of my thoughts, enacts different forms of silence on how I say what I say.

"Words
fall like rocks at your feet
and stay there."
—Katha Pollitt, from "There," *Antarctic Traveller*

• • •

Now I know: white is blue. Antarctica is not white. Look closely at the snow at your feet, even more closely at the snow out beyond. Where I say white, think pale reflected greys and incremental blues. When you ask which blue, think bruise behind lace. When you think hue, think oblivion.

All we see is surface. What we *say* is white, a cloud.

• • •

Jan., 1997: Fuel: Some of these McMurdo midsummer days are as dazzling to the eye as a prolonged bolt of lightning. My favorite time within them is tending the seven miles of fuel hose that snake from town toward the depot of aviation fuel at Willy Field. The hose is full of food for internal combustion, a lightning bolt buried in the cloud of the ice shelf. The sun-warmed hose melts a trench into the ice and is covered by a crust of drifting snow. We drive alongside the hose, hauling it back to the surface as we go.

My home away from home, a life of machines and controlled lightning under a gently slanting sun, dazzling and forlorn.

Lightning has never been documented in Antarctica, amazingly enough. The tall clouds required for electrical charge are never formed in this cold desert. Only the native summer albedo of all this snow and ice seems electric.

• • •

Art And Antarctica: Each summer, I smuggle words from home to keep me company, to help make sense of this place. I've made expeditions into literature to lay claim to the language of cold open space. Reading Michaux, Gide, Kafka, Pessoa, Jabes, Simic, Celan, etc., I shamelessly lift lines and quotes, thoughts they planted in their own more temperate emptinesses. I will weld their words to this absence, conflate their texts with this white page. Much of it translated already from its original language, I translate it all once again into this unworldly context. I exile to the Ice these already self-exiled writers, in order to derive a literature of Antarctica's own. In my imagination, at least, they thrive.

"You are the task. No pupil far and wide."
—Franz Kafka, *The Blue Octavo Notebooks*

. . .

I write to explain. A silence has blown through me. These words are flags shivering in that wind, but desire, constant desire to explain, is the battle to reach out to, and escape from, this silence.

. . .

Intimacy: People up north always ask about the isolation of my Antarctic work. It's difficult to convey to them that individual isolation is almost impossible to find down here, and that as a community we are extremely busy with the ways and means of American culture. I find conditions claustrophobic, crowded. It's something like ship-life, I think: all our space is shared. In McMurdo, we sleep at least two to a room, and we eat on the cafeteria's schedule.

Life in a field camp offers a taste of cultural isolation, as it mostly places us out of range of the TV and email of McMurdo. But field camp life usually means tighter quarters, more intense cooperation, and a therefore greater sense of enjoined humanity, island-making amidst the isolating (rather than isolated) landscape.

It's a function of talent and initiative to find quiet time in Antarctica. Where to hide, and how long can I hide there? Cook for myself with stolen vegetables in my room, read in a building or tent that isn't used (much) after dayshift, walk out to the horizon, or watch a blizzard sweep through town from the cab of an unused bulldozer.

. . .

Here I am, at play in the fields of the void.

. . .

The Substance Of Cold: Take away any idea of Antarctica you arrived with, and take away the ideas you conjured up in northern conversation; take away the rooms that keep you warm, and the machines that move you between them; take away the calm sunny days in midsummer and anything else that keeps you from shivering, nose-wiping, eye-drying, cheek-rubbing, earlobe-pinching, lip-stretching, and arm-swinging to drive blood back into the cold corners of your body. Remember when you're shoving your fingers into your armpits/pockets/crotch, or praying onto them with a cloud of breath, that you are having the only experience of Antarctica that matters on an ordinary windy day. This is the common dialogue between cold and the body.

. . .

No autumn, no turning of leaves, no apples to pick or winter squash to gather. No crows to punctuate the dying off of forests. No dying where there is no life. No mixed blessing for us to feel in the sudden flight of birds to warmer places. Instead, how little there is to see becomes stark: our eyes, trained to complexity, start to worry.

. . .

Albedo: Albedo is the measure of how much radiating energy, i.e. sunlight, a surface reflects. Antarctica has the highest continental albedo on Earth. It reflects over 80% of all sunlight because it is so perfectly white. More importantly, the whiteness of the Antarctic absorbs so little energy that the sun cannot warm it. The Ice remains ice, remains itself, due in large part to its albedo.

I have loosely translated this physical term for personal purposes because I am interested in Antarctica's capacity to give reflection to thought. For eight summers in the century of human activity on the Ice, I have been busy with the idea that there is much more to say about Antarctica's play on the imagination.

As someone has said, every theory is an autobiography of the theorist, and this is the story of an "I" looking for a blank page. Not a new story, but on a new page, more blank than any other.

Here the geography is so singular that our presence is inseparable from our desire to see: here we are the only figure on the figureless ground we study. This is the bright ground that obsesses me. Where else on Earth could I find such marvelous reflection?

. . .

This place is nothing if not an erasure.

. . .

South Pole: Where else can you feel exactly like a dab of paint on the Earth, a cold steel pin on a map of the Earth? Where else can you feel so well the fragments of space and time wash through you? This hollow wind is cold, racing in from nowhere and continuing on to nowhere, convincing you that you are between Nowheres, physically and philosophically, making you feel both beautiful and afraid, even after you trudge back to the heat behind walls.

. . .

The Plateau: It's hard to say whether being on the Plateau makes the Earth seem tiny or infinite or both. I'm looking right to the curvature of the planet in every direction, nothing but a texture of rough frosting to note the distance, and it strikes me that this sphere beneath me is little more than a tennis ball. On the other hand, if I were to walk the seven and a half miles to the far edge of the white yonder I can see, then perceive the next increment and walk it, and so on and so on until I starve and freeze, I'd know in my dying moments that my increments would scarcely mark a minor portion of this rough manifold earth.

To be standing here, or even at the cluttered Pole on this borderless plain, is to be stretched thin by the imagination's constant quest for place and context: I'm in visual possession of an entire round horizon, and that horizon is only a drop of ice in the sea of cold oblivion.

. . .

Desire creates absence. The more we want, the greater the absence becomes. Here in this nothing we want everything. Which is greater, our emptiness or the emptiness we see around us? The void we feel or the loneliness we fill it with? True absence is not ours, nor ours to fill. But we continue to interrogate silence.

To little avail: what ignores us saves us.

. . .

Memory And Antarctica: Memory always fails against the cold onslaught of time. Ice is time in Antarctica: time is both immoveable and unstoppable, like the ice cap. See the small stones memory places before the inevitable glacier, hear memory calling like an orphan through the abandoned ghetto of its thoughts.

. . .

Frozen wind falling on a graveyard of frozen wind.

. . .

Nov., 2001: Odell Glacier: On calm "nights" in our little amphitheater of ice, we have strange hours of Antarctic noise, gunshots and whispers from the ice itself. At bedtime the sun passes behind the spine of the Allan Hills, shadowing the camp for a few hours. During the passage of this shadow, the ice sheds its stored heat and begins to contract, crack. The firework pops and snaps that accompany the cracking can be heard underfoot, or under our sleeping bags, or from hundreds of meters away.

Some of them, though, force a dense susurrus of air from the ice which can last much longer than the crack itself. Like the whoosh in the instant a peal of thunder begins, their breathy sounds hurtle past us like bottle rockets. But they're much gentler, like whistling brush-strokes fishtailing into our ears. Like the echoes of a bullwhip, like ecstatic snakes of air, they are the sighs that follow the glacier's shiver.

. . .

There is nothing the color of blood in this country.

. . .

What intimacy is possible with this place? Not as much as I feel. How much loneliness do I find in the Plateau landscape? Not as much as I feared. The proximity of my life to this death, and the fact that my shadow is constructed by what objects I carry with me, contribute to the suspicion that I am scarcely here at all.

· · ·

I am very much capable of joy, but I do not carry it with me. It is a craft, one I have to relearn every time.

At these latitudes, and when the only sign of life is human, joy is the easiest and hardest lesson to be learned.

· · ·

The cold insisting itself into you like love, and never leaving.

· · ·

"What being are you set on being?"
—Henri Michaux, *Tent Posts*

Difficult to answer in the Antarctic, because while the landscape opens me like a book, it provides nothing specific by which I can define myself. The land is foreign to us, and our work is alien within it.

Hard to belong, except wishfully, to the passion within the brief human history I am mostly passing through, balancing awe with a paycheck, a transient able only to propose a version of being that includes emptiness and transience.

. . .

"It was a most remarkable thing to witness a snow-petrel, small, light and fragile, making headway over the sea in the face of a seventy mile hurricane, fluttering down through the spindrift..."
—Douglas Mawson, *Home Of The Blizzard*

Dec. 15, 2001: As I plowed snow from the runway in a windy overcast post-blizzard day, I glanced up just as two snow petrels passed in front of me. Few things could be more surprising out here than the pulsing of wings.

Drifts have half-buried the runway and our camp in hardened snow. An enormous storm has reached all the way up from the coast to smother us. McMurdo has drifts several feet deep on its streets and airfield. We have to plow out what was our sparkling blue-ice landing zone.

And now through all this strange whiteness, beating upwind into the teeth of a blustery 30-knot wind, come even stranger fragments of albedo, 40 hard miles from the coast and food. I thought at first they were two chunks of snow uplifted by the machine and hurled by the wind, but no, they had wings, and were moving slowly up toward the ice cap instead of whipping end-for-end downglacier.

Snow petrels are among the most beautiful birds and seem like the perfect Antarctic totem. Pure white and graceful, they flutter over open water and the vast south polar pack ice for their food. Snow petrels tend to nest in the rocky outcrops and nunataks of Antarctica, sometimes more than 100 miles from the sea. Inland Antarctica, where no terrestrial life greater than lichen exists, is a hell of a place to nest.

In the time it took me to take the tractor out of gear, drop the bucket, and jump out onto the ice, a few seconds, they were gone. Focus came hard in the flat light under milky clouds, and it's harder still in such a light to find two creatures so camouflaged as to seem inanimate. The petrels might have been just upwind, flapping invisibly, or they may have veered well out of range. I actually looked down to see if they might be resting at my feet.

The brief experience was almost visionary, or at least unnerving. Did I really see two small pearl-white birds with rounded heads and oil-black beaks? Did I invent them to keep me company?

What better gift, in a day full of hardness (hard snow on hard ice between hard stone ridges under a hard wind and light) to have flash before me these two soft creatures? Hard-nosed birds, no doubt, supremely adapted, and a rare miracle to a tired eye.

· · ·

The ice sheet returns my stare. Each of us a small peninsula into the other.

· · ·

Dec. 26, 1957: "Silence is now my bitterest enemy. Like a sorcerer in a magic hat, it stretches its cold hands through the porthole of my cabin and chokes me. It's an audible silence, a white river of time with a slippery bed. I wonder what the others feel?"
—Juhan Smuul, *Antarctica Ahoy*

Smuul waxes poetic and lonely in his first days near the continent. He hears silence, despite the steady noises of boat, plane and helicopter. This poetic silence is a fine example of either the power of imagination or the power of Antarctica to demand answers from the imagination.

It's quite common, especially in first experiences of the Ice, to talk of an overpowering silence regardless of the noise we make. And I think this is an honest perspective. The silence comes not so much from an aural experience as from a visual one: we look out onto empty icescapes, find ourselves intuiting the silence that hovers right outside the portholes of our perception.

. . .

Penguin Love: Penguins = Antarctica? Nonsense. Do we understand Australia by its surfers? The Great Lakes by the houses on their shores? Our bodies by the dirt under our nails?

. . .

The back-up beeper is the birdcall of McMurdo Station. A hundred forklifts, trucks, tracked vehicles, and bulldozers cry out to each other, giving warning, marking turf. How many untold thousands of these beeps are sung out daily?

McMurdo is a mechanical garden, a foreign grove amid the native clear-cut. And its birds sing out stridently "Watch out, watch out! We are moving backwards! Watch out!"

. . .

Here is the garden of absences.

. . .

The more I stare, the less I see. But I write more and more, to encircle with a thin dark line of fine print the absence that expands before my very eyes.

. . .

Albedo: I am a wick, these words my flame. The ice is our white wax. We are a pale candle in this light.

I write against the emptiness, the more to express it. I don't warm to my words as much as I study the space around them.

. . .

Memory And Antarctica: The things we say about the Ice are mostly what inhabit the Ice. The coast and the Convergence harbor exceptions, but as science knows, these are diffuse lines between poorly-defined regions. Like memory.

There are few borders between memory and imagination. There are even fewer to be found as we gape out across the borderless regions of the Plateau.

And what frame do we have for dividing the past, or for dividing the past from the present, while summer sleeps with its one eye open?

. . .

Albedo: Black may be the color of space, but white is the color of time. All colors sinter into one, or none, just as all moments annihilate, or fuse with, each other.

. . .

For some, Antarctica is the great white dove, a symbol of peace—geopolitical hope—and when the nomadic ground blizzards sweep over the nations of emptiness that form the Plateau, I can believe it.

. . .

"Get rid of words and meaning, and there is still poetry."
—Yang Wan-li, *Heaven My Blanket, Earth My Pillow*

Get rid of ice and stone, and is there still Antarctica? The land *is* writ on the consciousness of the few who have wandered it. I think that this is Yang Wan-li's poetry: the natural rhythms of nature in the mind.

Without the ice, is it still Antarctica? Lord knows, but the species who named it will not be around to think about it. The window onto existence given to humans will surely end before the ice slides off the continent, or the continent slides out of the polar region.

Without poetry, is it still Antarctica? This is harder to answer. While each has little to do with the other, words and meaning are similarly detached from both.

. . .

You could show a movie on this storm. No soundtrack, no tune, just the static and howl of the whirling reels, the slapping of the brittle film-end against your face.

. . .

Albedo: Memory And Antarctica: What We Leave Behind: Now that I'm preparing to leave, the Antarctica of the imagination includes the memory of myself within it, and this is both the best and worst tool I have for mapping such emptiness. The memory of the self in a place is what gives that place boundaries; this is how we make a garden (in the mind) of a wilderness. The vast openness of the Antarctic challenges this mental operation, however, and makes it clear how our claim to familiarity can be a pretense.

The landscape of the mind I've inherited from my experiences projects small dark figures against the white backdrop. They are features that cannot take root; I imagine them (me) always moving, never part of the land, like the snowmobile at AGO 1 racing back and forth to briefly tame the white surface.

The albedo of Antarctica also deflects our image and our efforts.

However intense our time on the Ice may be for us, it is not a trans-figured land we are leaving. The ice is unchanged. Our memories root themselves deeply within us but cannot find traction on the ice. We are mapping ourselves onto the ice as much as we are mapping the surface for our use.

The fact that nearly everyone who has left the Ice is haunted by their memories of it shows how impossible it is to conclude the mapping. Like the topographic maps which draw a helpless line in the shifting sands of the Plateau, at their "limit of observation," the visitor to the Antarctic fails to bring the strangeness within comprehension. We leave behind the journeying part of ourselves, unfinished and in awe.

• • •

"A tranquil country, sealed away."
—Andre Gide, *Amyntas*

Sealed away inside me, Antarctica travels around my mind like a lake through a turbulent river. My thoughts run to it as if to a country I long for but cannot find. Tranquility amid anxiety, and from now onward we are traveling companions.

ELLIS AVERY

Seventeen Reasons
2003
(selections)

In 1999, Ellis Avery and a friend began a daily exchange of fragments in haiku form. The following selections are from daily haiku Avery wrote in 2003.

+ + +

1/6

Home. Home. My own mess,
the radiator noises.
Streetlamps, snow.

1/10

Loud, on her cell phone:
He's a great guy, you know?
I found a great guy.

1/12

What is that, a fake rose?
A cabbage bloom, with
outer leaves removed.

1/14

> Maxine Hong Kingston
> kept the red leaf I gave her
> in October!

1/15

> Night. One sidewalk drunk
> to another: *Let's get that*
> *hat back on your head.*

1/17

> She reads, her bare feet
> propped on the table,
> one toe painted red.

1/28

> The cars, the sidewalks,
> the outside steps: white
> with salt, not snow.

1/31

> Night, silver-wrapped
> sticks of gum
> scattered on the sidewalk.

2/5

> Across the street,
> red tenements wet with rain.
> I've lived here five years.

2/9

Icicles curving
off the little tin roof
of the takoyaki stand.

2/11

My back to the
radiator, my face to
the snowy window.

2/16

Old snow.
A draggle-tailed squirrel.
A tree trunk eaten into lace.

2/18

Snow upon snow.
Each of us alive,
so small.

2/20

Warm spot underfoot
by the bedroom door
where you meowed for breakfast.

3/2

The raindrops, bright
on each twig, like the promise
of buds.

3/14

    Eating hot curried mussels
    with my fingers
    in the dark.

3/20

    War, stomach cramps.
    Sleepless night, sluggish morning.
    Seltzer. B52s.

3/29

    Astor Place. He's sitting
    on his skateboard,
    sketching.

4/9

    The petting zoo
    in the snow. Llamas,
    looking sarcastic.

4/10

    Train roars overhead:
    a little snow drifts off the bridge,
    falls through sunlight.

4/15

    The shadow of a bird
    through the curtain.
    Sweet bean, bitter tea.

4/16

> Evening. Warm air. Bare skin.
> Women, rolled-up yoga mats
> under their arms.

4/20

> A girl with an orange
> cat in a birdcage. The
> gutter white with petals.

4/29

> Lisa's new Paris street,
> too narrow for cars. Moss
> furs the cobblestones.

5/4

> Paris café, alone.
> A man takes my picture:
> I'm local color!

5/7

> A cup of green tea,
> the quiet pivot between
> a bad day and a good one.

5/16

> Are they making themselves
> a bed of flowers, the squirrels
> in Sharon's garden?

5/18

On the lamps, plastic bags
with pictures of chandeliers.
I love New York.

5/23

My legs bent
to bend with hers, my pillow
tilted the same tilt.

5/25

Rain. The lush mint
has grown overnight. I dreamed
the twin towers were back.

5/26

Huge new plum leaves,
green instead of purple. The
New York rainforest.

6/6

Bulldog, ugly
at both ends. Your tail looks like
a bellybutton.

7/7

On the sidewalk
a pool of chocolate
around an ice-cream cone.

7/8

Ambling in the dusk,
she tells her cell phone,
Sorry, I'm not out yet.

7/9

Sound of cars,
cool breath of morning.
How to stop time: sit still.

7/17

I can die now: Sharon,
this quilt on the wall,
this unfinished poem.

7/18

Cloudy crescent moon.
It looks like your ear,
she says.

7/20

Night, the furred brown
rump of a mouse
diving off the counter.

7/23

After four silent years
the marooned dog howls
in the blue lightning.

7/24

Three hours early
to the airport. Three sparrows
in the hall.

7/25

Helsinki street trash,
two kinds of green: spent pea pods,
strawberry tops.

8/3

Only sturdy Finnish
children—and Sharon—will swim
in that cold lake.

8/11

New York doves don't nest,
they plonk a few twigs on an
air conditioner.

8/14

No power on the
Eastern seaboard. Cup one hand
inside the other.

8/24

She lets me stare at
the dress she made, bejewelled
with macaroni.

9/2

> Two thirds of the year
> gone. Rain yesterday,
> rain today.

9/3

> Smokers tucked under
> the café awning. Rain on
> my taut umbrella.

9/4

> On Saint Mark's Place, a
> procession of one, skateboard
> balanced on his head.

9/6

> These clear September days,
> the Empire State Building
> could be next.

9/9

> Landing with a soft flap
> on my windowsill:
> green leaf, brown edges.

9/11

> Memorials on
> the radio, relief:
> no new bad news.

9/12

> Hard wind,
> greenish moon.
> New season.

9/30

> My blue wool scarf
> balled up all summer:
> still creased.

10/3

> My mother's hair,
> glossy in the sun
> as her cab pulls away.

10/5

> Tap! Sharon at the door,
> tea on a tray?
> No, bluejay at the window.

10/7

> Three kinds of hot water:
> lemon-honey, green tea, bath.
> Get well Sharon.

10/8

> Two men in suits
> hail a cab, kiss open-mouthed.
> Only one gets in.

10/10

> Crossing 2nd Avenue,
> a book in my hand,
> my name on the cover.

10/20

> Pigeon on my stairway,
> smacking its head
> each flight up.

10/24

> Elderly doorman
> does push-ups on the railing
> in his suit jacket.

11/5

> On my airshaft tree,
> no leaves
> until March.

11/8

> Eclipse:
> a brown pane of glass
> over the moon.

11/9

> Falling leaves in the
> cigarette ads. Fallen leaves
> in the front hall.

11/14

> Why does the water
> in the toilet *do* that
> when the wind blows hard?

12/10

> Eleven days,
> and they'll start getting
> longer again.

12/15

> Falling snow
> the Köln concert
> Sharon's foot in my hand

MATT CARDIN

There Is No Grand Scheme:
From a Life Journal in Progress
(selections)

PART ONE (1994–1997)
Enchanting Metamorphoses

3/24/94, 12:20 a.m.

What is a thinker? An experiencer? A doer? A knower? What am I when I am doing or playing the role of these things?

I feel that I can somehow "bend" my awareness back on itself. I discovered how to do this quite by accident when I was in junior high school, and although I have forgotten about it for months and years at a time, I am now trying to learn to sustain the experience, because it is slippery and elusive.

It takes several minutes of uninterrupted concentration for me to slip into this state, and if I do it too often, it becomes harder to achieve, almost like a muscle that has been overexerted and cannot flex again until it has rested. When I do achieve that state of heightened self-awareness, which usually lasts for only a few seconds at a time, my main feeling is one of intense strangeness and wonder. I think, "What the hell am I doing in this body? What is a *person?*" From this vantage point, my normal state of consciousness seems like a form of sleep, and I am intensely curious about who and what I really am. I begin to feel that everyday existence is rather like a dream. This is the most prominent theme: the feeling that everything is a dream.

Then these very thoughts and reflections begin to distract me, and an instant later I am kicked or dragged out of the experience and back to earth.

After these episodes I invariably refer back to the many things I have read about mystical experiences, in order to see whether I now understand them any better. I consider the words of Jesus, Lao Tzu, and the Zen koans to find out whether they are any less opaque. Most generally, they are not.

4/3/94

I feel first and think afterward. Thoughts are a coda to feeling.

4/5/94

Sometimes (such as now) I feel as if it is impossible to care about anything, because the result would be unbearable pain and disappointment. Oppenheimer was speaking truth when he said the world is going to hell in a handbasket. And this is why I find it unacceptable to care: because caring is painful and futile. If we care, we set ourselves up for misery, and it makes no difference anyway. The eastern view that everything is as it should be may indeed have the drawback of devaluing any specific occurrence or action, but it is the only alternative to driving myself mad with despair.

Actually, there is another alternative, but I can't accept it because it just isn't true. Tonight at work, as a preface to something else, I mentioned to L. that everything is rapidly going to hell, and he responded by saying, "No, it's not." Then he explained that he honestly thinks the world is getting better, not worse. He didn't give any real reasons for his opinion, but I was quite surprised to find someone expressing this kind of optimism.

8/23/94, Tuesday, 11-something p.m.

The arrow through the heart—how vividly I can understand the meaning of the symbol. Not that I've had any great revelation of love recently. But I think the arrow through the heart is a symbol not only of romantic love, but of life in its essence. Life is suffering, wounded, tragic. And the piercing pain in the chest is more than just a metaphor. Sometimes I think it's going to suffocate me.

9/13/94, Tuesday, 11:00 p.m.

Sometimes one view seems plausible, sometimes another.

There is a position which holds that if I receive a sudden inspiration for a song, a poem, a story, and I happen to forget it because I don't have access to a keyboard or pencil or typewriter—don't worry. Don't clutch these inspirations as if they were nuggets of gold. Rather, simply wait until you have the opportunity to write, and then write another poem. Wait until you're near a keyboard and then compose another song. The act of creating is a manifestation of the rhythms of energy in the universe, and what can be recorded in tangible form at one time is no more valuable than what might be recorded, or forgotten, at another.

Then there is another position which holds the previous one to be nonsense. Some ideas *are* more important than others, and their loss is a real loss, something to regret.

Sometimes one view seems plausible, sometimes another. I've rehashed it so many different times in my head and on paper that it seems a waste of energy to write of it. Each position grows from a distinct worldview, and therefore is internally justified. How do I get *beyond* worldviews?

9/17/94, Saturday around 7:20 p.m.
(Reading *The Birth of Tragedy* behind Glen's theater)

My consciousness, my ego, is like a bee buzzing around inside my skull. It observes all that goes on outside and buzzes madly trying to figure it all out, but it has no actual contact with what it observes. I tend to get very frustrated when I try to grasp certain concepts in the books I read, because I try to analyze them intellectually. My intellectual life is a very large part of my entire life, but some things are closed to it. I am beginning to have a faint glimmering of understanding of the "non-linear," "lateral" thinking I have read so much about. In religious terms, acceptance of the idea that my conscious awareness cannot grasp and control everything, that this is not something to be afraid of—indeed, that the most important things in life are out of my control and in perfectly capable hands—would be called faith.

9/28/94, Wednesday, 11:20 p.m.

I had another "break" in my worldview today. I was at work and very near the end of Schumacher's *A Guide for the Perplexed* when I felt my attitude start to shift. I could actually *feel* it begin, and as always, I resolved to hold resolutely to my current view. But then, also as always, I suddenly realized, "Why?" and let the floodgate open.

This inner shift is always followed by a sense of elation. I am a *new person* immediately after a change of reality tunnels. I feel completely free, open-ended, and excited at the thought that I can and do believe *whatever I want*. Nothing is True. Everything is Permitted. Indeed. When I first became consciously aware of these perspective shifts during my senior year of college, I was aware of this strange elation. I can vividly remember my sense of wonder and excitement when I shifted from a kind of Theodore Roszak-influenced romantic naturism to the opposite pole of pure nihilism. My thought was, "Hey, I don't *have* to believe this certain way! I am absolutely free to change my mind!"

Then, of course, I shifted into true believer mode with regard to my new attitude, and remained there until the next shift. What I am now learning to do is to have fun with the given worldview of the moment while realizing its contingency.

It's interesting that this process I am describing, this fluidity of world-views, which completely disregards the possible existence of a truth which is true in its own right and which forces itself upon one and demands to be recognized as true—this process actually *encompasses* the idea of objective, exclusive truth, since some of the worldviews into which I regularly shift are ones that recognize and/or are based upon the recognition of such truths.

10/9/94, Sunday, 11 p.m.

I noticed things much more clearly than usual during the drive home from work tonight. My sense of sight seemed particularly acute. A few days ago it was my sense of *touch* that seemed particularly awake. As I sat in chairs or stood or leaned or lifted things, I was very aware of the feeling of objects on my skin, and of the pressure they exerted as they pressed into my flesh. It occurred to me that it seemed as if things were *telling me they existed* through my sense of touch. They were using this sense to remind me of their presence. Tonight the same impression overtook my sense of sight.

11/25/94, Friday, 7:35 p.m.

A passing note on music, life, and despair: whenever I listen to beautiful music, I feel joy and despair at the same time—joy at the beauty and meaning embodied in the music, despair because the rest of life isn't like this at all. I am filled with an aching desire to do nothing but lie down and continue listening, to be consumed by the music and, just possibly, drift off into oblivion. I suppose this might be condemned as a desire to retreat from life, a negative and escapist version of the Theravada Buddhist's desire for self-annihilation. But it's what I truly feel.

1/19/95, Thursday, 11:35 p.m.

For me, the most damaging single thought for any belief, the one that keeps blasting to pieces every faint glimmering of certitude that I might otherwise feel, is this: the mere fact that something seems true or right to me does not make it so. My perspective is limited. Every day I come in contact with multitudes of conflicting ideas and claims which I am incapable of judging. I have encountered the idea that human logic is a part of the world and therefore fundamentally related to it; that what seems logically true is in fact true—but I have also encountered the opposite of this view, which states that logic and reason are fine as far as they go, but they are by no means the only way of knowing.

But if they aren't, *what is?* What is the meaning of intuition? In the face of myriad conflicting claims to truth and the fact that each seems plausible at different times, what am I to do? There is no way of judging among them, for the very basis and method of judging is called into question, and I second-guess my second guesses. It's a hall of mirrors and I can never find the one objective vantage point from which to see truly, maybe because such a vantage point doesn't exist. I am, in effect, paralyzed.

3/13/95, 1:30 p.m.

The existential realization of my own finitude and inseparableness from my flesh-and-blood life is indeed tragic, nihilistic, fatalistic, etc.—but only from the viewpoint of the rational mind. And just who do I want to be? Do I want to cram myself into a single corner of my nature and identify with it alone? Pretty foolish, really. There is more to me than reason, and who is to say that there is a hard and fast division between the different aspects of me? And what is self-evident about the idea that reason is naturally superior? To the mind that thinks it, it is, but that mind is hard-pressed to offer reasons that are compelling to everyone. The rational mind, in speaking rationally, speaks only to itself.

8/11/95, Friday, 7:58 a.m.

The fact is, I can only understand things from where I stand. This recognition does not do away with objectivity entirely, but it does mean that there are various levels of it. I may try to encompass a situation with my awareness, and relative to that situation I may attain a certain degree of objectivity. But my awareness is never *completely* objective. It is always included within, comprehended by, a context of some sort. Objectivity runs from less to more, but it is never absolute. With regard to the fact of my very existence, objectivity is impossible. In other words, I am always aware *from* somewhere.

6/18/96, Tuesday, 9:15 a.m.

I'm becoming painfully aware of just how manipulative I am, or try to be, in my everyday interactions with other people. Instead of just letting others be what they are, instead of letting them speak and act naturally, I frequently try to elicit from them the responses I want. Having lived for many years as this body/mind, as this finite identity, I am intimately aware on a subconscious level of exactly how I must act and speak, given the facts of my physical appearance and particular personality, in order to elicit a desired response. If I want someone to laugh, I will act and speak in one way. If I want sympathy, I will act and speak in another way, and so on. I have noticed that some of the people around me tend toward this manipulative kind of interaction too, while others appear to relate to people on a more genuine level.

I am not doing anyone a favor by playing his or her game, by giving the desired response to his or her performance, nor is anyone doing me a favor by playing *my* game.

The funny thing is, I don't even know why I want certain responses from people. It's almost entirely an automatic process, from first feeling to finished performance.

PART TWO (2002–2003):
More Than One Can Say

11/17/02, Sunday, 11:35 a.m.

Weird apocalyptic feeling pervading things, pervading life and the world—lately it's gone from being something merely, or mostly, of aesthetic interest, i.e. a justified subject mainly fit for science fiction and horror entertainment, to being a matter of real existential fear. This, now, today, this era which goes back about a year or two, at least to 9/11/01, and actually a bit before, is an era characterized by a more serious fear and dread of the universal destruction of life and civilization than has existed since the height of the cold war. Before that, World War II was damned scary to most everyone around the world, and then the cold war brought once more an icy tension to life.

But today the feeling is significantly different. More than just a sense of physical danger and dread at the possibility of universal destruction in some great conflagration, it's a creeping, gnawing sense that things are degenerating into chaos, and that all attempts to stem the decay are just more frantic flailings that are doomed to inevitable failure. That's the sense I get from world news, local news, political statements, people on the street, family members. Last night my father-in-law said to me, "You know, this world is in sorry shape right now." That sort of sums it up for me.

Of course, I write these things from the viewpoint of a thirty-something, white, middle-class American who has never encountered this type of uncertainty before. If I had been born twenty or fifty years earlier, or had been born into one of several possible alternate ethnic groups or nationalities, I might have had this apocalyptic sense for many years now. Surely a large part of my current unease is due to the sheer unfamiliarity of feeling a real sense of imminent danger and chaos. The feeling is old hat to others in this world, and has shaped their lives from their youngest years.

But this is life as it feels to me today, being who and what I am via a combination of heredity, environment, and personal choice. I can only wonder how the feeling will work to shape me and others like me in years to come—if indeed there are very many years left for any of us to be shaped.

5/2/03, Saturday, 9:30 a.m.

Plot/thematic idea: God is an infinite being that suffers from multiple personality disorder. We, the 10,000 things and beings, are His/Her/Its self-projections. There is no final happy ending to our restless quest for wholeness, integration, spiritual fulfillment, for the Absolute that we reach when we attain transcendence is *nothing* in and of Itself. Its essence is formless, is in fact nothing more nor less than the desire/psychosis that leads it to dissociate into the 10,000 things.

7/11/03, Friday, 8:32 a.m.

Aphoristic writing, and indeed any other type of writing that is directly dependent on the author's immediate, fleeting intuition, insight, mood, or state of mind or soul, is the type of writing that makes the most demands on the reader, for it requires the reader to be in the same state of mind in order for the writing to be understood. You grasp an aphorism instantly, effortlessly, through a kind of intense, exhilarating inner identification with its meaning and truth, or else you do not grasp it at all. And you may grasp the same aphorism once and yet not again at a later date—perhaps *never* again.

More: you may *write* an aphorism, as a direct, explosive expression of something you feel and know with your whole body and soul, and later find that it is now closed, perhaps forever, even to you.

7/14/03, Monday, 1:58 p.m.

The sickly emptiness of having, owning, *collecting* things, *any* things at all. Once you have your items arranged and arrayed, what do they do for you? What do you do with them besides admire them and then want something else, something more, something you can't possibly name or imagine, but whose absence fills you with a kind of sickened, clawing desperation? The more you collect things, the more your desperate emptiness weighs down inside you.

7/18/03, Friday, 9:00 a.m.

A dream from last night:

A young woman—capable, intelligent, pretty, perhaps in her early twenties—is babysitting a young boy of around eight years old during a period of some mounting global crisis. Perhaps the crisis revolves around a series of paranormal or supernatural eruptions. It has already put the young woman on edge and given her a sense of unease, but the young boy is exuberant and playful. He asks her to accompany him down to the basement, where he wants to show her something.

They descend to the basement, where the young woman stands and shifts uneasily while the boy produces a rubber mask. He tells her it is a *special* mask, because whoever wears it turns *into* it; whoever wears it really becomes the monster it depicts. The mask is green and vaguely reptilian in appearance, with irregular, roundish eyeholes and a twisted, jagged hole for a mouth. The boy says he wants to put it on and show her what he means. She agrees to this.

He dons the mask and begins to hunch his body and growl in an obviously fake manner, just like any child playing at being a scary monster. The young woman watches and tries to appear amused despite her continued unease.

Then, in a split second, everything changes. The eyeholes in the mask twitch and stretch and come to life with a blackish-crimson glow. The mouth animates into a bizarrely twisted organic maw with some sort of whiplike, tentacular feelers coiling out around the edges. The light in the room vanishes, and in the pitch darkness the boy—or whatever it is now—lets out a hiss or screech as it moves in an impossibly jerky, monstrous, horrifyingly rapid manner toward the young woman. She screams in terror, her own mouth and eyes wide, and recoils.

Suddenly, the light snaps back on and there is her boyfriend, whom she had been expecting to arrive at the house earlier, standing in the doorway. He has descended the stairs and flipped on the light switch. In the electric illumination the boy is now just a boy again. He removes the mask as the young woman throws herself against her boyfriend, shaking and weeping in hysterical fear, and tries to explain what has just happened. The boy, for his part, becomes confused and starts to cry at the recognition of how horrified she is at him. Sobbing, he says he was only playing.

Recalling this dream right now, I remember that during it, I some-how knew with utter certainty that the monster the boy had trans-formed into was really him, was his real self, his true identity. He truly was that monstrous thing, and he indeed took the young woman down to the basement for the express purpose of doing violence to her. Moreover, his transformation into the monster was somehow connected to the strange supernatural crisis that had over-taken the outside world.

And yet, I also knew that he was sincere in his tears. He really was upset at the attitude of suspicion and horror that the young woman, and then her boyfriend, directed at him. He was both the boy and the monster, possessing the appropriate, natural attitudes and emotions for each of their respective identities, and in his little-boy-ness, in the boy aspect of him, he couldn't understand the woman's horror and was devastated by such looks and emotions being directed at him. In other words, he couldn't figure out what he had done wrong. He thought he had only wanted to play, even though his game was deadly.

7/21/03, Monday, 9:35 a.m.

The only lasting, substantial change in one's self, in one's outlook and sensed point of balance, the only changes that may accurately be termed authentic transformations, are the involuntary ones, the ones that arise *into* one's awareness and mood and outlook from the unconscious, from the wider, deeper, higher aspects of one's total self. Conscious decisions to modify this or that behavior or outlook or thought process are worse than useless, for they may fool one into believing that something has really changed, when in truth such conscious decisions and efforts at self-reformation are nothing more than expressions of the *current* state, the state that one desires to escape from.

Even the desire to escape a given state, to change oneself, may be almost wholly an expression of the despised state itself. It's all rather like a vicious, self-perpetuating feedback loop, like a spiritual/psychological cul-de-sac with a fake "Exit" sign posted above the brick wall at the end of the alleyway.

7/24/03, Thursday, 8:33 a.m.

In my past journals, many years' worth of them, I was always trying to reach some sort of fundamental resolution, to arrive at an articulated philosophy of life that would be permanent and would encompass me and *become* my life. And I did this even as I was sometimes writing about the fact that no theory can ever encompass the theorizer, the existential subject.

There has been a fundamental, ground-level shift in the way I regard this activity of writing down my thoughts and impressions. I am now almost sickened with a kind of weary disgust, a sense of hopelessness, when I think of writing in these pages with that former goal standing in back of the effort. This journal is now more the equivalent of footprints in the sand, a record of my passing simply as it has occurred, not as I have tried to reify or consolidate it into any sort of verbally expressible meaning.

7/31/03, Thursday, around 12:15 p.m.

The appreciation of a given author's work, in the form of an intense, immediate sense of identification with it, may be due as much or more to an effortless, intuitive resonance with the author's *voice* as it is to any particular content or thematic focus. Thus, learning to appreciate the work of an author with whom one does not share this affinity is a matter of learning to understand this author's voice or style, his or her manner of speaking on the page. A work may be written in a foreign tongue even though it is penned in one's native language.

8/1/03, Friday, 9:15 a.m.

Maybe an abiding sense of contentment with the simple reality of the present moment comes only after one has so grievously exhausted oneself with efforts in the other direction that the very thought of expending even an ounce more energy on the search for a lasting, "codified" happiness of the abstract kind automatically fills one with a great weariness, and more, with a positive sense of loathing and disgust.

Such present-moment satisfaction arrived at in this self-damaging manner is not at all an affair of bubbling joy and lightness. It's just a deep, quiet, soft sense of recognition that this is all there is; that this, whatever "this" is, is it. And both the "this-ness" and the realization or recognition of it are empty, internally colorless, subjectively hollow, not in a disillusioned or bitter sense but in the sense of having *no* sense, of simply being what they are aside from all those former attempts to make them into more or other, or to find reality and satisfaction in some fabricated elsewhere and elsewhen.

Again: contentment with the present moment comes when the search for something else is recognized—immediately, intuitively, effortlessly—as a source of suffering; or rather, such searching is recognized *as* suffering, as being the source and expression of suffering itself.

8/12/03, Tuesday, 3:53 p.m.

There is an ideal landscape that resides in the mind. It rarely, if ever, surfaces into awareness, instead remaining shadowy and misty and undefined in the twilight borderland between the conscious and unconscious minds, where it acts as the unarticulated fount and focal point of that infinite longing, that inconsolable wound, whose passion wells up from time to time.

Occasionally, unexpectedly, an outer vista beheld with the physical eyes will conform in great measure to that undefined inner one, and suddenly, as you drive across a level expanse in autumn with russet colors painting the earth and sky, and with smooth ponds lying in cool sheets amidst farmer's browning fields, the longing rises up and locks hands with the outside world, and you can hardly bear the burning pressure of the unfillable sweet craving that at that moment seems to be the only true thing in all the universe.

8/14/03, Thursday, 4:16 p.m.

This voice that comes out whenever I try to speak my truest, deepest thoughts and feelings, this voice that sounds so pretentious and artificial and contrived in my own ears—this isn't my true voice, the voice of who I really am. But it's all that anyone will ever hear.

9/1/03, Monday, 9:14 p.m.

Philosophical thought should end the moment the pen leaves the page, or the moment the impulse to reflect and philosophize has come to an end. To try to "live" one's philosophy is tantamount to trying to live a scripted life. Philosophies grow out of life, not vice versa.

My adult life has been a witness to the awkwardness and stiltedness of trying to live a philosophy instead of having one's philosophy created and actuated in the course of living itself.

The danger, one feels, if one is a congenital philosopher, is that one will slide into inauthenticity or become foolish or brutish, or otherwise somehow spiral down to a sickeningly low level of morality and intellect, if one consents to live too freely without also turning back to one's reflective thought processes and trying to bring one's life and the world into alignment with one's philosophical principles and conclusions. And the supreme irony of it all is that by doing this, by insisting on trying to live consciously from and for a philosophy, one becomes more foolish, brutish, and inauthentic than one had ever allowed oneself to fear or suspect.

Philosophy as the articulation of the wisdom that one arrives at—or that arises into one's life—through the act of living and paying attention. That is, this must be, the only kind worthy of attending to. And even this is best forgotten as soon as one has finished thinking or reading about it. To do otherwise, to cling to it, is to betray its deepest principles.

YANNIS RITSOS

Monochords

(#300–336)

*Yannis Ritsos (1909–1990), Greece's most popular
poet, wrote the sequence of 336 monochords (of which
the last 37 are printed here) within a single month in
August 1979 while in exile on the island of Samos;
they were published by Kedros in Athens one year later.
The following is from a new translation of the complete monochords by Paul Merchant.*

+ + +

300
The sawdust that fell from your hair, I find in my poem today.

301
Under the still page, a great wind drives the ships on to the rocks.

302
The trumpeters came down from Mycenae without a word.

303
A secret light multiplied in mirror fragments.

304
Repetition: confirmation of an undefined significance.

305
Declaiming in the Market, among the scales, broomsticks, butchers' stalls.

306
They've gone. Solitude. The blue sky takes a deep breath.

307
They broke the drums and hid them in their manuscripts.

308
Dead city. The heralds came. Broken statues.

309
Everyone has a little story. Throw some more lime on it.

310
The white chapel on the mountain still holds your secret, my country.

311
Swimmers, a rowboat, summer, a body, the guitar against a tree.

312
Impoverished evening. Down by the ocean the roar of engines.

313
Soldiers, boots, curses. Mother, say a prayer.

314
Summer islands without bookstores. Wet towels on the line.

315
Late evening, distant voices of children, women, and lost years.

316
The new moon came out above my poems.

317
I have no secrets left. They've lit the lamps down by the harbor.

318
What were you going to do about the wild geese and the shuttered
hotels?

319
I carved a stone with care; threw it behind the door.

320
The old woman came from Myli with a basket of tomatoes so she
could enter my poem.

321
What rhapsodies the youthful old man played for us on a single
string.

322
Back then, a dilapidated garden gate took up the whole city.

323
Pale morning orisons. Corpses on the sidewalks. Black rocks.
History.

324
Pictures, lamps, memories, a train, dreams, words above all.

325
Petros barefoot, Alexis in sandals, you in buskins.

326
He still loves beautiful things. His wickedness shows when he
speaks.

327
Sun-drenched irresponsibility. Sunday. Marble stairs down to the
garden.

328
What a great tan we got on vacation, from the sun and amnesia.

329
Quiet night creatures, smelling the roses, patrolling the walls.

330
With a piece of chalk I drew on the blackboard the moon's golden eyebrow.

331
The sound of drums, distant voices, smoke. And statues in the hospital corridors.

332
A pair of iron pliers swinging in infinite air.

333
Vowels, consonants, vocalizing, consorting, falling silent in profound impartiality.

334
Now they've taken off his muzzle how can he speak?

335
You, Greece, blessing my bread and my pages.

336
So you'll know—these monochords are my keys. Take them.

- Karlovasi, Samos, August 1 to September 1, 1979

KAREN AN-HWEI LEE

Anthropomorphism
(on blindness, glass, & orchids)

(selections)

WITHERING BUT NOT FALLING

A poem was finished on a spring afternoon. I laid it aside. A year later, I found it in a childhood closet, forgetting why I thought the past was a safe hiding place. It could have been lost, almost thrown away. I was glad to see it again. You're not such a bad poem. I often grow fonder of poems once thought lost, no matter what rough shape they're in. It's you again. I thought you'd left.

EPIPHYTE

You write a fragment called *epiphyte* and lay it aside, whispering roots of an orchid drop from the veined arm of a banyan, an orchid perched in air sends down air-breathing roots loose and voiceless as uncut hair, remember the translucent roots of the elephantine orchid flourishing on the wall of a house where you once lived as a child, a house with a courtyard of red tiles where you heard black crickets and not the whispers of a potted orchid thirsting for rain but one breathing freely in the garden.

TO NARROW SHOULDERS

She lifts her face over narrow shoulders. Is this who I am in the evening, she wonders, river of water-based ink, is this the hand, is this a staircase in the distance, are these the words to utter above cool shoulders of wavering rivers.

POISE

Close your eyes.
Your arm is the radius.
Make a circle with a piece of chalk.
A solution exists.

WHAT POETRY IS

Notions with skin on, words as fish skin.
Am I one degree off from my heart?
Surgery requires much patience.

EVERY YEAR

Swallows return to ruined arches of the mission after wintering near rivers on a southern continent. The birds have done so for at least a thousand years, says the blind woman, an instinct for home like invisible stars inside each one and the children of their children, pointing to God.

RELATIONSHIP OF LIGHT TO BLINDNESS

The blind woman touches painted muntins in the window, *what are muntins*. White hyphens holding in panes. You dusted the windows, she says. Were the windows closed before rain? Yes, I heard the forecast. It's going to rain, she says, I can tell by coolness of light falling across my open eyes.

RAIN FLOWERS OVER BROKEN STONES

Birds are flocking up in cold weather, late afternoon changes tempo, low clouds move in from the bay and open ocean, if an earthquake happens, dust from the earth seeds the clouds and gray rain flowers over broken stones.

A GENTLE BASIS FOR LIVING

I see her holding a pencil. I see flowers taken out of a paper case. A drop of bleach and honey in water helps the flowers last, or is it an aspirin. I see her feet in her yellow garden clogs under the table. I see nothing through the window. Noon. I see a white hyphen in one part of the glass.

APPARATUS

The deeper the image of truth, the fewer words.

GRIEF

Systole. Listen between the heartbeats. A thin woman passed under a window above the alley and asked for a bottle of aspirins. The dream wasn't about hot weather, says the blind woman, not a whole ship on fire or sailing too close to another. A woman's heart is broken and she's dying. Diastole.

SIMPLICITY

Soft place where she sleeps sounds like the sea. In this part of the coastal mesa where she lives, the ocean sleeps under innumerable grains of sand. I wrap up the blindness in a parcel of cloth, ash of hunger in human words, open the parcel and blow the ash into the sea. *Eyes, be healed in the name of Jesus.*

WITHOUT FALLING IN LOVE

A man and a woman. Pale grievances formed a shadow, why they had not fallen in love.

RECOVERED POEMS

In time, as one moves on from what was written, the heart moves naturally to fill leftover spaces if words are missing in old poems.

PRAYER

Internal architecture of grace.

CLOCK UNDER A DRESS

I hide a yellow clock under my dress. You have so many clocks in your house, says the blind woman, why not take one to school? I can't, I reply. What if someone stole it. A stranger would be running off with my heart. You gave me this clock, remember, a hundred minutes or a hundred summers ago, and a hundred yellow butterflies passed through its hours. You pressed your hands on them.

PERMANENCE

I wrote *flower* instead of flow and remembered a child writing the word years ago, flour, and didn't erase.

HEARING BUT NOT SEEING

Remember the hillside rose terrace in late summer, says the blind woman. We walked for hours searching for it. I could hear the roses shouting their perfume into the burning arroyo wind. A waterfall was eclipsed by the eucalyptus grove. Lost, we couldn't see, neither you nor I. We walked for miles in the burning wind towards the sound of water. A talent for transparency.

LIGHT AS THOUGHTS

Nearly seed, she noted, freshwater cultures in pale tones, small and light as early morning thoughts, a mother's day gift from her youngest daughter living on the coastal mesa, sent along with a box of handwritten letters.

ROYALTY

Queen bee, one day she would wake up with stripes across her torso and wings attached to her shoulder blades, paper wings covered in pencil. Pure house of paper would emerge from this body.

BOOKS IN A LINEN CLOSET

The blind woman thought of this. It's a linen closet of books. She taught me how to brush each closed book on all sides and also brush the place where it sleeps. We keep our books in a linen closet.

LONG-FINNED VIOLET

Long-finned violet fish, one with ten stripes instead of two, sails around a stone quietly. Soft inside her world with large eyes, a patient woman waits, but the fish never swims into her net of words. I see the faraway darkness inside the woman with the net. Faraway darkness, long-finned at the edge of the field where inland water meets the sea.

MORE THAN ONE NAME

I was sleeping on a wood floor. Night carried floral scents through the open window, night-blooming jasmines, same ones tipping the wind when I walk to the mailbox around the corner, says the blind woman. Jasmine or jessamine, as a child I knew a flower could have more than one name.

FLOWERS WITHOUT NAMES

Hot arroyo winds sweep down the mountains to low sidewalks where fruit trees send little white petals across the sand valley in corners of school yards where snow blooms forth in desert winter and children pretend their words are visible in air, flowers without names.

WHAT IF YOUR LIFE FOLDED OUT

You can say sea foam, says the blind woman. I can see the red shade in raspberry, the foam in sea green a shade apart from the room with a garden window near the wavering gingko trees. What if your life folded out like an open book, what colors would it be, in pieces like broken airport glass.

THROUGH LONG CORRIDORS

I thought of long white flowers, long stalks of water directed on gurneys through long corridors.

ROUTINE

Every day, she opens her window around one o'clock.

LIVING AWAY FROM THE SEA

Strangers in their flesh carry the earth in a different way, without intuition of the sea, its salt mutability, reformation and splendor.

Motionless hills are their oceans of unbounded journeys. Smooth trees keep no salt in their uncreviced backs. Sand grains in winter streets are not blown in from dotted lights along a shore. Women's dresses, the way they flutter, are different.

YESTERDAY INTO YESTERDAY

You sweep the corners in the morning. You clear all the upper points of the room. You even sweep the front walk where ash rain fell, sweeping yesterday back into yesterday.

GUY GAUTHIER

Journal Fragments

Some of these fragments were first spoken into a tape recorder and later transcribed. The text is preserved in its original form, including occasional typos, crossed-out lines, and unconventional punctuation.

+ + +

Feb 12, 1997

(On the way to work) I wonder what it's like to be a pigeon. To have a beak, and feathers to keep me warm. *(Stop)* To be a pigeon in February, pecking at grains on the sidewalk.

March 2, 12:25 am

Jennifer was dancing by herself, and, seeing me there beside her, said by way of explanation, I'm dancing to the song in my head. Dancing to the song in my head, I repeated, that's a great line. I'm going to write it down.

June 30, 1999

Seen from the window of a bus: leaves in the wind. *(Stop)* The smell of a freshly lit cigarette.

August 5, 1999

Leaves on the wet sidewalk. Leaves turning into a yellow powder.

Aug 8 9, 99

On the bus to Beth Israel. Crisp, clear air. The rich sail past, behind tinted glass. The buildings are rock solid. The walkers in razor sharp focus. Hostess Cake. Wonder Bread. I'm out there, with Jennifer, on the cutting edge of depression. Why am I always exaggerating?

Aug 10, 99

Yellow cab dropping a passenger, or picking one up, I forget which, I only remember a blinding flash of yellow.

August 18, 1999

(Walking the dog) Now, as it gets darker, the sky is filling up with stars. *(Stop)* The headlights of a car swinging through the trees. *(Stop)* And another. In the silence of the night, I hear the cars coming from a long way off. *(In the back yard, behind the lodge)* I've caught the moon behind a tree, radiating through its black leaves. *(Stop)* It's one of those moments that makes you feel alive. *(Stop)* Several minutes ago,

a dog was barking in the night. Now I hear only crickets. *(Stop)* One of those moments charged with the electricity of life.

August 21, 1999

The sky is overcast, and the light, filtered through the clouds, has a touch of grey about it. *(Stop)* A very light rain is falling, and the grass is wet.

Aug 21, after the play

It was still raining as we drove back to the inn. We were driving through a cloud, wisps of smoke clinging to the grass and trees, in the glow of my headlights, it was a luminous haze, lit up like neon gas.

August 22, 1999

A cold, grey morning. The pine needles hold water like a fine tooth comb. *(Stop)* I shook them, and the water rained down on me.

Aug 22, Village Square

The smell of burning leaves. Of damp, smoking leaves. The flag hangs limp from its pole. Yesterday I saw fields of ~~ripening~~ corn, and sunflowers bending, bending ever so slightly in the breeze. You want to feel those leaves? Jenny said, then you can write about how they feel. I felt the leaves. They were furry and soft. And again, the smell of burning leaves.

~~Tree trunks green~~ The bark of a tree...green with moss, or algae, the pages of my notebook curling in the breeze, red leaves in August

August 23rd, 1999

Walking in the cold morning air, with a Mozart concerto, and the sound of a car going by on the road. *(Stop)* The grass is wet, and there's not a cloud in the sky.

Aug 23, 99

Hummingbirds, yellow jackets, flies—I have a whole menagerie buzzing around me,

Sept ~~4~~ 5, 99 [date corrected on Sept 6, at 8:30 pm]

I'm writing on a window sill overlooking the bay, but I can't see the water, it's too dark, only the lights across the bay, and my reflection in the window, I can see through myself, I'm transparent, behind my forehead, car lights are streaming across a bridge, and there, through my shoulder, branches are swaying in the wind.

September 9, 1999

(Walking to the subway) There's a light fog hanging over the city. So light you might almost mistake it for haze. *(Stop)* This morning, on West St, I couldn't see the World Trade Center. I couldn't see the Jersey shore. *(Stop)* My shirt is sticking to me like an extra layer of skin.

99-10-10 12:47

Fragment of a dream: I had swallowed a worm, it had flown into my
mouth like an insect, and a second worm flew into my mouth, and
the two worms were fighting, they were twisted around each other,
locked in mortal combat, and I could see them, as if I was looking
into somebody else's mouth, their heads were huge and frightening,
their lips orange and red, I could see their eyes, they were like snakes,
and their tails reached down into my stomach, and I was concerned,
and others were concerned that in their fierce struggle, they might
secrete some deadly toxin, and I started coughing violently, and their
two heads were sticking out of my mouth, and I, or someone else
pulled them out, like long, thin spaghetti noodles

Other fragment: I was defending Rimbaud (who hardly needs to be
defended), insisting on his greatness, but it wasn't Rimbaud as we
know him, it was a strange and unrecognizable Rimbaud, and the
world that didn't believe in him was also strange...it was like a hazy
cloud, with dark, hazy boundaries, perhaps it was the fact that the
world...was running without him, he was only a name, a dust jacket
on the shelf, they were ignoring him, he wasn't the spark, the piston
that drives the engine, is that it? is that the whole...fragment?

Nov 2, 1999

There's a grey drizzle on the East River. A tugboat making foam.
And gulls flying in its wake.

Sipping my soup in the cold wind.

The tunnel lights ~~fall~~ flash on my notebook.

At the library,

A sight that makes my day: wet leaves moving like surf in the wind.

A woman, the magic of her, under an umbrella.

Nov 8, 2:30 am

I reach into the dryer, and start pulling out Karen's clothes. I see crumpled dollar bills. I take out her slacks. Her sweater. More dollars. They're all over the place. She's got me laundering money in the middle of the night.

Nov 10, on the bus

A smell of bacon in the autumn air.

Dec 10, 1999

I'm so disgusted with myself, and the life I lead, I'm shuddering with disgust, I hear a bird singing, and rain falling,

The only thing I remember about my dream...is the vague sense that it would have been worth remembering, but the phone rang, and by the time I got back to bed, it was gone.

Dec 29, 1999

Fragments, I said to myself, as I was wiping my ass.

00-01-09 22:23

I was washing the dishes, and I could see, outside the kitchen window, that it was starting to rain. The cement tiles in the courtyard were glistening. I thought of going back to the computer, and writing it down. I could see myself writing the words, "it's starting to rain." But I wasn't sure the impulse would last long enough, would still be there when the dishes were done. I'm going out now, with Frisky, in the rain.

Jan 15, leaving Stanley's place,

Hazy grey buildings, in a faint echo of sunset.

At dusk, in Brooklyn: the white vapor of my breath.

Young woman hobbling on a cane. Her hair long, black, and curly.

January 15, in the evening

It's cold, and the air is very still.

Feb 14, 00

I'm still a bit drowsy. For all I know, I may still be asleep. This could be a dream I'm having. The wind shaking the windows. The cars that sound like surf. A dream.

February 19, 2000

The branches are glazed with ice. *(Stop)* The snow is brittle, and cracks under my feet, like ice on a puddle of water.

3/15/00 [maybe 3/16]

Reading poems in the subway, and walking home in the rain. *(Sound of rain falling on the street)*

March 21st, 2000

(Driving to the hospital) Haze over the Hudson. *(Stop)* Grey bristles. Trees like puffs of steel wool. *(Stop)* It's hard to steer in the wind. But the waves on the river were like a glimpse of the ocean. *(Stop)* As long as there's breath in my body, I'll do everything I can to protect her, and keep her safe.

(Return trip) To see the world through a haze of poetry. My vision clouded with dreams.

March 23rd, 2000

(On the West Side Highway) Gull flapping its wings over the docks. *(Stop)* A slight haze. The river water calm, glassy like a mirror.

~~Aug 1, Lake of the Woods~~

~~We happened to find some cabins on the lake,~~

~~The soft lapping of fresh water~~

A sound I haven't heard in years: the soft lapping of lake water on the rocks. A sight I haven't seen: long-leaf pines swaying gently in the breeze.

What's that? Jennifer asked, as we swam in the lake. Those are seeds floating on the water, I said. Seeds falling from the trees on the shore. She saw a spider skating on the water. When we got out, dripping wet, the boat dock was burning our feet.

Clouds in a blue Ontario sky.

They hover, hover and dive: dragon flies in the fading light.

The red sun. The black pine needles.

Twilight on the boat dock. The faint, the distant cry of a loon.

8/1

I see the lights of a cottage across the lake. The lights streaking over the water. *(Stop)* A dog barks in the distance. *(Stop)* I see the glow of headlights long before I see the truck. *(Sound of the truck roaring past)* Insects flutter around a light. *(Stop)* The light has a faint hum in the silence. *(Stop)* The trees reaching into the night sky...black silhouettes surrounded with stars, and the glow of headlights in the distance, the hiss of tires on the asphalt, *(a rush of air, the hum of tires: I let the tape run, to record the sound of the car going by)* nothing is quite more mysterious than dark, leafy branches in the night sky.

(Stop) In the distant sky, a flashing light. *(Stop)* Trees transformed by night, and light in darkness. *(Stop)* Northern lights shimmering in the sky over Ontario.

8/2, (Red Deer Lodge)

The color of morning on the water. A gentle wind from the north.

What are these insects doing here, in the land of long winters, and short summers?

8/3

How would I like to die? Slowly. Lingeringly. With the passivity of a tree. To be still standing after I'm dead, like those trees I saw in the swamp, hollowed out by termites,

To be standing in the street, like a wooden statue, with people walking around me,

To die like a fir tree at the foot of Mount St. Helen, a tall fir incinerated by the blast, my branches burning, rocks smoking at my feet,

an ashen husk, towering over the young trees, and the red, the purple flowering weeds,

Aug 12, 2000

~~It's~~ It was raining. Jennifer was drawing letters on the trunk of the car. I'm just writing on the rain, she said.

The road is the color of the rocks along the shore.

00-12-23 02:25

I've just watched Mission Impossible 2, drinking beer, and eating corn chips. I'm bloated, tired, and ready for sleep. I just wanted to sit here for a moment, and write a few sentences, it makes me feel better, to know I've done something, to know I haven't wasted the whole day,

April 13, 2001

The sidewalks were still wet, and there was a smell of rain in the air.

I wonder how much longer I'm going to live.

April 29, 2001

Today, I'm wild about poetry. There's poetry in the sky, in the trees, and the blinding glare of the sun on the river.

01-11-11 02:09

It was cold, and I was comfortably wrapped in my thoughts. I could see the world through the window of my own mind. I could see a lone star, the only one bright enough to penetrate...New York's haze of lights. I was wrapped in the thought of reading Olson and Zukofsky. Of spending a lazy Sunday afternoon reading poetry.

01-11-29 12:40

This morning, there was a chill in the air, and the streets were wet. There was a fine drizzle, a light fog of rain, and something was stirring inside me, dim recollections of morning mist, memories of wet sidewalks, I couldn't put my finger on it, can't even now, but...I knew I had felt this rain on my face before

November 29, 2001

Wet leaves on the sidewalk. Bare branches reaching down into a water puddle. *(Hurrying)* I missed my stop on the subway. I was reading one of those subway poems. The words were dripping with meaning, and suddenly, I realized that the doors had closed, and I had missed my stop. *(Sounds of traffic, snatches of conversation)* A smell of fried fish. *(Stop)* Blonde in brown coat, talking on cell phone. *(Almost at the door of the club)* I feel the rain on my face.

Nov 29, at my desk

(In a low voice) To ease into a dream. To live and breathe poetry. That's all I ask.

01-11-30 11:04

There was fog on the river. I couldn't see the lights of New Jersey. The trees in the courtyard, swimming in yellow light, were beyond my power to conceive. You can't imagine something l;ike that. I'm not even sure4 you could photograph it.

01-12-15 19:18

As we drove back, the sun was laying a carpet of light across the river, and the branches were black against the yellow sky.

December 17, 2001

(Walking home from work) White streaks of light on the wet pavement. *(Stop)* Raindrops trickling down a car window.

December 23rd, late at night

(Walking the dog) It's raining, and the sidewalks are shimmering with light. *(Stop)* I can only see the rain in the glow of the streetlights.

March 8, 2002

(Walking the dog) A white haze hangs over Wall St. *(Stop)* The buildings are like mountains in the mist.

02-04-28 03:26

It's very late and I hear the sound of rain, a light patter on the window panes, I'

Early morning of June 16

It's almost 2 am, but only 11 in Seattle, I hear somebody laughing outside, I think it's a woman, and the hiss of car tires like raging surf, it's like I'm in some kind of movie, and I can't figure out what the plot is, it never stops, the hissing of tires bound for parts unknown,

July 20, 2002

We're climbing into the car, sound of airliner tearing through the air, coasting towards a stop sign, turning onto Utopia, hot feel of sun, red light, the glare in my eyes, specks of dust floating in sunlight, a sudden jerk, a woman's hand on the wheel, holding a cigarette, she flicks the ashes out of the window,

CARLOS V. REYES

Mazemapping
(selections)

Lost Mapmaker

I'm drawing maps to master the art of losing myself.

I'm drawing maps of subways, so I can follow the movements of the underground people, my fellow subterraneans.

I'm drawing maps, cutting them up, and piecing together a world I want to live in.

I'm drawing maps of landscapes I've visited in dreams—cities with shifting streets and forests with wandering hills, dreamscapes where the earth is as fluid as the sea, where one has to navigate as circumspectly as on uncharted waters.

I'm drawing maps to commemorate my fugitive loves: This is where I first saw him... This is where I fell... This is where we walked, this is where we flew... This is where I died, again and again... This is where...

. . .

I'm searching for a map of the gaping chasm between lovers, an

echoing abyss that only gets vaster as their bodies draw closer—
when their skins touch, they're sucked into an insatiable hole.

I'm searching for a map of the strata of grief underlying all my loves:
the progression of love is a regression of griefs—the greater the love,
the deeper the grief.

I'm searching for a map of life's passing, enfolding everything I've
lost to time—elusive fragments of my irretrievable autobiography,
dismembered memoir of the countless lives I've lived and haven't
lived.

I'm searching for a map of the shadow world where the darknesses
within communicate with the darknesses without in an obscure language. I'm trying to learn its black vocabulary, so I can move more
sleekly in the gloom.

I'm searching for a map of the secret passages connecting my separate labyrinths, my crazy mazy selves.

I'm searching for a map of what comes and goes without a trace—
elusive vectors too fast or too slow for the unvigilant eye.

I'm searching for a map of a moveable country, a portable roaming
I can call home.

. . .

I lost my maps. I'm running away as fast as I can before they find me
and give me new ones.

I lost my maps. I'm going to throw my watch in the river.

I lost my maps. I'll hide behind this tree till another traveler comes along, then I'll steal his maps, his name, his face. Every time I want a new life, I just lose my maps.

I lost my maps. All my life, I've been struggling to find my way back to you. Suddenly, I'm overwhelmed by other possibilities.

Since I lost my maps, instead of skimming the surface, I've been digging underground. Some people think I'm trying to get to China, but I'm not—I'm just digging.

I thought I was trapped in a labyrinth, but when I lost my maps, I realized I *am* the labyrinth.

I lost their maps. Now I'm drawing my own maps with my feet.

I lost my maps. I've forgotten the names of my mother and father.

Since I lost my maps, I've taken to traveling slowly enough to learn the names of flowers and trees—*every* flower, *every* tree. When I meet a cluster of daisies, it's not unusual for us to spend the greater part of the day making introductions.

I lost my maps, so I ask everybody I run into questions. I'm not trying to find my way—I just like asking questions.

I lost my maps. I'm scarcely making any progress toward my almost-forgotten destination. On most days, I don't even cover any ground—lying on the grass or on a big flat rock warmed by the sun, I just watch the clouds drift through the sky's unmappable blue.

After I lost my maps, I followed the river to the sea, where I watched the seekers come and go.

Since I lost my maps, things have been changing places whenever I'm not looking. When I go to sleep at night, I know I won't recognize where—or who—I am in the morning. These involuntary displacements used to vex me, but now I look forward to seeing where I'll be transported. Lately, I've even been learning how to change places with my eyes open.

I lost my maps. Maybe I'll finally stop going around in circles.

When I realized that the shortest path between two points is never a straight line, I lost my maps.

I lost my maps. Now I travel like a gambler, following the dice I throw before me.

The Swelling Laboratory

I'm experimenting with…

Invisibility
I'm writing my selves out of existence.

Catatonia
I'm playing dead to trick my haunted body's ghosts into coming out.

Pornography
I'm studying carnal conjugations that disturb the flesh beyond reason.

Desire
At the heart of each craving there beats a pulsing pain.

Mixtures
I'm mixing a bit of me with a bit of you to make a strange brew.

You
I'm trying out your hands, your eyes, your sex, I'm borrowing your mouth to see how it tastes.

Telephones
Electric silences knot distant tongues.

Masks
Each of my faces lets a different voice sound through.

Fire
I'm burning away my second skin to bare the raging flesh beneath.

Emetics
I'm throwing up my mother and my father.

Hunger
I envy the ascetic's beautiful hallucinations.

Poisons
Many of my selves are poisonous to me; it's hard to tell which ones.

Catastrophes
For the love of accident.

Reversals
I'm shuttling faster and faster between opposites, till they become contiguous in me.

Doubling
With two of me, I'll be able to see my habits as if they were the customs of another country. Why stop at two?

Autobiographies
A Portrait of the Artist as His Mother, Autobiography of a Virus, A Day in the Lives of an Illegal Alien,...

Perhaps, Maybe
Perhaps the only thing that's real is maybe.

Parturition
To give birth to other worlds.

Clouds
I'm dispersing myself into a polymorphous mist.

I'm experimenting...

The Promiscuous Garden: Eccentric Epistemology

Epistemology

Every scrap of wisdom I've scavenged deserts me when I need it most, leaving me with folly's tears that drip, drip, drip from my leaking eye sockets, bony waterclocks. If I didn't weep, how would I keep time?

Time

I love to make up explanations for things—this is because of that... It's a harmless pleasure...until I start believing my inventions.

Inventions

Maybe there's no exit from this expanding labyrinth, but I'm determined to map the convolutions of my maze—a map of the lost, by the lost, for the lost.

Lost

I'm bending my body into a bow and sharpening my passions into arrows that I'll shoot into the unknown.

Unknown

We assume that everything that happens behind our backs is reasonably continuous with what we see before us, but again and again we discover that we've grossly misrecognized what's right in front of our eyes. Wouldn't it be more reasonable to believe that the world is tripping funny dances behind our backs?

Behind Our Backs

There's no reason to believe in love, but I've always had a soft spot for the incredible.

Incredible

I only want to write the impossible, especially when I'm writing on myself.

Writing on Myself

I'm cutting myself open to unleash my fabulous genealogy—the singing beasts in my balls and eyeballs; the delirious machines ticking and whirring in my buzzing skull; the ferocious flowers blooming in my belly, promiscuous garden.

Death Journal

Media vita in morte sumus.

March 2, 2002

3:17 AM

I trust the world with my life—why don't I trust it with my death?

5:11 AM

Old age, disease, suicide, accident, murder,... How do I want to die? (There are as many ways to die as there are to live.)

7:47 AM

An unworldly afterlife bears no attraction for me. I wish, however, that I could believe in metempsychosis.

NOON

How many people die without discovering the limits of their suffering and joy?

4:29 PM

If it comes to that, how will I kill myself? (My sense of decorum dictates that I die "cleanly"—no blood on the floor, no brains on the wall.)

6:29 PM

If deathdays were celebrated as well as birthdays...

8:33 PM
Here in this living-dying moment, death and life are not enemies.

10:19 PM
When they say you have six months to live, they're also saying you have six months to die.

MIDNIGHT
I am a cosmic accident; my life, a gratuitous dicethrow.

April 1, 2012

She died today. No tears.

March 3, 2034

Sixty-four years old. If I had died thirty-two years ago, what difference would it have made? If I live thirty-two more years, what difference? Today, what difference?

_____, 20?? *(Last entry)*

Give everything away.

March 3, 2070

What is remembered? Who remembers?

March 3, 2470

Nothing. No-one.

March 3, 1970

8:12 AM
It's a boy! (Bloody beginning of my lives and deaths.)

Feb 6, 1990

We could have all died. (How many times have I nearly died without even knowing it?) The van was totaled. Death's fingers brushed my face, clutched my hands gripping the steering wheel. Something should have happened.

July 4, 2002

The *San Francisco Chronicle* announced nine deaths today. What will my obituary say? (What will it not say?)

July 5, 2002

I've never contemplated suicide. What does this say about me?

July 6, 2002

I don't want to write my life away.

July 7, 2002

Dying of AIDS is the worst death I can imagine. Nobody blames anyone for getting cancer.

July 8, 2002

I'd rather kill myself than suffer too much. But how much is too much?

July 9, 2002

I will be childless for life.

July 10, 2002

A voice recorder on my deathbed.

July 11, 2002

What will I leave behind? (I know the faint ripples my living made will rapidly fade away till the small circle of time's water my life disturbed is still again.)

July 13, 2002

How many more lives can this body live?

July 14, 2002

Writing is my transmigration-machine.

July 15, 2002

Life is the only thing worth dying for.

July 16, 2002

Sunrise
If I was told I only had a year, six, three months left to live, the only thing I'd do differently is pay more attention. (This would change everything.)

July 17, 2002

Sunset
You only die once.

July 18, 2002

It doesn't disturb me to picture my dead decomposing body. What discomposes me is trying to imagine the *labor* of dying.

July 19, 2002

Death is not the enemy—it's forgetting. But who can survive a life without forgetfulness?

July 20, 2002

Life is a breathless parenthesis. Why do we run toward death?

July 21, 2002

I want to write a joyful *Portrait of the Artist as an Old Man.*

July 22, 2002

I feel more and more as I grow older. This terrifies me.

July 23, 2002

There's no such thing as an uneventful life—life itself is *the* event.

July 24, 2002

Death defies explanation. Why do we expect life to be different?

September 4, 2002

Every night for nine hours, I am dead. (Every night for nine hours, I'm neither behind nor ahead of myself—unconscious, I'm going at the speed of life.) Is sleep the closest thing to death or the furthest from it?

September 7, 2002

If desiring ceases, how will I know if I'm alive or dead? If my body isn't stretching toward you, how will I feel it?

October 31, 2002

Whenever I come to hear of something another person has said about me, I'm always taken by surprise: partly because I'm amazed anyone is thinking of me (not because I'm modest but because I'm self-centered—I take it for granted that everyone thinks about themselves as singlemindedly as I do), and partly because the sudden awareness of another's gaze (all eyes exterior to me are evil eyes) throws me outside myself, placing me in the uncanny position of being beside a self I don't recognize. Thus, few things are more chilling to me than imagining people speaking of my dumb, purely external existence after I'm dead—like a mute photograph, my life would be shrouded by an irrevocable silence.

November 28, 2002

My life is not mine. (I cannot count the stars.)

December 31, 2002

Outside the little world of my life-and-death, the universe keeps on expanding.

In the midst of death we are in life.

DARBY McDEVITT

Horizon

The train tumbles forward from *Danmark* on down. Onward to a loved one waiting afar. Consider the work in progress.

On the fold-down tray-table a plain white paper napkin. Border dimpled filigrees. Consider adding a line to the napkin. An ink line with black pen on the paper napkin.

A horizontal line. Left to right running quite to infinity. A millimeter thick top to bottom. Hard to see. Just. Exactitude. No nearer parallels. This would be the right line. A fine line. A fine day's business. Call it a horizon separating top from bottom. Air from earth. Sky from land. Halves from one whole. Do it.

Done. Left breathless. Pause to catch a swallow of atmosphere. Tobacco smoke and cooked food filling the atmosphere. Life churning the atmosphere. On a train quite comforting the life to be felt. Contrasted with the work in progress. Flee to that life. Abandon the work.

Agony of underused thighs. Rise up off haunches and stretch. Peep up the fore length of the long train cabin. Peep down the rear of same. Life becomes sometimes a bore unadorned. Regain the seat. Consider the work.

The napkin here. Still plain almost clean. But for the line. A strange accomplishment to smile at. Neither happy nor dissatisfied. Profess a certain further curiosity. Press questions further. If unsatisfied with the line what would satisfy? What would be the purpose? Neither happy nor sad. Satisfied unsatisfaction. Occupy what instant next with what glorious wonder?

Wait. The same mistake of old. Thinking about thinking again. Now groping now reaching now straining to open the box of the mind to peek in from a vantage within the box of the mind. First paradox of the day. And so early! Not an easy job of housecleaning. Biting the inside of the cheek and smiling, despite the cheek, despite the mind.

Consult a clock. The little hand says late. Forgotten to? Yes forgotten to eat again. Life again intruding. Feel joy feeling hunger knowing the work has been prodigious despite poor health and other setbacks. Stomach grumbles. Must eat but quietly there beckons the work.

Revisit the work. Consider adding color above the line.

Say a soft uniform pink unbroken smooth. Say with cranberry juice left alone in plastic tumbler. A tiny pool. Mixed with water this light pink gives a lilting glow. A luminescent rose lit from afar poured across the top half of the plane. Urge to drink down the smoothness would be the greatest compliment. Better to solicit praise from the mind than from the outside. Train shudders eliciting deep feelings of comfort. Admiring the rosy mixture now. Yet cannot concentrate.

Abandon the work for hunger. Having remembered food it is now impossible to forget food. Devour something!

Stewardess passing by pushing cart so hail her. Order peanuts and yellowish lemon drink while considering the work askance. Refreshing yellow for thirst and possible use in the work. The work! The stewardess close by so display it. What resembles a spill is art. The work seen by the stewardess she smiles asking, Can I take that? No, is the reply, This is the Work In Progress! Exeunt stewardess surprised and annoyed. Now left alone with peanuts, yellow drink.

Consider the work as a stewardess. Stand turn bend blink now. Consider it from here. For all success it may yes appear to be a bit of garbage. O well. Forgive the stewardess and forget. Sit again. Poise again above the work, yellow drink in hand. Add it.

Out the window the wind picks up and dark clouds ripple, roll between the sun and personal property. Fascinating the effect no light has on lighted things. Killing the original colors of the work for a time. Discouraged. A wish might have coaxed the sun to stay. Or might not have as there is no magic in the world but the work of the world. Magic!

Abandon the work for further refreshment. Sip refreshed.

For the first time consider the sleeping passenger adjacent. Without saying so say the passenger is beautiful and worth wooing. But why always only beautiful ones worth considering it seems? Would it were not so but it is. Or not. The faults of the world begin with the beholder so who is to blame? Now remember the loved one waiting afar at the end of the line and blush.

Turn away at a loss. Consider the work.

Consider adding imagistic representations of past fruitful discussions on the subject of erogenous zones and romantic satisfaction into the corpus of the work. What might be added to achieve this effect? The illustration of non-physical nouns is a challenge. One worth trying. Go!

Abandon the work.

Go to sleep to continue the work in hours. Yawning. Wondering. Hoping loved one will love the work when done. Drifting. Sleeping soon so well.

Hours later train rumbling on so waken. Blink off blur. Consider the work from a distance of three inches.

Consider adding imperfect ellipse approximating a circle. Consider adding two dots within the shape parallel to the horizontal line drawn first. Consider adding another horizontal slash within the circle approximately the length of the distance between the two dots but a little beneath. Does this look like the face of someone known? A wife or a husband or a father or a mother? A boss or superior? If unemployed, a former boss or former superior? Close enough?

Consider the consequences for creating representative images? What are the rewards? The losses? Consider a statement spoken by a layman art-lover viewing an original Warhol silk-screen: At least he could, you know, really draw, you know, realistic looking faces and stuff.

Should realistic looking faces and stuff be drawn and stuff as a pre-requisite to other stuff like art stuff?

Consider the plane with the horizontal line and the two colors above and below and the space retained as representative of a human face. Is it anything? Like an earth or a sky or a face from any angle? When the representational figure's body is added just below the face, will it represent something as being represented, or merely represent itself? All?

Abandon the work.

Deeply sleep in the small seat fetally cradling one calf. Wake rested and confident with the work still ahead. Smell cigarette smoke in the cabin and smile. Inhale. Stretch every breath to last a decade. Every movement of every cell in a body signifies a miracle sent from the mind in heaven to the body on earth. Or not. Abandoned long ago, Dualism is best when betrayed.

Consider the work. Consider the color below the line. Add further yellow below the line.

Once added note how hue still not-so-yellow. Almost white yet. Strange the way it works. Below the line the situation is severe. Many have faltered and died below the line. Difficult to describe the color there. Below the line is a tone a shade a hue which if viewed peripherally and under incandescent lights glowing at a cool 2800 K resembles a situation seen somewhere else, some years before, unrelated to the work in progress. Close examination of the color makes a problem of the whole. The whole-half. Everything below the line.

After acute visual perception it might be said that the two colors taken together with the line amount to a whole world. Hermetic aesthetics. Is this possible? It is not. But this is the dream. Knowing heaven cannot be painted, the attempt is made. Knowing love cannot be sung, the singing begins. The subject is assumed. The result is false. Occasionally admired. The process is true. Consider how often a lie has sent a man on his merry way. He hoping to do the right thing the right way. It is common. Finding him later embarrassed or killed along the way. So common.

The jury once out is back. The process has authority alone. The labor, the sweat, the voice. Yet priority to sell the process dominates the day. Bids it buy alcohol and stuff and food for family and impressive gifts to woo loved ones who need no wooing into bed. New crisis of purpose.

Abandon the work. Consider it.

Consider the line. Call it a horizon. Believe the illusion rendered and escape. Run in. Distant pale horizon so far from where all sit. Within the work consider the time it has taken to travel from here to there a distance of zero miles zero feet zero inches. Weeks months or more?

Consider unfettered joy for the time lost and gone forever. Future happiness to come coming on. Loved one waiting in *der Leipziger Hauptbahnhof* eager for anniversary three. Feel a love for the loved one and smile and shiver. Consider the work as part of life but as a gift it will not do. Better buy a rose this time. Better do it.

Feel the new joy where has it been? Watch the time pass where does it go?

See the horizon? Consider it.

OLIVIA DRESHER

Moments & Confessions
2002

January 14

Sometimes everything seems off
and all the world around me begins to tilt.

January 15

The relief of watching the birds
Just *that*

January 16

The wind remembers

January 17

They tear down houses because they're too small
They tear down houses because they're too old
They tear down, they tear down

(written in bed on a small tablet, in the dark, 5 a.m.)

189

January 20

Aphorisms: drops of blood from my life

January 23, 9 p.m.

~ the eye inside ~

(looking at the ink inside this fountain pen, before writing)

January 24

Tell me more than I know,
always more…

February 1st

There's something sacred about this form of writing.
It's like whispering or praying.

February 3

Dust, dust, everywhere.
But why does it most love to collect underneath the little table
in the kitchen? Why *there?*

February 9

A dream of a spider, a big black one with a huge round belly that had white spots all over it. It kept following me.
I could never lose it.

February 11

It all fits together: thinking, feeling, dreaming, fearing, doing.
Five children fighting and playing under the same roof.

February 12

Now and Never

February 16

That West Coast feeling in the air. That nostalgic feeling when winter starts giving in to spring. (Why does this time of year always remind me of walking home from school in the early 1960s?)

(2:30 p.m...front porch, briefly)

February 18

Lack of intimacy with others is a death sentence.

(noon, naked after a bath, putting on lavender lotion)

February 20

Why do people look at me when they look at me?
And why do people not look at me when they look away?

February 22

I go to bed with the radio on, again that ritual (as in September 2001), and I leave it tuned to NPR all night long. I go in & out of sleep, in & out of the news stories, the only light in the room coming from the old-fashioned radio on the corner table by my bed.

February 26

The *Past* and the *Future:*
Twin ghosts of *Now*

February 27

Lost
in the Found

March 1st

Still remembering the film about Shackleton's Antarctic expedition… The soundtrack was the ice speaking.

March 2nd

Proof that I've never grown up:
all the questions I ask.

March 3rd

To imagine is to do something intangibly.

March 4

Patriotism is the opposite of free speech.

March 5

Thoughts of-the-moment and essences of the day:
I want to capture these here
before they disappear.

(1:30 p.m., looking out my office window)

March 7

If you never touch anyone physically,
is it like trying to live without a body?

If you never reach anyone's heart,
is it like trying to live without a heart?

Is it enough that he allows me to press my nose & lips into his hair, while he sits at my desk working?

(lost in thought while driving on Brooklyn in the U. District…)

March 9

It's possible to love someone's pain…if you're in love with the person.

March 10

Living alone for many years is the feeling of living in a monastery.

March 14

The minutes are tingling like chimes in the wind

March 17

My mind is a tornado in my heart
My heart is a tornado in my mind

March 18

Link the leaps

March 21 (eve)

The crows…*hundreds* of them in the trees
at the edge of the Arboretum at sunset.
The *sound* of them…and hundreds
more flying toward that sound and those trees.

March 25

I saw him outside on the porch, talking to himself.
When I asked him what he was saying, he said:
I'm having a conversation with the air.

March 26

There's nothing that smells more earthy than raw potatoes being
washed, and there's nothing that tastes more earthy than whole grain
buckwheat pancakes.

April 1

I can't imagine sanity.
I can't imagine it.

April 4 – Noon

All I really want to do is meditate on God
(or the absence of God, which ends up being the same thing)

April 15

And the grass keeps growing…

April 17

Who do I write to/for?
No one I know.
Only strangers, the unborn, and the dead.

April 24

Tomorrow is now
and now is yesterday.

April 26

Instead of being intimate with a human being,
I intimately hold books in my hands…

April 27

I wish there was a God to pray to.

April 29

Everything is a substitute for something else.
Where's the real thing, then?

Pain is the real thing.
Because there's no substitute for pain.

May 3

To be celibate with someone you're in love with
is almost like making love.

May 10

No way to say it
except *this* way.

May 23

I secretly embrace *everything*, sideways.

June 6

The light lingers in the evenings and the sky glows;
that's all that matters now.

June 20

All the days and nights I haven't written in here...
No, that's an illusion.
I've been writing with invisible ink.

June 26

Walking down Broadway, I pass two blind men walking on the same side of the street within five blocks of each other. I close my eyes for a few seconds and keep walking, just to see what not-seeing is like. Then when I open my eyes, everything looks like a miracle.

June 27

Written on a piece of notebook paper tacked onto a telephone pole:
LOST BLACK CAT
extremely scared of everything

July 1

When I write in this notebook
or when I read someone else's notebook
I don't imagine faces, no
just infinite layers of what can't be seen

(brushing my hair, looking into the bathroom mirror)

July 3

A spider so small and delicate
it looks like a tiny piece of light-brown lace
I'm looking at it right now
It's on the window ledge in the kitchen
above the sink
(oh how fragile beauty is)

July 4th

Every time I need to write
I hear a bell ringing
An old church bell out of the past
high up in a tower

(looking up at the half-cloudy sky, 11:00 a.m.)

July 7

My words are photographs of thoughts and feelings,
photographs of what can't be seen.

July 8

Memories are a playground in the summer.

(lost in the leaves)

July 10

Right Now
Right now what are most people in the world doing?

(watching the freeway at 1 a.m.)

July 11

What's a bigger mystery,
the past, present, or future?

(drinking orange juice after midnight)

July 22

Thoughts are intangible heartbeats

July 24

I can't make silence
the way I can make words

Silence is a womb
Words grow inside it

When we speak
we give birth to words

July 25

What are whispers?
The sound of words breathing.

August 1

Love is a dance
Friendship is a walk

August 2

Life is a vacation from death

(washing my hair at night in the clawfoot tub)

August 3

There's no end to Now
It keeps going on & on
until 20 years have passed
then 30 years, 40 years, 50…
A lifetime is just one long Now

(putting old clothes from the 1970s onto hangers in my bedroom closet)

August 4

It hurts when I can't put thoughts and feelings into words

*(cleaning the rust stains off the corner sink in the bathroom;
they won't come off)*

August 5

All my life pouring out, pouring in

August 8

Sometimes short poems I've written many years ago surface in my head and I chant them as I go about doing what I'm doing. They come up for air, they speak themselves, here's one now:
Life is / Life is rough / Life is a rough draft / Life is a rough draft on a raft / Life is

August 10

Sometimes when I listen to people speak I feel very small, I shrink, I become invisible. I see their mouths moving, *their mouths are moving*, and words come out, words and more words, all kinds of words, with tones and meanings attached. Words don't bounce off my skin, they're like bullets, they enter. Words can kill, and then they resurrect me. I go on living because of them and in spite of them, without one *visible* scar.

August 22

If I ever meet him, I don't want to speak to him with my voice. I want to hand him fragments written on little pieces of paper. Or we could remain invisible and slip notes to each other under my front door.

September 8

What I did today...
I read 20 manuscripts. It rained and I smelled the air. I closed the upstairs bedroom window that hasn't been closed for over three months. I put fresh water in the birdbath three times because it kept getting filled up with feathers. I thought about the impossibility of God. I thought about the impossibility of Life. I saw that the leaves on the trees are turning golden and falling already. I thought about Mt. Rainier, hidden behind the trees and clouds. I thought about my hair turning gray and how it happens so slowly because it blends into the brown the way summer is now beginning to blend into fall, but fall doesn't get gray hair, just golden hair, imagine if we got golden hair as we aged, I thought about that today. I thought about Berkeley in the '60s and how those times are gone forever. I thought about what I can't imagine, trying to imagine it.

September 12

I don't write *about* my life; I write *from* my life.
Perhaps I'm not even a journal writer.
What, then, am I?

September 13

In the mornings I pick up trash in the neighborhood—hamburger wrappers, cigarette butts, bits of Styrofoam lighter than air.

September 14

A Sighlence of Words

September 16

I'm a terrorist of curiosity.

September 23

I can't stand to be anywhere
but *here*

(peeking at the sunset over the city while closing the curtains)

October 1st

How do I know what I know, how do I learn what I learn?

He was tutoring late, and asked me to feed his cats, so I went to his apartment. After I fed the cats, I started snooping around. I snooped everywhere—inside his personal notebooks, at his notes from his class reading, in his closet, in his bathroom, in his refrigerator (I saw a near-empty jar of spaghetti sauce turned upside down and not much else). I looked at the recent CDs he had made, and found a few he had taken from my house to copy. I looked at the clothes he had hanging on his indoor clothesline. I smelled his worn shirts, in a heap on top of his orange dresser. I read an old birthday card (a cat card) his mother had sent him. I stopped looking, in spurts, and soaked up the feel of the room. I examined the cracks in the kitchen ceiling and tried to determine if they're getting wider. I looked out the south-facing bay window at the desert area where the old shady tree was recently cut down. I heard people going up and down the stairs. I heard echoes coming from the empty apartment across the hall.

Then I began to read something he had written on a pad of paper that was sitting on the table where he eats. It was hard to read because it was a rough draft and many words were crossed out. I tried to determine if it was written with me in mind or not, if the "you" he addressed meant *me* or the ambiguous "you" that often appears in his writings. His words were flashes of lightning from his mind, his words made everything in me stop and freeze into a stunned passion. I could feel hot tears at the door of my eyes, but they stayed right there, on the brink. He wrote about the tragedy of male/female relationships, the impossibility of love, how he can feel sorry for me (me? was the "you" *me*?) but he can't give his heart to any woman.

I went to my car and drove around and around in circles in the neighborhood. I didn't want to go home but I was hungry. I wondered where I could go to eat. I looked for a restaurant I could park near without squeezing my car in too close between two other cars. I kept not finding a place and kept driving around until I decided to stop at the little Indian restaurant.

I brought manuscripts in with me to read. Everything in the restaurant felt wrong. I almost didn't stay. But I sat down at a table that faced the front window. I put the envelopes containing the manuscripts on the table. A fruit fly kept buzzing around my table but I let it. It was getting dark outside. It felt very autumny.

I wanted to go home but I didn't want to go home. I felt aimless. It was the first time I'd felt aimless in years. It was that old feeling from 30 years ago. The owner brought my food—some rice and vegetables —but the rice smelled funny. Everything smelled funny, like plastic.

The darkness outside looked like black water that the city lights were shining into. I could still feel his words but I couldn't remember them exactly. He was tutoring the young students at the university while his private writing was teaching me, giving me secret lessons in darkness...

October 3

I learn intuitively, I can't learn anything directly, and I learn by taking my own steps, and by letting my footsteps be heard, and by hearing his footsteps, too, like footsteps up a flight of stairs at 3:00 a.m. when it's quiet and I can't sleep, and I hear them now, his footsteps going up the stairs, and my footsteps going down, I hear them.

October 5th

How dark
the not-quite-dark is
right now,
this early evening
in early fall

October 22nd

The simple moods
are a clear blue sky,
and a secret is a bird that hauntingly flies by

November 2

What are my fragments?
Parachutes that open as I fall through the night.

November 4

Blinded by the sun of my own longing to see.

November 8

Maybe only that which doesn't exist is perfect.
Existence is chaos, imperfection.
Non-being is perfectly still, and goes on forever
in every direction in space and time.

November 10

They sold the house and cut down the bamboo forest. And now
there's just the little white house next to all the other little white
houses that have had their trees cut down.

November 11

I'm a witch. I'm a witch that fell from the sky, and I have two broken
legs, and a broken heart, and an imagination that likes to pretend that
I'm not broken and that poetic fragments can put everything back
together again.

November 12

Seattle is Paris in the winter
Seattle is Japan in the spring
Seattle is America in the summer
Seattle is England in the fall

November 13

Autumn leaves and letters…

I've been writing letters in my head
while raking leaves in the dark.

November something

I couldn't hear the freeway this morning.
The fog hugged it into itself.

(in bed, 6:30 a.m.)

November 18

Perhaps I need more Zen masochism in my life.

November 20

I don't understand what life has to do with death and what death has
to do with life. Especially when they crash head-on with each other.

(making up my bed, at sunset)

November 22

No windows or doors in eternity.
No escape.

No way out.

(looking out the kitchen window while washing dishes)

November 23

I stayed up all night reading her words. I couldn't sleep. I'd read, then turn off the light, toss and turn (my heart was pounding), then I'd give up trying to sleep and turn the light back on and read some more.

Her writing is simple and kind…why, then, did it stir me up the way it did?

November 26

It's snowing where he is
and he's reading philosophy.

November 27

My mother is here. She's sitting at the breakfast nook, watching me wash dishes. She looks like a 20-year-old with gray hair, young and beautiful and natural, with her hands under her chin and her elbows on the table…

November 30

Fog is rain that whispers

December 12

It's windy and rainy. I didn't eat all day, except for orange juice and a few almonds. Then for dinner I went out and had vegetable chowder soup and an udon noodle salad with peanut sauce. And peppermint tea to drink.

December 14

Dark, rainy afternoon, 3 p.m. I peek into the living room window of a remuddled bungalow as I walk by. A TV is on in the center of the room but no one is there watching it. The images shoot out of the screen, through the living room window, and enter my eyes. *America*, I think, *on a rainy Saturday afternoon...*

December 17

Language is a wave that covers me and then recedes back into the sea, leaving just sand and broken shells at my feet. I walk in the sand, I pick up the broken shells. *These.*

December 18

Imagine a journal that's about secretly reading someone else's journal. Imagine a journal that's a secret about a secret.

December 22

Only the dead are old.
The living are always young and naïve.

December 23

This morning I swallowed a spider, a tiny spider that had crawled onto my toothbrush during the night.

December 28

Some days I feel close to everyone because we're all going to die.

(hearing the nails being hammered into the addition being built next door)

AMY S. F. LUTZ

Primary Allegiances
(selections)

Secrets of the City

It took me three years to find out about the drinking water. When I caught giardia for not boiling, my landlord said, "That's all?" He said, "Just wait." He said the PCBs would make me sterile.

By then everyone else knew about the sodomy laws, the tire factory, the bats over city hall and the cats that were brought in to kill them. My landlord said "Look up," and there they were—so much like the m-birds in a child's picture that I wondered what we had really been drawing all those years.

Expiration

Spring came in February that year and stayed. It happens every century, the meteorologists reported, characterized by a general state of disbelief. We didn't believe it. We lay awake at night, listening for heaters that never came on. Mrs. Vaughn stamped on her flowerbeds to keep her tulips down and when that didn't work she dug them up as they sprouted and carried them inside in clay pots. The branches rippled with new leaves. We were afraid for them, expecting every morning to wake up and find that winter had returned and scraped away the bits of green like spinach stuck between its teeth. We wondered if the trees would then stay leafless all summer.

At dusk, the ambulances drove slowly through the silent town. We saw it is possible, to die from holding your breath.

Tangents

One hundred years before we hiked out to Wolf Cave, washerwomen walking past the exact same spot were attacked. As they ran, they threw pieces of clothing out of their baskets for the wolves to pounce on. This was how they escaped. There are no wolves in the cave anymore but you look for evidence, gnawed bones or rocks that you insist on calling "fossils": "If I had a flashlight the fossils would be easier to find," you say. "I bet that fossil-hunters have already picked the place clean." I think about the wolves, about Atalanta pausing for apples and I marvel at how easily distracted we are. Last night, you whispered, "You weren't my first choice. I don't know how this happened." But as you scrape through pebbles tracked in by our own boots I know you understand the irresistible temptation of a smooth skin, a damp sleeve.

Spoils of Victory

My problems are not like other women's. You left the beautiful nymphomaniac for me, instead of the other way around. That is a lot of pressure.

I believe it when you say that what matters to you is not what matters to other men. But whose idea was it to have sex in a phone booth and on the shoulder of a highway? I imagine the gravel pressed against her back gave her skin the rough, pitted texture of a grapefruit, but that isn't something I've asked you about.

I haven't cut my hair since you told me you like it long. I know from her pictures that her hair was never long enough to tie around your waist like I can. Even if she could, it was too pale and fine. I can tell it would break as soon as you started to pull away.

Horseshoes and Hand Grenades

It's the same everywhere. Across the country, your building was emptied because of a bomb scare and you spent your afternoon eating onion rings at Houlihan's. You didn't even stand outside and wait for it to blow. I couldn't get in touch with you to tell you about my car, the gassy stench that drove me to the mechanic, how I started the engine with the hood up and fuel sprayed everywhere. It could have exploded, the mechanic said. But I just watched the mist glaze my windshield and thought about the lovely arcs of Bernini, pennies tossed for good luck.

Wedding Night

We weren't invited to the wedding but the bride came to us afterwards, searching our yards for her lost cat. The new husband followed slowly in his car; we woke to the glare of headlights trailing like comets across our pillows. When we came to our windows we saw her in bright and exquisite detail; not even her guests saw her so completely: the ridge of icing under her fingernail, the glistening lipstick smudges on her cheeks, the dirty lace along the bottom of her dress from the bare spots in the grass. She called to the cat in a voice shrill and unrecognizable with effort; she didn't seem to care if she disturbed us. We thought about going out to help her look, taking our flashlights and our porch lights and turning our neighborhood into a brilliant spider web the cat could not escape. But we didn't. The only excuse we had was how self-contained she seemed: with the spotlight, and the costume, we would sooner have addressed an actress on a movie screen. After the car rolled past we stood blinking into the darkness, but the yellow spots in front of our eyes would not fade.

In the morning, we stood outside and peered around our azaleas and our rosebushes, just in case. All we found were holes the size of pencils that her heels had left in our lawns.

Genesis

The night of your conception, I couldn't sleep. I lay in the dark, listening to the rain and the cars on the busy road. It was a rainy night, but according to the weather report, we didn't get the worst of it.

Or maybe that wasn't the time. Maybe it happened the next morning, when your father and I made love with our mouths turned away, scraping our teeth against each other's shoulders. I don't know; something was keeping me up that night.

Most men, I think, are kind in public; they keep their cruelty a secret. But your father is inside out. He tormented me in front of my sister. He said that our children, of which at that time we had none, would love him most.

After my sister left, we made love to the sound of the rain. Downstairs, the dog pulled a five-pound bag of sugar off the kitchen counter. Your father tucked the blankets around me and went to sweep it up. When he returned I sucked his sweet fingers and he was careful with his cold feet.

WILLIAM STAFFORD

Aphorisms

This selection of William Stafford's aphorisms, first published here, is chosen from every year of his daily writings between 1951, when he was a graduate student in the Iowa writing program, and 1993, when he died at his home in Oregon.

+ + +

1 October 1951
When he saw the leopard jump, he knew he was poor.

15 April 1952
So light the bird, so heavy the mountain.

16 May 1953
Off a high place, it is courtesy to let others go first.

28 February 1954
It is legitimate to crawl, after the wings are broken.

4 August 1955
To be happy only with unattainable things.

8 October 1956
Successful people are in a rut.

29 April 1957
The world is an old place. Everything has already happened once.

24 November 1958
Every mountain has that one place when you begin to know it is a mountain.

15 February 1959
The cost of epics may ruin all this world.

6 June 1960
Before you have your dreams, your dreams have you, and every day pushes a night before it while the wilderness follows.

31 December 1961
Lost pioneers were the ones who found the best valleys.

20 December 1962
There is such a thing as helping history to get along with its dirty work.

5 August 1963
The relish in that blemish.

18 July 1964
Traits we dislike in a friend are sometimes good in a teacher, alas.

8 January 1965
I dreamed no way out.

26 March 1966
A day is all one person needs: it is long.

11 June 1967
If there is a trail, you have taken a wrong turn.

12 November 1968
Daylight is fiction. Dark is where fact lives.

14 June 1969
You hope. But you know.

4 January 1970
My kind of faith is that most mountains won't move.

28 July 1971
We found out the earth is only a star.

23 July 1972
Some leaves don't try very hard. But the sun shines anyway.

9 April 1973
A zoo is where one kind of animal imprisons other kinds of animals.

26 July 1974
It is not the sound of the ax that cuts the tree.

8 June 1975
Selling your poems is a little like selling your prayers.

24 January 1976
The ideal teacher—someone who can't talk.

23 November 1977
Everything I say is really inside parentheses. (Except that everything put in parentheses is really outside.)

12 June 1978
Maybe we're just worms, but we eat the mulberry leaves of experience and turn them into silk.

1 July 1979
By the sound a pen makes you can't tell where it is going.

28 February 1980
The Sun is thousands of times bigger than Earth; I block it out with my hand.

2 May 1981
Water is always ready to learn.

20 May 1982
Philosophers, Rabbits: Different ones take different paths through the brambles.

4 January 1983
You can be drowning and like it if the water is warm and soothing and people keep cheering and hugging each other and waving little flags.

3 June 1984
No matter how well or loud you speak, none of the stars will stop to listen.

7 December 1985
Now is ours. By our breath it lives. The forest grows out of its own brown leaves.

6 March 1986
Why should I worry? I have pens and plenty of paper.

23 July 1987
I love tomorrow, it stays away so well.

3 November 1988
Like a frog at a moonrise, I am impressed but not reverent.

13 April 1989
I hear the clock's little teeth gnawing at time.

6 July 1990
Any person you meet may carry destiny and sometimes you catch a glimpse.

22 May 1991
A rejection slip: "This is too good for our readers."

1 July 1992
Truth comes near, my teeth chatter. A fierce demand has taken hold.

16 March 1993
At first it's not much of a river.

JENNA EVANS

Diary
(selections)

September 19, 1987 – FLORENCE, ITALY

A lizard climbing up a wall. Yellow stare of cats from under cars, under orange streetlamps. The night air clung to our skin like a wet hot cloth. And then this crackling electricity that ran between us. I felt like a thunderhead in summer.

It was scary to look into Polly's eyes. Now I have a fever so I'm drifting above the rooftops, held up by the noises from the courtyard. If this baby stops crying, if this woman puts down her dishes, if these cars stop driving by, I will fall to earth.

Later

No. I want to describe life exactly as it is. I am alone, cooking fried potatoes for dinner. I am listening to reggae, to which the high ceilings lend an echo. I wash the dishes and break a saucer neatly in two—it can be fixed—and get water all over the filthy tile floor. I push my hair off my hot forehead and go into the bathroom to see if I still look ill. I do.

There are three ripe peaches on a spotted plate. There are white gladiolas in a glass vase. The ashtray is full of cigarette butts, though

Polly doesn't smoke. Sometimes sirens go by.

I am eating my fried potatoes out in the backyard. You can hear everyone in the building talking & shouting & eating. I watch people on their balconies and think: I will think of this someday and miss it.

September 25, 1987

Polly and I were sitting on the edge of the bed holding hands. We were being silent after a long supper of talking. I saw her hand. My hand saw her hand. I said: I feel like it's our wedding night—there's been all this love & bonding & affection and now we are suddenly realizing that we are two people and can see exactly what that means, and we don't really know each other because a person is so big, how much can we possibly know?

I said: Look at your hand. Your hand doesn't know me.

Our hands, a tangle of black & white & silver, rested on her white lace skirt.

She said nothing. Then I said nothing. It was raining outside.

September 27, 1987

Right now I'm sitting on a freezing park bench. I am cold but I will not move because I am a glacier. A glacier bound to the ground by heavy shoes. Polly makes me feel shame and so I must dress myself in heavy shoes, solid shoes, so that no matter what happens to make me start straining my awkward wings, I cannot fly away, I will stay rooted to the earth. An icy bird. A glacier with frozen wings. Heavy black shoes. It is good to be cold—it makes a woman beautiful, to have features carved in ice. Opaque & glittering & flightless.

September 30, 1987

The air is chilly & pale & blue because my breath has frozen it solid. Because today I am a Medusa. It is the only defense I have left. I will look at men on the street and watch as they freeze into statues. A thousand stone satyrs littering the street. An orchard of empty men.

My clothes are as white as the arctic and black as the sea. I laugh and birds fall from the sky like hail. This pleases me.

Polly and I walk through a beautiful park at the top of a hill. There is water and clear light and green trees and from somewhere the smell of smoke. I panic, remembering how it feels to go from ice to animal. Somewhere there is someone who could melt me.

No. No. I am alone and stony and graceful. Polly does not want to melt me, she has made that perfectly clear.

October 1, 1987

I telephoned America tonight. I read in the newspaper that there was a massive earthquake (*trema*) in Los Angeles. Bent over a laborious Italian dictionary, I deciphered words like "death," "tragedy," "collapses." Each word sent a sharp thrill through my body. Imagine: everyone you love buried under the rubble of a thousand Hollywood apartment complexes. To be so cut away, so free, that you're just sent drifting into the universe like a big hollow bird. Sailing & sailing through cold black space, with no need to be understood. Sailing.

October 11, 1987

We took a bus through some very beautiful countryside to Siena.

Siena: The streets of Siena are very narrow and shady and have names like "Della Deformata," "Via Malcontenti" and "Via Termini." The buildings are dark & crumbling & intricate; in fact the whole city looks like some huge instrument of perverse Catholic torture. When you stand in the central piazza you can feel the soft black dust of fascism left over from the war sift down onto your shoulders.

A Bus Ride: On the way home I rested my head in Polly's lap while she sang to me: "My mama done told me/when I was in pigtails/my mama done told me, hon/a man's gonna sweet-talk/and give you the big eye/but when the sweet talk is done/a man is a two-face/a worrisome thing who'll leave you to sing the blues/in the night...."

Italy: Italy has the consistency of a soft heavy fruit. Italy has the consistency of the body of a drunken woman. It smells like incense and sounds like hoofbeats. Everything has a damp richness that verges on decay.

October 12, 1987

What is the only thing more lonely than walking alone in a beautiful city in an autumn rain?

What is more lonely than a row of wet black trees with round yellow leaves that fall and stick to the wet black asphalt below?

The only thing more lonely is taking a taxi alone in a beautiful city in an autumn rain, and the radio is playing that cheaply mournful music that taxi drivers play in every city, and the rain is hitting the windshield and dripping off your glasses, and your breath steams the window.

October 14, 1987

We had a nap yesterday til two and then we went to the British Library and everything in the world was something to laugh about and we found Ibsen's *Ghosts* for me and the librarian was giggly and probably had been sniffing glue, and when we crossed back over the bridge to the center of town the sunset had turned the Arno an impossibly soft marzipan pink, and we looked for the English/ American bookstore and on the way we found a shop selling household appliances so I bought my love an early Christmas present of a toaster, which made her laugh and clap her hands and jump up & down like a little kid, which made my heart swell full of love, and then we found the bookstore, and I bought Marilynne Robinson's *Housekeeping* and she bought Dylan Thomas' *Under Milkwood*, and we were all laden with bags, and then we did evening prayers in the doorway of the most mysterious place in the world, a tea-shop-cum-astrologer's-reading-room (with red velvet draperies in the window) called MAGO MERLIN, while behind the locked door someone, presumably Merlin, played a piano in a highly eerie & erratic fashion, and then we went to the Piazza Della Signoria to drink our wine and tell jokes, and then we went to the cinema and smoked dope in the ladies' room until we were falling against the walls, and then we watched *Fantasia*, clutching each other & uttering tiny giggling moans, and then we came home and had a million pieces of toast with cream cheese & butter & hot coffee, and then we got into bed and Polly read me the Dylan Thomas play in a series of wonderfully shaky Welsh dialects, and then we lit a candle and lay in each other's arms, and then we made love, finally mutually and so finally really passionately, and then we fell asleep, and it was good, no, it was perfect.

October 15, 1987

Things that I think are good: white Tuscany wine, Bessie Smith, Italian figs. Polly doing morning prayers, looking dazzlingly beautiful. A certain vague pain that excites—maybe youth.

I feel as if this whole Italy trip is going to make me want something, and I'm not going to know what it is, and Polly will not be providing it, nor will this country, and I will go home and Adrian will suddenly not be good enough nor will America—it will all be unfulfilling. I wish I could pinpoint this feeling. I wish I could cry, but sometimes there is just *no* way to feel sorry for yourself.

October 21, 1987

I'm trying to avoid thinking about returning to L.A. totally homeless. I take the two red Japanese paper lanterns from my suitcase and hold them in my hands, making the paper rustle, and think, look how pretty these will look in my new apartment. And I can build a bunch of shelves for my record collection, and put all my little clay sculptures out on a coffee table. Maybe I can get another cat.

November 9, 1987

I thought I was dreaming because the water there was blue. Actual blue sea water, not just reflecting sky, but blue in your cupped hands, like bubble-bath. Little blue waves rolling into caves that dripped with stalactites, caves streaked with pink & green, fringed with garlands of purple algae. Caves that made our voices echo and the boatdriver said that the water was fifty miles deep there and that you could still see the bottom so we looked and he was right.

The cliffs ringing the bay were striped white & grey, dotted with tiny silver-green trees. Our little boat chugged through the blue water and cut a silver path for me to trail my hand in.

Some people Polly babysits for took us there, Porto de Venere. They were being grownup in that day-trip, slow-walking way so Polly and I played with their boys, doing loud war whoops and piggybacking them up the steps to the ruins of the castle. Playing follow-the-leader along the edge of the water, we found in each and every docked boat a family of scruffy kittens. They lapped the stagnant water at the bottom of the boat and crawled up on the seats to greet us.

Later we went to some rich & stuffy family's house and the children grew restless on the champagne-colored carpet so Polly & I ran outside with them into the dark. The house was on a mountainside overlooking a misty green valley dotted with fairy-lights. We played ghosts and horses-and-chariots and some obscure Italian games like Tok-Tok (which is far too good a game to explain) until the grownups had finished grownupping and then we piled into the car and Polly & I sang them blues and there was a harvest moon, or almost.

Yesterday we wandered along little crooked streets fringed with olive trees. A man pestered us as usual (we were pretty nice but when he left he muttered "lesbians!") and we ate cold mushroom pizza that was crawling with bacteria and got sick and laughed and talked about the interesting new twists to our relationship. I climbed a tree and got pine resin on my gloves.

We passed through the famous Boboli Gardens. There was a hideous fountain full of brackish water & dead goldfish & coins, and some frescoes dripping with seashells & bobby cherubs & globs of pendulous cement.

We made love and I kept thinking god I can't believe I'm feeling so much, and when I was coming I said, *Look at me*, and today she told me I had looked to her just like a wild horse and that all that night she'd dreamt of muscular wild stallions, black, gleaming and kicking up dust as they galloped away from her.

November 10, 1987

I don't know what to do when I see beggars here. In L.A. they're like crazy super-citizens, aggressive & dreamy & fierce. Here they're almost all women, they sit against the walls with kerchiefs tied around their heads, holding out cups. They always have a very young child with them. They just sit and wait. I never have any money with me and so it hurts to make eye contact with them. Which leaves only the option of walking by very fast very upright like all the other bastards.

A city of soldiers and men and dogs. I'm sitting in the center of the Piazza de la Republique. There are white & gold & purple & blue lights shining in the wet pavement. There are hundreds of people walking fast, carrying closed umbrellas. There is a smell like hot raspberry jam. Cars hiss and splash. Women with young sons and expensive shoes drop crumpled bits of paper on the ground. There is no music anywhere.

A city of soldiers and men and buses and rain.

November 11, 1987

It is chilly and cloudy and there is a smell of woodsmoke and a dull clanging of churchbells. I passed a shop window lined with dead grinning piglets, each with its forelegs stretched before it as if leaping, each with a yellow apple balanced atop its head. The Arno is slow, opaque, mud-colored. I'm unwashed and shameless in a black dress, with filthy hair. Still the men on the streets look at me as if they would like to cut out my sexual parts, to core me like an apple.

I'm writing in the British Library. I came here because it's warm and dusty and wooden inside, and it faces the river. I keep trying to make a line-drawing of Polly and I making love but it always comes out looking simple and obscene.

November 16, 1987

Stepping into Venice, especially after being trapped in the black wedding cake of Florence, was like stepping into a marvelous dream.

Soft pink crumbling buildings with patches of faded red bricks. Ash-grey buildings weeping black rivulets from the cracks and domes. Lavender marble, streaked with damp living green, and shocks of green growing out of black statues. Pink and lost-green paint peeling off driftwood shutters. Faded scuffed pale-blue wood, very dry, with water lapping against it. Delicate purple heather growing out of ancient stone walls. Small brown rats swimming across the canals, white birds circling overhead.

We just walked & walked & walked until our feet were aching. A pixielike boy with bright blue eyes and a soft Irish lilt stopped us on a little bridge, ostensibly to ask help with directions, but really, he confessed, he'd seen the pink triangle on my jacket and was desperate to speak English with someone gay; he'd been traveling for months. We muddled over maps of Venice (which are useless, it is not a map-able place) and he promised us a place to stay the next time we're in London.

Ten million tiny gold mosaic tiles in the cathedral, each one placed by hand. The soot and dust of five hundred years. Gargoyles with black caps of grime. Brass horses.

I made love to her in the rickety *pensione* twin bed and woke up to the sight of her peeing a tiny amount, awkwardly, into a tiny glass & then emptying it into the sink & then peeing another tiny amount. These are the moments love is made of.

The next day was clear and bright and I bought bongo drums from a Moroccan street vendor and a teeny fake plastic gondola with Christmas lights inside and was happy.

MATT HETHERINGTON

Fragments from Notebooks (1990–1999)

The train station and its tunnels are like the roots of a tree spreading underground.

• • •

To live as though one is not part of any era...

• • •

Laughter has nothing to do with happiness. Laughter comes from momentary revelations. The larger the revelation the longer and harder the laughter.

• • •

Oh for some great man to crush me in his enormous hand and drop me on the ground!

• • •

Thoreau—man who the animals came out to see.

• • •

The ducks quack underwater. Under the wave of the stars we walk and talk.

• • •

Generally, we are most impressed by someone telling us something we already know.

• • •

He has the perfect sincerity of a man who has convinced himself of the truth of a lie.

• • •

Sometimes you continue to lie only out of curiosity.

• • •

Illusion—there is nothing but what you leave behind. Truth—there is nothing.

• • •

Light is both a wave and a particle? The parallels in the self...

• • •

If a person wins the lottery, it's acceptable for them to be idle for the rest of their life, but not if they are poor and have won nothing.

• • •

Dancers—like dogs wagging their tails.

. . .

Sometimes I love her the most when she's walking away from me...

. . .

The ultimate aim of the wise man is often the contentment of the fool.

. . .

He says: "I'm lost in my future."

. . .

The most political thing you can do is astonish someone.

. . .

He doesn't water his plants—he just likes to watch them die.

. . .

How almost every act can be seen as an act of cowardice—the turning away from the void.

. . .

We spend eight hours a day dreaming. What's wrong with a couple more?

. . .

Interstate trains—full of people starting books they'll never finish.

. . .

I keep feeling I am traveling across a face. Here: a dense patch of beard, there: a shiny expanse of bald nose.

. . .

Eternity is in love with the productions of dusk.

. . .

The idea that as a writer I judge the worth of other writers by how much they make me write.

. . .

It's the ashes of the fire that glow longest.

. . .

The further I am from home the better things look.

. . .

Want to get away from people? Then walk beside a freeway.

. . .

If golf is a bad excuse for a walk, then fishing is an even worse one for sitting down.

• • •

One day you'll be an old man with hair in your ears.

• • •

If wisdom stays inside the body it becomes poisonous.

• • •

People are people people.

• • •

God won't really be dead until every church is a museum.

• • •

Music is beautiful in proportion to how much it is like a kind of flight.

• • •

To be a poet is to embrace one's own singularity and insignificance.

• • •

A narcissist is a lonely exhibitionist.

• • •

Not the fulfillment of the promise (which would only mean the desire for another promise), but the promise itself.

. . .

The artist: an imperfect *bodhisattva* (the one who can never accept final enlightenment until all are freed from suffering, which is what the art attempts).

. . .

Why do I love you? I love you because you simplify my self.

. . .

Perhaps the greatest moments are when one laughs and weeps simultaneously.

. . .

Brevity: because I can't bear myself very long.

. . .

If one wants to love one's reflection, the surface of the water must be still.

. . .

Sometimes I smile to myself simply because I'm not dead.

. . .

We are engaged in the gloriously tragic task of perfecting ourselves—tragic because we are already perfect.

. . .

Thinking nothing is more productive than thinking small thoughts.

. . .

The certain writers (especially Blanchot) that I can only read lying down...

. . .

The profound idea put in the novel seems to me like putting a wild animal in a zoo.

. . .

Intelligence is a kind of impatience.

. . .

Pain too deep to get hold of.

. . .

Aphorisms leave more time for *action*.

. . .

Shall I sit or drift? Write or dream?

. . .

We are only as distant from each other as we are from ourselves.

HELEN RUGGIERI

A Year Along the Allegheny
(selections)

I've walked the dikes along the Allegheny River for years, taking notes in my head, making poems. I thought I would write things down. I wanted to keep a written record of the value of this time, this nightly commune with myself, with the world out there.

+ + +

September 24, Saturday

It's getting dark earlier, earlier. Twilight hovers over the path, ground fog rolls up from the river, clinging to the low places. Crickets raving in the brush, the smell of drying grass. Asters are like ghost flowers in the twilight. It is so still our passage is like an earthquake, our lumbering a disruption at least 5 on a seismograph.

September 30, Friday

We went fifteen minutes later tonight and it was dark. We walked through woodsmoke and the faint scent of skunk. Soon the time will change and we'll walk in the dark with only the stars to watch.

Strider runs up, a shadow materializing out of shadow. You can't see him, then the white of his nose or the blaze on his chest appears, a strange white in the dark.

October 7, Friday

We went about 7:15 p.m. tonight and it was dark. A sickle moon hung in the southwest just over the hilltops with Saturn at her heel. Coming back you could only see planes crisscrossing the north/south boundary twinkling warning lights. The silvery trunks of the river birches and clumps of white asters are just about all that can be distinguished. Two blocks away West State traffic rushes and honks. Here is all dark, silence. How lucky we are to have the dikes. The nursing home windows were lit up like small screens, TV sets predicting the future.

November 12, Saturday

There were mists rising from the pond and you could see the white puffs of expelled breath. The Pleiades are up in the northeast, a fuzzy clump. Across the river headlights made a halo over the trees and disappeared. The dark ground from which thought forms—huge white umbels of boneset that have escaped the frost.

November 16, Wednesday

Not much to see—silhouettes of trees, lighter gray of the path against darkness. I became aware of noise, a rumbling, and on the right was a jet, the rumbling falling down over us, and on the left, across town, a train going by, but both the same, the far away rumble, a transportation song in stereo.

December 1, Wednesday

A cold wind blowing and a lip of light over the long ridge to the south—must be Bradford some 15 to 20 miles that way—it's the only thing over that way for a hundred miles or more. The deeper into winter we go, the worse the wind, the darker the nights. Red says the dark is beautiful too. You turn from sight to other senses—woodsmoke floating, wind rushing by your ears and the stars so far away, the patterns clear, distinct. I think sometimes I don't look out at all, but burrow into the darkness of my character. A Christian might call it sin, but I mean the things about me I'm not aware of. Small black holes in the fabric of consciousness. They're like astrological patterns I have to understand and name. Then I'll know them, but not before.

December 2, Friday

The night is dark, the path a gray smear. I find my way by using my feet, not by using my eyes. Woodsmoke and stars. Spotlights from B.J.'s Wholesale Warehouse opening over across State Street bisect the field where the lupines grow wild in the spring. It's the dead end of the year. Christmas threatens. I'm concentrating on one black hole per night and by spring I'll be a clear white light. Neon maybe. I'll have constructed an astrological chart. I'll know where I'm going. My life like some spiral nebula, circling back on itself, smaller and smaller. In the nursing home you can see only the small nightlights, the bluish blinking of a television. They are building a chain link fence around the place. Most of the posts are in place. Do they want to keep us out or the folks in.

December 7, Wednesday

Ford is 60 today. It snowed and the dikes were covered but the path was open still, uncovered, a dark streak through the new snow. It was brighter than usual because of the snow, clouds moving rapidly to the south, the wind, a damn cold wind bringing lake effect. There were dog prints, sneaker prints, jogger prints. I thought that if I could get it right, explain it correctly, if I could understand how thinking changes, how you can go away from yourself, or concentrate on yourself, I could defend winter. I don't think I can. I can feel it but not say it.

December 17, Saturday

A thick evening, the ground icy, the fence around the nursing home finished except for the gate. Tonight I have to fence off disappointment from my life, my character. Chi balances what's out there and what's in here and doesn't let one disrupt the other. A full moon up there, but we can't see it behind the clouds. A great metaphor.

December 22, Thursday

The year has turned. Winter comes sunny, mid-40s. The semester follows the year. Going, going, gone.

Winter

we are all rooted
in the same yellow clay
darkened by generations

of maple leaves
like an old lesson
we hear the wind a long time
before it touches us
we wait under the same moon
and the stars wheel as they do
owls glide silent and dark
over frost-scored weeds
and further and further
into winter we go
one by one our lovers drift away
until there are only
those of us left
who write the same poem

February 13, Monday

So cold, so very cold. Wind chill in the minus twenty something.
Very short walks these nights—up to the gate and back following
tire tracks someone's made—someone with a key to the pumphouse
gate. Now that they've blocked off the road, you have to walk down
to get to the pump station. All the fishermen used to park down here
and the lovers.

March 3, Friday

Very dark tonight. You couldn't tell where you were walking, just put
one foot in front of the other. The moon is a sickle on its back with
the shadow of itself in its arms. The sky is very black, the stars
bright, Mars to the southeast.

March 5, Sunday

32 degrees and a slow steady rain falling. All I thought about was the sound of rain on the umbrella—the now. Li Young Lee said there are three topics for poetry—love, death and food. I thought language too, and the dark ground out of which the poem grows, the sea of symbols from which it emerged. Myth, science, god, consciousness.

March 14, Tuesday

Another wonderful warm day—71 degrees and the moon almost full, just a sliver off. The landscape is elemental—no color or shade but the lay of the land, the hills, stands of gray trees. The twin paths on the top of the dike spread into the distance in their odd perspective. The powerlines shine in the sun like an alien spider web—huge. The tower of the Friary rises as if we were in Renaissance Italy.

March 17, Friday, St. Patrick's Day

Dark tonight and cold again. No trace of the full moon low in the east, huge, hidden under thick banks of clouds. All is quiet, snakes sleep in their rocky dens hiding from the old Christian. They say there are no poisonous snakes on the north side of the Allegheny. Perhaps St. Patrick drove them south.

March 19, Sunday

In the light! Overcast day and twilight was just a hazy pearly gray. We walked down through the tank lots—trash everywhere exposed —even the paper casing of a Roman candle. Some ground pine was greening up on the dirt pile they made to block off the access to the road. And one beautiful gold coltsfoot in bloom.

BIANCO LUNO

The Philosophical Notebooks
(selections)

Notebook VIII: 1992–1993
rosary esophagus

When my ex-wife left me I came close to killing myself.
I groveled before her, unable to breathe because I couldn't hate her
without seeing my own wretched image.
That May the cherry blossoms and the weather were especially
lovely.

. . .

Two women in conversation in a café.
I can only see the face of one and barely hear anything.
Her expression alternates between amazement and nodding acknow-
ledgment or approval.
Do I ever have conversations where I can make use of such faces?
Or am I just unaware of my substitutes for them?

. . .

There is no going back.
If there ever was a golden time it is irretrievable.
Without sounding too hopeful, we must come to embrace the
darkness more and more.
Yes, we lie ourselves to the grave but it appears to work.

. . .

Cold morning sun, like faith.
Like Bach.
I have not lost everything.
I can still remember the rapture of what it was like to believe.

. . .

Not between a rock and a hard place, but between a rock and something that will turn the rock into powder.

. . .

The irresponsibility of the truth will make a boy out of a man.

. . .

My earliest ambition was to be a corner grocery clerk.
Returning the can of paprika my mother had sent me to get, I observed the clerk reading comics.
I showed him the bugs crawling in the can and he said it was okay to exchange it.
He seemed to have a nice job, and, as far as I could see, had an important role to play.

. . .

"I don't know what you're talking about."
You lie, or you reveal some truth.
Tell me, which is worse?

Notebook IX: 1993–1994
a variety of cockroach

The reason why I write in the morning (and sometimes upon waking in the middle of the night).
Toward the end of each day, it seems to lose point.
In the idiot morning everything happens as though it had never happened before: the darkness is strangely inconceivable.
By afternoon I feel chased, alerted to the special circumstances of the minute.
Each one has earned the mortal appellation "now" by then.

• • •

Like any little boy's mother, I will have my heart broken.
When he leaves me, when he dies, this always half-feral cat.
As a survivor I will have a tangible sorrow to chasten me.
I vainly scramble through these abstractions to brace myself.
The old logicians' joke about the inexperienceableness of death, hence our immortality ("When I am alive, I'm not dead; when dead, I am not.") has this much truth in it: Death is an event only for non-participants.

• • •

Children have to be very young before I am able to sense their innocence.
I wonder if I've ever seen a child that young.

• • •

A lie can sometimes—by dint of its naked beauty—be converted to truth.
How else explain all this around me?

. . .

I committed a heinous crime this morning.
Early, on my walk to the university, under the bridge I pass, a man
slept against a stanchion next to his shopping cart.
While he sleeps I approach and pull from my wallet a bill and slip it
under his blanket.
When he wakes he will go to the nearest convenience store to buy
an alcoholic anodyne and shorten his life a little.

. . .

It is better to err on the side of perfection.

. . .

The intellectual passion seeks always to discover and explore
uncharted regions of its unrestricted universe of discourse, scale
exotic peaks, move about obscure ruins, plumb still deeper
trenches...
How many adventurers make it a part of the plan not to return?
Is there a responsibility to report back?
At the very heart of the desire to take these risks is the coy wish to
be relieved of this duty.
When it sometimes happens, news never reaches us.

. . .

On a bus: "Nobody gives a damn about the truth except when it gets
in their way!"

. . .

Hope is immanent.

It can be embodied.

A news photographer in Rwanda captures the image of a cholera stricken girl, legs almost too thin to walk on, struggling to reach a refugee camp, collapsing every few steps in the dirt—and above, in the same frame, on a rock, a patient, observant vulture.

A poster girl.

The photographer wept helplessly after taking this picture and, having taken enough, a week later, took his life.

The girl, we are told on the radio, did reach help and probably survived.

The vulture, because there were thousands like her, also did well.

• • •

Owing to the shortness of memory, hope thrives all around.

• • •

The ideal life.

One in which so little is needed that if it were lost the event would go unnoticed.

• • •

But always, I distort the language, don't I?

Shall I never learn what words are intended to mean?

Feel their longing to embrace, to kindle mindless warmth?

I must be asking that we behave freely as animals yet think like gods, but neither with bad conscience.

Or better, both with the same conscience.

The blood that races through our veins races for a reason, with purpose, not to say, a vengeance.

A definite distance to go.

The truest of all our goals.
The intent behind all our intentions.
Toward that day when it will not race anymore.

Notebook X: 1994–1995
what you don't want to hear

What is truth?
The positive and complete exposition would consume a lifetime.
For practical purposes (the only ones you can ever excuse yourself for having) truth is special to you and valuable almost in proportion to your reluctance to hear it.
It is, in short, what you don't want to hear.

• • •

At the moment, the autumn sun feels very kind on my skin; I live in a very beautiful part of the world; I have reason to be happier than anyone I know.
Through my window: at this latitude even the fallen oak leaves cast very long shadows on the walk.
It is 59 degrees F.
With an old shoelace my cat and I dance about on a carpet recovered from a dumpster behind a lawyer's office on the eve of the rains that now will soon wash the dust from his fur.

• • •

Those philosophers who prize clarity—what would they think of the dust and cat fur congesting my lawyer's carpet?
Isn't the fragrance offered by blossoms of that rude thing "truth" quite enough, in itself?

Yesterday I was reminded by the carcasses of two animals in close proximity to each other on the street: Another squirrel, opened up by a wheel, and a pigeon, its neck broken on a curb.
Also, last evening I was revisited by my old pain.
A very quick visit, thankfully.

• • •

Long ago, many years ago, I began this journal as a suicide missive. Though the intention has remained determined, a thousand diversions, remarks deemed necessary, confessions, pleas, commentaries, face-saving excuses, etc....
No sentence wishes entirely to complete itself.

• • •

I have come to learn the sentiments of the critic so well I cannot even momentarily empathize with her without seeming to mock her in the same act.

• • •

Wake up, stretch.
To which god shall I pray today?

• • •

Reasons against suicide:
(ordered by whim)

1. Life still amuses.
2. Compassion for loved ones.
3. Plain fear.
4. Cowardice.
5. Uncompleted projects.
6. What people will say.
7. Strangers will paw through my private midden of belongings.
8. I will be forgotten by most, remembered by few and then only painfully.
9. I will miss a good bit of gossip, news, events, opportunities to vote or not vote.
10. On my shelf, too many books left unread.
11. I might set a bad example for others,
12. or forgo the chance to comment on my own death and be misunderstood without the chance to further contribute to the confusion.
13. I would dearly miss early morning walks on sunny winter days.
14. My beloved cat.
15. Sometimes nursing my bitterness at the world is positively enjoyable.
16. The waste: what lies in store for us after death will keep, the food in my refrigerator will not...

Notebook XI: 1995–1997
iridescent blossoms

Suicide, *n.* ...the occasional child is fed such poor lies by its mother that they fail to hold up a proper lifetime.
But we expect the child to work with these lies, to make them durable truths.
But the material, the lies, could have been better...
Could they?

• • •

We have all been abducted by aliens.
If not sooner, this is revealed to us at the moment of death.

• • •

Humanity, *n*. …characterized by a mastery of pleas and prizewinning excuses.

If Nature gave out awards to her species for "best in" categories, we would certainly get it for self-delusion.

• • •

Sunlit alleys, wisteria growing over back fences…

• • •

All lies as white?
—at least this is how you must come to forgive, if you bother, in the aftermath of your awakening.

• • •

It is not that the truth is too difficult to say or that we don't know it or any such thing.
It's that it was exhausted in its simplicity and brevity long ago and that life is too urgent and too ample to not lust for filling itself with something and lies are so fetching and available and everywhere throbbing with hope.

• • •

255

The sun sparkles on the snowy ground.
After a week of being ill, I seem to recover while shoveling the walk.
By their constant renewal my plans reveal nothing of their desperation.

. . .

Just the faintest intimation of death, a whispering in the heart, a murmur…
I discovered I had one today.
The two women doctors looked at me with concern in their faces—professional and perhaps otherwise.
They seemed to be wondering at my reaction.
I don't know what they saw in my face—it would have been nice to have been handed a mirror as in a barbershop—but they continued to wait expectantly.
I smiled and said, "I'm always this way." I was amused, a little thrilled, remembering the Louis Malle film from many years ago, thought how poetic an ailment, how appropriate, I felt a little proud.
I don't think if I had been a pregnant woman (they told me, by the way, that this type of eddy in the flow of blood in the heart is more common in women) I would have been more at ease at the center of a production.
One of the doctors was in fact pregnant and had some sort of leg injury; she hobbled about on a crutch.
She praised the younger resident for her acumen in hearing this one: it was almost not there, way, way off in the distance like the plash of wavelets on a hull or shore invisible or indeterminate in the still fog of night.
The barest speck around which to collect moisture for a precipitous event.
I recall the movie again. It was a gentle take on incest between

mother and son, as legitimate a human relationship as might be conceived, as pure as we are likely to encounter in a lifetime.

The feeling was of a Japanese garden, an intimate landscape cultivated for repose.

It was near the end of what must have been a long day for them and my two busy doctors were resting in their silence.

. . .

To be first to go or the survivor. Which is worse?

. . .

Depression, *n.* Consciousness—sometimes lingering, sometimes fleeting—of truth and its brutal impartiality. At an earlier time it was synonymous with melancholy.

. . .

Bach as a means of healing a wounded mood, one special afternoon's temper, knocked askew by a long series of suppressions begun early in the day.

The bruise has yet to run its course of colors.

The music, the cantata, *Ich habe genug*, sets me back to the time when I could not have been hurt this way.

Notebook XII: 1997–2000
the world is my Vienna

There is no hope either for the individual or for the lot of us.

No reason for sadness, however.

Sadness, as its opposite, requires no reasons.
But when available, it will train itself upon them as wisteria on a trellis.

．．．

Even in our best lies, the truth oozes out.

．．．

There isn't enough spillage in his life for him to rest content.
Obsessing on efficiency to the point of art is the last excuse for what he does.

．．．

She went home to her apartment to nibble on the indecorous biscuit of her existence.

．．．

A child should be spoken to as though it were a god, fully cognizant of the wiles and vagaries of adult excuses and justifications.
When it is told it cannot do something, it should be informed as to why *anyone* is ever allowed to do that thing, if anyone ever is.
If it is suggested that a child cannot have a requisite capacity for judgment on the matter, then we must be prepared to explain how it is ever determined that a non-child can have such a capacity.
And we can never say that this happens magically at a certain age.
We are addressing a small god to whom the lameness of our excuses looms very large.
If the child is curious, then it will have the wherewithal to understand, if *you* have the courage to explain.

And then it will be out of your hands what the child does.

If the child is incurious, there is no hope because there was no god in the first place.
Only another liar to add to our vast and proud collection.

· · ·

What would have to be true for the view from here to be mistaken?
...as modern birds are from dinosaurs, this is how different from what we are now we will have to become, the evolutionary link virtual and a construct in time for the satisfaction of a distant curiosity and for a contemporary solace.
Picture dinosaurs on the verge of extinction waking to consciousness and stilling their runaway despair in a vision of their descendants gracing the skies of a future world without them.
The lengths to which Nature will go to remain naïve.

· · ·

You begin to live fully when you have been almost dead.

· · ·

Men kill themselves for one of two reasons.
(They are not the same.)
Because they cannot live with themselves or because they can live with no one else.
Weininger was an exemplar of the latter and much scarcer sort.

· · ·

Never content with what is possible.
Because what is possible is nothing.

The impossible, at least, has never lied.

. . .

Facts so obvious oftentimes we fail to notice:

1. There is no God, but there is most certainly a hell.

2. We will die later today, tomorrow, or the next day, etc.

3. Sometimes, it seems, I am *not* in pain.

. . .

To the extent we are *not* wise, there is drama and less melancholy.

. . .

A tiny wren picks at crumbs, swept from the tabletops to the café floor, the doors wide open to the cool summer morning.
This bird is out of proportion to its importance.

. . .

There is something fundamentally ill with a culture obsessed with finding cures.

. . .

Women and men arrive at and depart from wisdom in different ways.
Male wisdom, at its height, is negative, quintessentially Socratic: it consists in achieving the conviction that one does *not* know.

For a woman the corresponding conviction is that one does not *need* to know.

This is not negative because it frees energy in the direction of action in contrast to the male state of aporia.

(The negativity I speak of is relative to *this* world, not some other less bounded one.)

Men are busy up until (if ever) they reach this state.

Wisdom, for a woman, is the beginning of enterprise.

. . .

In a cashier's face I saw God briefly.

Her eyes counted change.

All of this suddenly explained and I understood.

The movements of galaxies and her fingers over keys.

I put my change away.

There used to be a God a long time ago.

And maybe again a long time from now.

Now—where I am always at—here there is only bewilderment and stupidity surrounded by treachery.

I don't know that I am complaining.

My harsh judgments may convey the impression that I know what would please me.

I don't know, and it would not matter to me—if the change was correct.

The explanation she embodied for an instant was adequate.

. . .

Science was my first love.

My fourth grade teacher called me her "little scientist" because I had

read every science book in the elementary school library and knew the names of all the moons of all the planets and what their atmospheres were supposed to have consisted of...
I knew so much then.

Things I no longer know how to do:

- Vote
- Answer someone who asks how I am
- Understand someone who tells me how they are
- Believe
- Accept responsibility for anything less than everything
- Say sincerely, "I don't know..."
- etc.

It is not likely that I ever knew enough.
To say that it is the desire that has been lost does not help explain.

• • •

I don't believe in God because, to date, I haven't had to.
God forbid I should.

• • •

The next best thing to silence is to open one's mouth and say something no one can agree with.

• • •

Friends can be sorted from enemies by the nature of their misunderstanding.

. . .

I continue to tread water.
On one or two occasions I have almost drowned.
There is still no land in sight.

. . .

Sanity, *n.* The successful suppression of truth.

. . .

So many ways the world *could* have been.
Yet it *is* this way.
I would fall on my knees, the dignity of reality having been stripped
away at the thought...
but to what, to whom?

. . .

When consensus starts, thinking stops.
And "agreeing to disagree" is an agreement to what?
...fatigue besets both sides; conviction, let alone truth, nowhere in
sight.

. . .

Long sentences?
Or short ones?
The latter will be misunderstood and the others ignored.

. . .

To care about others is to have enlarged the self, not to have left it behind.
It is to treat one's disease by sharing it.

. . .

Corruption among its leaders is a sign that a *representative* democracy is working.

. . .

The patience of thinkers who expect to live a long time.

These philosophers who splash about at the shallow end of the pool. Who never learn to swim.

CATHERINE EDNIE

Gemtactics: A Journal
(selections)

We play at Paste—
Till qualified for Pearl—
Then, drop the Paste—
And deem ourself a fool—

The Shapes—though—were similar—
And our new Hands
Learned Gem-Tactics
Practicing Sands—

—Emily Dickinson, #320

+ + +

20001009

This is all something that can be done. All of this is something that can be done. I will not write questions. It can be done. Art can be done. Three letter words can be done. The mystical does come to earth. There are oceans. Yes, there are oceans and oceans. Sweet is the taste of time. Every midnight there can be champagne. There are hazelnuts. Gathering is something we can do.

I want playtime. It can be done. I am as happy as a clam. Leaving is possible and arrival is possible. Short poems can be written representing beams of light. Poems can be written that resemble small golden bears, honey bears. Hexagons in wax are to be gazed at and restored. Energy does flow. There are blazes on the trail, blazes on my forehead. The burn scars remain, occasional fatigue, but no pain this year. The body has a knowledge. I don't fight this direction. I sink into my unusual difference, I bathe in the glass teapot.

20001015

I used to be a computer programmer who tried to write poems. Now my face is corroded and I can't keep any secrets. My eyebrows permanently raised, lids fretted, the skin of my forehead transparent and textured, thin as thin silk. I still don't understand. I don't understand why humans dehumanize. I don't understand beauty, loss of beauty, then beauty found in the unlovely. I don't understand the burned girl, laughter, the dead man who kissed the earth, or the why-we-are-here.

I still haven't been able to write about nothing. Tonight I saw that nothing came directly from war. And war came from dehumanizing, and dehumanizing came from silence. And then back around, a swift circle back to silence. The silences between the stars and the silence at the back of the choked throat. So I cried.

What's astonishing to me is the permanence of iconoclasm. The sirenity of the new. It's a force within me as big as god. It can't be killed and it can't be trashed. It's always whole and it's always there no matter what I do. I'm no longer allowed bitterness, no longer allowed despair, no longer allowed doubt. I'm allowed to make words, I'm allowed to gesture, I'm allowed to follow, and I'm allowed to wonder how people do their laundry. The new astounds me every single day, I can't turn away, I'm awkward in your grasp, my kiss missed your lips, I'm sorry for my slips, I have to serve you, grandeur.

20001027
from my house

Awe is hard to experience without feeling like a phony.

Awe is hard to experience when you are trying to take the marvelous for granted anyway.

Awe is hard to experience when you are lost in the woods looking for clear directional signals and you come across something like, say, a pearl necklace or a nice pair of suede shoes.

Last year, 8/31/99 to be exact, a sentence came to me out of sleep. I didn't understand it and I thought it was strange, but I was practicing listening, so I wrote it down.

"There were messages from Alcestis almost every day, from her rat cellar under the eaves."

20001228
akaday

I'm in a museum. A big long rectangular room, like the Guggenheim in Soho. I have a headache and a stomachache. I'm surrounded by abstract art of the emptiest rectangular form. A pure white painting. A pane of glass mounted in a stand. A blank sheet of paper. A TV screen showing only snow. These works of art are vaguely aggressive in their arrangement. They box me in; no matter where I turn I face one of them. I have about a square foot to move around in.

I admit right away that I don't understand them, hoping to defuse my perception of their stubbornness, their withdrawal. It doesn't work. I'm still getting upset. I try to show them my harlequin socks and shoes, but they don't care. The ceiling, floor, and walls start to join in on their side. I'm alone. My name is Enchantress. I make believe I see many tiny harmless flames floating and playing. They move freely in and out amongst the barricades of the artworks. I like their shapes. Maybe they are enough. I invite them to burn patterns into my eyes.

20010101

I love Charles Simic. I realized tonight that whatever makes me love Charles Simic is the same thing that makes me dislike Mary Oliver. I'm sorry not to like Mary Oliver, because she is supposed to be a good poet, and very popular. There has got to be something to her, or something lacking in me? I wrote a poem once about disliking Mary Oliver. It was unsuccessful. I'm afraid at times I start trying to write like Mary Oliver. Danger! Danger! It's not me.

I read some of Charles Simic tonight in *The Poet's Notebook*. I was a little shocked, a little delighted, a little laughing. Then I went off to scrub the bathtub. I started thinking thoughts like "I don't trust any poet who doesn't scrub the damn bathtub." I don't know if Simic scrubs his bathtub or not. But that's the kind of thinking he causes.

> It's a desire for irreverence as much as anything else that
> brought me first to poetry. The need to make fun of authority,

break taboos, celebrate the body and its functions, claim that
one has seen angels in the same breath as one says that there is
no god. Just thinking about the possibility of saying shit to
everything made me roll on the floor with happiness.

Form in a poem is like the order of performing acts in a circus.

My second-grade teacher in Belgrade told me more than forty-
five years ago that I was a "champion liar." I still remember
being mortally offended and kind of flattered.

I was reading *The Poet's Notebook* because I realized that's what this
journal is.

The head of a poet is more like a town dump than a town
library.

20010107
It's January. Seven days into it, it hits me.

I wonder if recipes can be copyrighted. Today I blithely copied one
and sent it to my sister, unattributed. They have a less rigid existence
than some other forms of writing.

Recipes are transformational. They can be made. I think they are
superior to poems in this way. A poem can never get so close to
reality.

I know my way around my kitchen. The floor supports me. I collab-
orate with the appliances.

I rescued the barley. It had congealed into a nasty grey glob, neglected
in the crockpot. Here's how: I scooped up two or three chunks of it

and stirred it gently into vegetable broth. To cure its blandness, I added mushrooms sautéed with garlic and butter, salt, and a touch of sherry. Edibility! This would never work as a recipe because it starts with failure.

I stripped an orange of its natural skin and then I couldn't eat it. I tried to save it in a plastic bag, poor substitute.

My son wanted to know why we didn't name the dog "Gustave."

20010112
Empty chairs

I sort of lost my job
a pale blue
sort of
diffi
culty

Chair gymnastics
An inaugural parade of folding chairs
Not enough seats
Musical chairs

Chairs stay alone in the house all day
without barking or chewing anything

Chair-ity
Chairfulness
Chairvoyance

The chair can be a friend to you

20010125

I like to write on the bare edge of meaning. I like to taunt meaning, tease meaning, make meaning moist, and then dry her tears. I like to dance. I like to write along the edge of the snowflake where it vaporizes into ice. I like ponytails. I like passion, passionfruit, and passionplay. I like to scan the sky, I like to see the sky as an empty garden, I like to stroll in the sky. I like life to be populated. I like a greedy, silly, glad, large populace. I like populations of objects. I like humor that comes in from the side like a weasel. I understand the need for employment. I like multiplicity more than anything. I do not want to hesitate. I want to concoct. I do not want to retreat. I want to grab. I do not want to be the passive voice, I want to sing, sing, and sing, and grab, and smile. Smile at the snow towers, smile at the rocky ledge, smile at the artificial, smile at clothes, smile at the telephone, smile at tomorrow.

I love:
Isabel Allende
Remedios Varo
Clarice Lispector
Alice Walker

20010309
Dream images
Teacups with saucers

You can't go looking for water unless you have a container. So I go looking for a container.

What we know about these teacups:

they are stacked on an open shelf, chest-high
each has a saucer
maybe fifty of them
some have color, but subdued designs
some have stripes
mostly white
mostly uniform
mostly extremely shallow
they would only hold one or two swallows

I try to handle these teacups. When I touch the set of cup and saucer at the top of the stack, the whole stack becomes unbalanced and jitters sideways into the next stack. Somehow I avoid a domino effect and manage to stabilize the stacks.

The teacups are charming. Do you collect teacups? I collect teapots.

Teapots are more stable and hold more liquid.
Teapots are deep, teacups are shallow.
Teapots are enclosed, central, warm, and seem more fragrant.
Teapots are more securely attached to their lids than teacups are attached to their saucers.
Teapots hide the tea, protect the tea while it's young.
Teapots shelter the tea, while teacups display the tea and let it get cold.
Oh the tea gets cold no matter what.

I reject the teacups. I'm really hungry and really thirsty, but they are just too unstable. And too shallow.

They are just too shallow. I'm so thirsty I'm going to need a bigger container. Delayed gratification in dream imagery.

20010322
Ideas

Most of my ideas are hairy and wild.
I don't even recognize them as ideas
until they have taken me hostage.
Sometimes they hang around
for a day or two.
I usually manage to trap them
and remove them to a wilderness area.
Sometimes they can be domesticated,
but only if I'm very daring
because they smell funky
and have big sharp teeth.

ESTHER ALTSHUL HELFGOTT

Anna's Last January

Wed. Jan. 3, 1996

It's wrong to wonder   even for a second
if someone's going to die/when.
It sets a precedent for
living with the dying,
as if the person's
no longer alive—
as if she's dead
before she
is.

Thurs. Jan. 4, 1996

I wonder:
what earrings
you wear
when
your mother's
dying.

Fri. Jan. 5, 1996

Today after seeing Mother, I had a third hole pierced in my right ear.
I went with Irina. She got both ears done. I don't think I should be
wearing earrings. The mourning's already begun. The mourning
began a long time ago. This is a diversion.

Sat. Jan. 6, 1996

I take my earrings off.
Scott says, "You can wear them, Mom.
Grandma's still here.
We aren't sitting *shiva* yet."

Jackie sits silently
singing
her grandma
a song. Ian calls.

I wish my father
were here.

Sun. Jan. 7, 1996

Seventy-nine pounds of wrinkled skin.
Somebody could make a crinoline out of her.
Or a lampshade.

Mon. Jan. 8, 1996

She fights off death
as if it were a capitalist plot,
one more bad idea,
like corporations, profits
and taxing the poor.
I wonder when

the funeral
will be.

Tues. Jan. 9, 1996

The nursing home staff
thinks she's dead,
acts like it,
throws her in bed
with no water.
Oxygen off.

Wed. Jan. 10, 1996

How
    long
        will I
            have her
                here
                    with
                  me?

Thurs. Jan. 11, 1996

They put her on a mattress
on the floor,
because
she took herself
out of bed
to go to the bathroom,
because
she refuses to be who she's not,
even when she's not.
When she tried to get back in bed,
she slipped to the floor,
sat there   a sweet little doll
until somebody found her
beside the bed on the floor
a sweet little doll
on the floor.

Fri. Jan. 12, 1996

(final nouns & adjectives)

They sound like the grunts I made
the first time I had sex
with a neighborhood boy pressing
my nineteen-year-old body,
a hundred & seven pounds
of frightened flesh,
into our honeymoon bed.
I wanted to go home,
and so does she.

Sat. Jan. 13, 1996

I love being here:
sitting with her as she dies
as I sat with her as she sewed
singing to me:
as she made my dollies'
clothes. She looks at me
and knows I'm here,
takes my hand, says:
"My throat's dry."
I give her water—
even though
I'm not supposed to.
They say she'll
die a worse death.
I don't believe
them.

Sun. Jan. 14, 1996

Her mouth
's open
wide
as a tennis
ball.

Mon. Jan. 15, 1996

Guarding Mother

I will
guard her
against
all harm.

I will
watch her
until
my eyes run
dry.

I will
swab
her mouth
with a
saliva stick.

I will
hold
her hands
until
warmth
comes.

I will watch
her
breathing
until
it stops.

Even then,
I will watch.

Tues. Jan. 16, 1996

I don't want to be here
when she dies. I want,
instead, to be at a poetry
workshop   making words
of her death. Lying to
myself   that art's all
there is, after all.
The body doesn't
matter.

Wed. Jan. 17, 1996
(fifth full day without water)

Anna's Last January

The plastic snake splicing her face,
wrapping itself around her ears,
sticking its prongs into her nose,
slinking across her chest.
The sour smell smacking my face,
the gurgling in her throat,
the space between breaths.
Her watch still on—
as if she can use it.

Thurs. Jan 18, 1996

I sleep on the floor next to her bed.
It's cold. I think I'm homeless.
17 hours here.

Her breathing. Is
me.

Fri. Jan 19, 1996
(3:30 a.m.)

She's lived another day.
I can't...

Sat. Jan. 20, 1996

. .

Sun. Jan. 21, 1996

.

WILLIAM PITT ROOT

Knocking at the Gate:
Notes on Poetry & Related Matters

The swan is traditionally a poetic emblem, the goose a barnyard watchdog. Yet what's a swan but a goose with good PR and the presumption of class? And the smooth gliding of poems is propelled by the churning, just out of sight below the surface, of webbed feet caked in dung.

• • •

We don't look into a poem for the poet—we look there for lost parts of ourselves.

• • •

"I write poems because I've never learned to play blues harmonica or flamenco guitar, and I've had to make words my instruments or be riddled with the silences of a music I could not otherwise tell." Since this appeared in print, twice students have given me harmonicas. I love them for their literalism, and I bless them for gifting me.

• • •

Success in the craft of poetry, as in the art of striptease, is, in equal parts, the suggestion of what is hidden and the inaccessibility of what is disclosed.

. . .

Vowel sounds are made nearest the heart, starting from the lungs and gushing upward and out; consonants, on the other hand, are made at the interface between self and non-self, at the front of the mouth—lips, teeth, tip of tongue. Vowels then are pure feeling-sound, a matrix sculpted into thoughts only by torturously intricate deformation during exit. Hog-callers, poets, singers, lovers, cantors, muezzins—vowel-howlers, one and all.

. . .

Isn't it the mind's capacity to overflow its forms that drenches existence with significance?

. . .

To the literalist anything that moves is moving.

. . .

Personality and character: The first we develop to get along with our fellow human beings, the second to get along with our secret gods. It isn't difficult to tell which poets have gods to deal with and which are content with social devotions.

. . .

We do not bring the wolf into our living room unless it is domesticated, nor do the impulses behind a poem find a place in polite society until they, too, are muzzled or taught to display their fangs only in a classic grin.

. . .

Assumptions about the legitimacy of detachment, which make criticism respectable in our world, would, in any indigenous culture, constitute a state of unbelief which would instantly disqualify the suspect from any further dealings with the spirits aka the arts.

. . .

Light is obedient to laws of refraction and reflection. Vision is subservient to the heart's ability to bear what it has seen.

. . .

"Just because I teach English," he cried, "doesn't mean I'm an English teacher."

. . .

Syntax just may be the most intimate aspect of a poet's work. It is there—rather than in image, idea, or diction—that we learn directly the complexities of a mind and the convolutions of grace in a spirit.

. . .

At its best poetry enchants reason in all its fetters with imagination in all its freedom. As a woman with the gift of dance ensorcels the stockbroker, as the sea embraces the rocky coasts. Even the hunting cat, all business, is enchanted by the bird, all grace.

. . .

In a culture where people would rather hear songs than sing them, no wonder commerce replaces community, and idolatry succeeds creativity.

. . .

The too earnest flog an art of unimaginative candor.

. . .

The eye is the window to the soul, as Blake famously declared. It's no accident that the word for our organ of vision and the word for our first person singular are homophones, sound-alikes: eye and I. The more we see the more we are, the more we are the more we become a part of what we see. That the sense of individuality and the sense of co-existence increase proportionally is only apparently a paradox. To explore individuality to its ultimate stages is to lose all sense of separateness from what we sometimes are encouraged to think of as the Other, the non-Self.

. . .

By illusions we may not learn Truth so much as what it is in our lives that rings most true.

. . .

Life as we know it is entirely an act of imagination.

. . .

If in dreams we rehearse our audience with the infinite, in the arts we merely knock upon the gate.

ARTHUR WINFIELD KNIGHT

Swimming in Sand:
The Imaginary Autobiography of James Dean
(selections)

Isobel

The ocean smelled like poppies in July. I'd go to Venice's Pacific Ocean Park late at night when the sky was colored with hazy neon and red brake lights. I'd watch people eating corndogs and clams while they stood next to the great roller coaster that rocked and shook the dark, and I'd follow teenagers along the boardwalk as they held hands and laughed. I'd see old men in worn suits leaning against the funhouse, trying to make it through one more night while they passed a bottle back and forth, waiting for the light. Cops watched me watching.

I'd spend my last nickel at a small coffee shop on the boardwalk in the early hours before dawn because I liked to talk to the waitress. Isobel would wipe the counter with a dirty rag and try not to get any grits into my cup. She had dark circles under her eyes and read all the movie magazines. She was a philosopher of trash. "I wonder how the stars look so beautiful all the time when they're so miserable," she said. Her life didn't seem so drab when she watched others. It gave her purpose.

Hollywood

I like to drive into the copper-colored hills at dusk, past the huge letters that spell out HOLLYWOOD, as if people would be lost if the name weren't there to remind them where they are. Many of them are lost anyway. You can see old men and women sitting on their faded stucco porches, watching the sun go down, their feet stretched out before them in the burnt-sienna sunlight. The rich are getting ready to have cocktails in Beverly Hills or Brentwood, but there are no cocktails for the poor. No dinners at the Villa Capri. The poor drink cheap wine or unsweetened iced tea out of old jelly glasses, their hands shaking. They might have dinner once a week at some flyblown Italian restaurant where the sidewalks out front are cracked and huge dandelions grow out of the concrete. There are a few cheap hotels where nobody but people named Smith and Jones sign the register, and there are some cheap apartment houses for aspiring actresses, but most of them have faces like stale beer by the time they have been here a year. The lucky ones make it back to wherever they came from. Hollywood almost looks beautiful from the observatory at Griffith Park as the sky deepens, turning ocher, but it's an illusion.

Buster Keaton

He was out of work, out of favor, when I met him. Keaton had a face like a burst white bag. Everyone in Hollywood knew he was an alcoholic, but he said, "I never drink—unless I'm alone, or with someone." He stood there weaving, in the middle of Rodeo Drive, then he began to shadow-box, as if he were reenacting a scene from one of his silent films, but his timing was gone and he faltered, stumbling. A surly cop with red hair shoved him into the back of a patrol car.

Producers had called him a genius when he was making pictures like *The General,* but that had been more than a quarter century ago. Since then, he'd been in and out of psychiatric wards, and he always needed a shave, smelling of bourbon and beer. He'd do a little dance for a dollar. He'd become a symbol of everything that could go wrong in the lives of the rich and famous, and everyone in Beverly Hills wished he'd go away.

Ghost Rider

I'm hitting a hundred when I come down the hill from the Palisades to the Coast Highway on my motorcycle, leaning over the handlebars, a ghost rider. I know the cops won't be able to spot me. I'm invisible. I pass rows of Edward Hopper diners with no customers and forlorn Signal and Shell stations that have been shut for hours, their signs creaking in the wind and salt air. Giant bird-like machines pump oil out of the damp earth, moving rhythmically, their iron beaks rising and falling, as if they were prehistoric creatures keeping time to their own deaths. The lights in most of the cottages along the ocean have been out for hours. The waves wash huge pieces of rotting kelp onto the beach in the rusty moonlight. I like it because it's so lonely.

Rape

"It is always the same nightmare," Pier said. I'd hold her for hours, feeling her tremble, because I knew she was afraid to go to sleep. She'd been raped by an American G.I. when she was a teenager in Italy. The soldier forced her to lie down in the rubble of a bombed-out building near Rome. She remembers lying on some pulverized bricks, remembers the dust hanging in the Mediterranean air. Remembers the bricks cutting into her back and buttocks. The soldier couldn't have been much older than Pier. He had blond hair and baby-blue eyes, and she remembers he was sunburnt. Even in her dreams, she can see his nose peeling. He showed her his .45 and said, "You know I can kill you with this," cocking the pistol, before he pushed her skirt up over her face so she could barely breathe. But she heard him. Felt him. When it was over, the soldier gave her a Hershey bar and said, "My buddies died on Anzio Beach for you people. Their bodies turned the water red." She could feel the blood congealing on her thighs. "I hope you appreciate the sacrifices we've made."

Venice

The air on the Venice boardwalk had always smelled of boiling hot-dogs, candied apples, popcorn and hot funnel cakes with powdered sugar, but the only thing I could afford in those days was a cup of coffee.

I took Pier to the small shop I used to frequent, because I wanted her to meet the waitress. Isobel had loved movie stars because their lives seemed so tragic, but she didn't work there anymore. No one knew where she went, and no one cared.

The sky over the Pacific had turned from a greenish-blue to brass with strips of crimson along the horizon. It had begun to rain by the time we ordered. The side of Pier's face was rippled with the shadows of raindrops running down the window, and her skin was a faded pink in the late light.

Some seagulls that were the color of dirty dishwater hovered above the gray waves. Pier and I bought snow cones when we left the restaurant. We walked along, our lips purple, in the warm rain, and the wind blew from the east.

"When I was growing up, people told me a wind from the east meant bad luck," Pier said, "but everyone in Italy was superstitious." She held my hand. "It's been a perfect day."

"I still wish I'd been able to find Isobel," I said.

Salinas

The wind blew the dust across the lettuce fields late each afternoon in Salinas. The men who picked the lettuce wore bandanas as they hunched over, going down one row, then up another. The wind always blew. Biting into their backs. Into their faces. They called lettuce a stoop crop, because you had to bend over to pick it. The sky was the color of a dirty parsnip, but most of them couldn't see the sky.

The dust swirled down on Salinas like dry rain. It seeped between the boards of the bunkhouse where I was staying. Kazan had sent me there to learn how the people talked. It was easy. They dropped their g's and their vowels had the sharp sounds of consonants, and their conversations never changed.

The men wore bib overalls and patched jeans, and the girls had fragile, bird-like bones and worn, calico dresses. The drugstores sold out of Ben-Gay every week and the bars were filled each Saturday. Okies and Mexicans, the lettuce pickers, stood around in small groups under a hostile sky. They were always on opposite sides of the street. Only the dust prevailed.

Mendocino

The sun, when it appeared, was as light and dry as pale sherry, and the wind shook the old buildings along Main Street when it blew across Portuguese Flat. There were some magnificent groves of ancient redwoods surrounding the town, and the sea was primordial, but you could smell the burning wood from the pulp mills in Fort Bragg, a few miles north, when the wind was right. The sky would turn plum-colored from the smoke, and tiny particles of soot would whirl down on the town, covering the general store and the bank. The bells above the church clamored in the foggy dew, and you could hear the leaves from the huge eucalyptus trees trembling in the wind. We wore coats and sweaters most of the time we were there because it was always cold. Jo Van Fleet's skin seemed translucent in the soft aqueous light, and her lips were the color of faded rose petals when we stood next to one another, rubbing our hands together, between takes. Mendocino was one of the most gorgeous places on earth, but I wondered why anyone would want to live there.

The Burning Cow

We saw a burning cow run through a field alongside the highway shortly after we left Lone Pine. The cow's udders swung and blazed against a caramelized sky. Pier asked, "Who'd set a cow on fire? Who could be so cruel? What does it mean?" I'd never heard her ask so many questions, but neither of us had ever seen a burning cow. We watched its legs collapse, then it fell to the earth with a huge thud, its feet caught in some barbed wire. The cow mooed terribly, and we could smell its burning flesh when we got out of the car. I felt Pier tremble as I held her. "We've got to do something," she said, "the poor creature is suffering," but we just stood there helplessly.

Emotional Wrecks

We told each other our sad stories. Mine always began with the death of my mother, but Natalie's began with being a frightened child in the small northern California town where she'd been raised. Her mother had been a ballerina, and Natalie had been forced to take ballet lessons when she was still a toddler. "I could barely walk and there I was, trying to perform entrechats," she said, "while American soldiers were going off to die." Natalie remembered saving the tinfoil from chewing gum wrappers and watering the Victory Garden in her backyard to help the war effort. There were rows of tomatoes and the corn was so high she could get lost in it. She remembered the air raid warden coming down her street each evening, making sure all the lights were out in case the Japanese attacked. She said, "We all had to wear dogtags when we went to school so our little bodies could be identified if we were blown to bits, although no one told us that. I just knew, somehow. It was as if I had extrasensory perception. I hid under my desk, crying, every time I heard a siren or whistle. Wind and rain still scare me, and I still cry easily. Everything's so close to the surface. That's why Nick claims I'm such a good actress. He says we're supposed to be emotional wrecks."

The Old Country

I watched her go. She was wearing high heels and a pleated Pendleton skirt and her burnished hair hung down over her shoulders. It was just before the coming of complete night. I watched her step down from the curb and get into the Buick that seemed too big for her. Watched her light a cigarette while the car idled, her hand shaking. The tip of the cigarette glowed when she inhaled. I wondered if she was still crying. She'd told me her mother wanted her to date someone respectable. Someone Italian. Someone Catholic. A nice boy, like Frankie Sinatra. Or Vic Damone. Someone she could have bambinos with. I hated crooners.

Pier's voice had been carried away by the wind as we stood on the porch in front of my house. The sky over the Hollywood Hills was red, but there were always fires during the summer. Pier had said, "I hate my mother, but I can't disobey her. It's the way I was raised, Jimmy. Things are different in Italy. You have to understand." We were living in the freest place on earth, but we might as well have been in the Old Country. I waited for her to wave, but she didn't look back as she drove away beneath the burning sky.

Natalie

She came to me the afternoon she learned Pier had gone. "I'm sorry," she said, "I'm so sorry." We became instant lovers. She sat on my lap, her legs spread, in the front seat of my Porsche that first night. I could see the lights of the city over her shoulder, far below us. She had great dark eyes and small breasts, and I understood why everyone loved her. She was only 16, but she was already sleeping with Nick, who was in his 40s, and with one of the supporting actors, but it was Hollywood so no one cared, as long as she didn't have to stop work on the picture. I don't know how many people she'd slept with before that, but neither of us were counting. We were both casualties. Natalie said, "You'll see, everything will be all right," her breasts pressed against my face, but we both knew we were going to die young.

Vic

The baby weighed eight pounds, thirteen ounces, and it was delivered by Caesarian section at Cedars of Lebanon Hospital in Los Angeles on the 21st of August, a Sunday. Pier and Vic named the boy after Vic's closest friend, Perry Como, who was also a crooner. A Catholic. Italian. All the things I wasn't, which was why someone else was going to raise a boy who belonged to me.

When Vic came over to my table at The Villa Capri, he said, "It's a boy," and I nodded because I couldn't say congratulations. I'd been drinking since I'd heard the news, so everything seemed bleary. Vic held a bottle of champagne and smiled. He was the kind of guy who'd have to shave twice a day if he didn't want five-o'clock shadow, but Pier's mother thought he was perfect. He was a smiling fool.

I wondered if Pier had told him I was the father. Probably not. I thought about telling him, but we'd all suffered enough. What good would it do? I sat there rigidly, holding a martini, until Vic went back across the room to join his friends. It was one of the worst nights of my life, and they were all laughing.

Highway 1

It's already midnight when I pass the castle William Randolph Hearst built on the hill overlooking San Simeon and the Pacific. I like the squeal of the tires and the smell of rubber burning as I accelerate, then downshift, then hit the gas again. I can corner at 80. I like the feel of the night air in my face and the scent of cypress. Trees bent by the wind grow impossibly out of the rock, illuminated by my high beams as I head toward Big Sur. The two-lane highway twists hundreds of feet above the ocean, and the moonlight's brilliant and playful on the cold waves. I could disappear into the pale darkness forever. Some people say I'm chasing death when I drive like this, late and alone, but I'm just living fast.

JUDITH AZRAEL

Aegean Light

Today the ants are carrying flowers along the dusty roads. The wind is making love to every leaf and blade of grass. Oh teach me that my heart is empty. Teach me equanimity. Teach me loving kindness.

. . .

The brown donkey is crying and will go on crying until wild crimson poppies grow beneath his feet. I want to go home but I have forgotten where I come from.

. . .

The past keeps slipping away from me like spare change that I toss to the beggar women of Athens with their mournful eyes and their prayers that follow after me. Today the clouds are flocks of sheep huddled beneath the trees. The stone walls are patiently waiting and will go on waiting for a thousand years.

. . .

I long for you and roses go on singing in the crannies of the rocks. Mules sway by with stacks of red bricks on their backs. I remember when my mother was young and beautiful. I was the light flickering in the almond trees. I was the sea running to the shore. I was still unborn. I knew nothing of this life.

• • •

There is nothing to hold on to anymore. I move away from the mountains to the olive groves and flowers. There are tears in my eyes but what does it matter.

• • •

The sheep clamber over the stone wall to graze in the meadow. A lizard lifts its head in the sunlight. This day has no beginning and no ending.

• • •

I see sadness in your eyes and all the flowers are swaying on their stems.

• • •

Tonight the wild goats come down from the hills and the air is filled with the scent of thyme. The sky is a chapel with its door flung open and all its candles glowing.

. . .

Here I am in this land of mountains and braying donkeys, where the wild geraniums sing their song of desire along the dusty roadsides. I climb to the top of every hill past women picking capers in the fields and roosters crowing proudly, past goatherds with their flocks of goats. Where will all our dreams lead us but back to this dusty earth, back to these rocks and thistles, back to this sea so blue the sky turns pale beside it.

. . .

When I entered your shop in Koufonissi, you played me music, blues and jazz, and we sipped our drinks and silently listened as if it had always been this way. I found Sophia standing in her garden and together we watered the thirsty flowers with fresh water the boat had brought that morning. At night the electricity went out and the stars shone so brightly I knelt before them.

. . .

All day and night the meltemi blows. Prayers fly out of the chapel windows. Thoughts sweep away like a flock of bright birds. I am left as clean as a bone.

. . .

Where are all the beetles going on their slow pilgrimage over the dry earth and stones. Where are all of us going. I climb the footpath higher and higher until I have entered the sky.

. . .

Along the footpath to Kastro I call your name and white doves startle into flight.

. . .

I descend the wide stairway into the valley where goats are sleeping in the shadows of the stone walls. The wind is singing about weeds and dry grasses and figs ripening on the trees.

. . .

Goat bells are ringing in the mountains, a xylophone played by the wind.

. . .

At Ayia Anna a rooster is crowing. White houses sleep in the sun and bougainvillea spills over the walls. From far below the sea waves its deep blue kerchief and departs on a long journey.

. . .

The wind is sighing like a forsaken lover and all the stones are crumbling into earth. There is no reason to say goodbye. Some day all our dust will rise and dance together in the air.

PHYLLIS KOESTENBAUM

oh I can't she says

(selections)

The following fragments are from the book oh I can't
she says *(published by Christopher's Books in 1980).
The book is essentially a dream journal, reproducing
dreams as they were first experienced, with little or no
revision.*

+ + +

There are working dreams and dream fulfillment dreams a psychiatrist says. My psychiatrist.

Beverly says have you tried cutting them up and reshuffling them.

• • •

a girl on the phone in a movie ticket booth is expected to do calcu-
lations in her head   3 digits multiplied by 3 digits   oh I can't she
says   I start to multiply for her

• • •

It may take the whole summer to get through *the man who loved children*. It may take the whole summer to get through this. I'm writing a book.

. . .

John Berryman: a dream is a panorama of the whole mental life.

I am reading him this summer.

. . .

Dreams change as your understanding of them does.

. . .

to be faithful to the dream   not invent   not try to dazzle   to trust the dream is poetry   let the dream grab my arm   let it write   as a blind one walks with cane, and dog   frightened   trusting   I am frightened   anyhow, what do I know of language   not much

. . .

I want to write poems, my life is not a poem, I am writing my life.

. . .

we're sitting on a bench
Dr. Fry and I
looking over magazine pages of my drawings of insects
drawings, not poems
my father never read to me

. . .

Ian and I give our handwriting to a computer. Mine comes back YOU LOVE DEEPLY AND STRONGLY. I believe I love deeply and strongly. I believe the computer.

. . .

a house of gardens, floors of gardens, too many to take in at once, water one garden it grows lush, on the next floor the garden could be dying, a house of gardens

. . .

between naïve and intuitive
closer to naïve

. . .

A woman leans out the window, she claims it's the 3rd floor but it looks to me like a low 2nd. She instructs Lissy to position herself to catch a breakable ornament like bone china. Miraculously Lissy catches it.

Being fragile, how do you survive.

. . .

Janine says after I read her section 66, You mean, The thing is not to let the *writing* matter so much. Of course that is what I mean. I didn't know it was what I meant. Now I know.

. . .

what happens next matters as much as what is happening now or what happened before   I am learning to give up   I am learning to look ahead

. . .

Robin dreamed we burned a bookstore down   it was a used book bookstore   we asked the man for an old book   he brought us pornography   Robin said I was powerful in her dream, not as I am in the car in San Francisco when she has to tell me how to get where we are going   we burned his store down   I say, Robin, how do you feel about me being powerful   I tell her, maybe we are burning down our past   our fathers, our Jewish fathers

. . .

I have almost used up another cartridge working. Working. And the silver pen squeaks, it is at the end. Working. My third pen has a wobbly point. Working. One wrong write and it will break. Working.

. . .

Too many interruptions. I am panting for the end.

. . .

My mother is not thin in the picture attached with pushpins to the wall of her living room. She is thin now, very thin. My mother is dying.

. . .

When dream meets life I can pause.
I have used dream to find life, dream
to take life away.
When dream meets life, I can pause.

Low tide, the island can be walked to, but hurry
though I need to take my time.

. . .

I have finished *the man who loved children.*

. . .

I said I wouldn't hurry the end.
I lied.

. . .

The end belongs here.
Once it's ready why hold it in.

. . .

I have the end but it is not the end, because I have it more and more
comes.

. . .

We were to take an airplane but it's foggy and the flight is delayed.
I'm not even packed though it's 12 and the airplane was to leave at
12. It could leave momentarily, the fog will lift. I tell someone to get

me all my underclothes for packing, underpants, nighties, even dirty underclothes. I have the feeling the suitcase is full and I will have to jam this stuff on the top. I don't want to go without it. The fog is lifting but not completely. What matters is sun is beginning to squeeze through.

. . .

In yellow house with smudged yellow garage door lived 6.
Lived mother, lived father, lived three brothers and sister.
Now there live 5. Next week will live 4.
who I am
who I
am
am

. . .

The first night in 6 months there were no dreams to write down.

. . .

I have passed the end.

. . .

I have a foreboding. Lightning rolls in the sky. The neighbors on the front porch feel it too. I grab my red binder of poems after I grab something else. My notebook. Or this. Mrs. Gilbert is in her house and animals, teeny cats or animals that are not cats but look like them, are climbing the walls of her house. The ritual is to close and open the doors just right, they are climbing all over me, get them off me, she's daft, Mr. Gilbert, will you please help me.

. . .

I would be whole.

. . .

We get a cab. We don't want to go over the bridge, we want to stay in downtown Brooklyn. We're going over the bridge, it's good we got a cab, I wouldn't like to drive over the bridge. A woman asks a question. The attendant won't answer, as if speaking on bridges is illegal, like parking. A car almost sideswipes us. Driving across bridges is dangerous business. A car drops some papers, maybe pictures, I see the woman inside that car as we pass. Her eyes stare. What does she see. She is staring at something in herself. Peter tells the cab driver to return to Brooklyn.

. . .

The poem forms, reforms, daily it becomes a different whole. The poem became something in the reading to Janine. Today I work on it and it is something else.

. . .

The baby I have beaten, when I haven't, maybe the baby shows who I was, what I was feeling when the baby was a baby. The baby could even be me. Who I was when the baby was a baby. Not doubletalk. Not doubletalk. I don't want to think symbol, but symbol is the streetlight, with halos.

. . .

Lynn Wachtel in a Peter Pan collar white blouse with tight cuffs and a pink bow, dreamy and young, her hair long and black, her dog-black eyes. My father or mother, someone makes a comment on the fact, not opinion, fact, of her being pretty, she is being compared to me objectively. Yet something tragic has happened to *her* not me.

. . .

Walking north on a dark crowded Bowerylike street, almost the smell is possible. And I get my purse stolen, I didn't get much money stolen, but besides the affront something was taken I'd rather not have. It could have been my pen.

. . .

Then I walk down natural steps the color of raw dirt. I am being told, maybe by Stella, that I take the long way to go to the city. Long means wrong.

. . .

I don't want people reading this who will know more about me than I do.

. . .

I'm a bus driver who doesn't know the way, who drives an empty bus, the passengers in the bus are irritated with my driving, I don't know how to drive the bus, I could be going to the ferry, I could be driving through towns I have driven through before, really driven through, towns I long to see again.

. . .

I am writing a sort of fiction. No, Robin is right. Don't name it, just write it.

. . .

The end is a place to stop.

. . .

I have put in time, time was the risk. I hoped it would work, but I'd have gone on anyway. Inevitable. It had to be, had to be invested in. Now more a small death than a birth. We used to make paper boats my brother and I. Sail away. I'm tired, even bereft.

. . .

It would have been a waste to dream and have only the unconscious benefit.

SCOTT SUSSMAN

The Clever Antics of Lizard
(selections)

Innocence

Angels whisper warnings
which I am too human to hear.

. . .

To: Bart Arnold
Re: essays/torture/hell

For me, reading and writing outweigh teaching in the same way that
love outweighs like. I do teach, once in a while, and I like it, but
despise assigning homework, giving grades, and other educational
duties. I especially deplore reading essays. Essays are torture. If
there's a hell and I'm going, I'll be down there grading essays.

. . .

Substitute teaching a kindergarten class

I get there, the bell rings
and all the five-year-olds come in,
hang their backpacks in the closet,
then sit on the carpet in front of me.

The syllabus says:
1 Take roll
2 Count up to ten
3 Recite the A, B, C's

But before I can say a word
a little boy raises his hand.

"Yes?" I ask.

With a serious face
he says,
"I have a bunk bed."

"Nice," I respond, "great…"
but am interrupted by another hand
held high in the air.

I call on a small girl
who says with sincerity,
"My cousin's seven."

Now almost all the hands
are in the air and I say,
"Hold on! Hands down!
Everyone put your hands down,
I still gotta take roll!"

...

To: David Takahashi
Re: bought a bathrobe

One idiosyncrasy involved with living in a garage is that the bath-room is in the house. I save empty water bottles, gallon-size, and when it's an emergency or I'm too lazy to make the trek through the courtyard, down the corridor and around to the house, I piss in one of them. In the morning or later that day, I place it in the dumpster in the alley. I suppose it's not sanitary, and probably illegal, but worse things happen in the world.

Our complex consists of eight duplexes and garages surrounding one courtyard/parking area. Garage electricity comes on at night. I can plug an extension cord into our kitchen during the day but it's like waving a red flag to the landlady. Nevertheless, that's what I do on the weekends. Weekdays, I either return from work and other activities after the power is already on or else I occupy myself with other endeavors until it does.

During the week, I wake at four in the morning. I say a prayer, exercise for thirty minutes, and then go into the house, taking my keys, a towel and, when it rains, an umbrella. Then, pinching my boxers under an elbow and carrying my lunch in a plastic sack, I lock the door and return to the garage with the towel wrapped around my waist. It used to be a cold, dreaded walk in winter, until I bought a bathrobe.

. . .

Tuesday, April 16, 2002

Bradshaw,

Do you know that Chinese proverb: It is impossible to know the results of your actions? It seems to me that if we knew the future, we could change it and, therefore, it would be impossible to see it, right? For example, if I knew that I was going to crash my car while driving home today, I would either not drive home, or else go a different way and then the future I had seen would not happen and so what was it that I had seen? Meanwhile, everyone else involved in the accident (other drivers, police officers and paramedics) would also have envisioned a future that didn't occur.

Maybe we *can* see the future but as it's always in motion because people can alter it, it looks blurry and so we think we can't see it. Like right now, if I imagine the future, I see a blur of black, white and gray like snow on a television screen. Is that it and can I change it like a channel?

What if we could alter the past? What if I regretted having eaten grits with sauerkraut for breakfast this morning and could go back and eat toast instead? Is that possible? By altering an action in the past, I would undo the aftermath that resulted from that action and I might even disappear because, heck, I could kill myself like that. Maybe eating grits with sauerkraut is the reason I'm still alive now because, had I poured myself a bowl of cereal, I'd have saved seconds, left earlier and crashed my car and died.

I was invited to a party tonight and the thing is: I get up at four-fifteen in the morning. It's difficult to enjoy myself at a party when I get up at four-fifteen because I can't stop thinking about the fact that I get up so early. Go to the party or not? What if the girl of my dreams is at the party? What if I don't go and therefore never meet the girl of my dreams and then die a lonely old fart? What if I go to the party, oversleep the next morning, arrive late to work, get fired and then end up sleeping in the gutter for the rest of my life? I might die a lonely old fart. The Chinese are right: It's impossible to know the results of your actions.

What's new with you? How're they treating you in there? Good? Bad? Ugly? Is it easier to stomach now that they let you out a few hours a week? Are you adapting? Starting to like it in there? I'll bet that by the end of a year you'll want to stay and they'll have to drag you out of there. You'll be screaming for more. I'm sure of it.

P.S. Happy Chaplin's birthday! (1889–1977)

. . .

To: Paul Shepard
Re: my pal, my pet

When I was a boy, I saw my puppy, my pal, my pet, Heidi the dog— with her furry black head and that pink tongue lolling like it was stretching to lick the ground—run straight into the street, hit the hubcap of a passing car, and split open her skull. It was my first experience with death and witnessing it in such a brutal manner confused me. I saw brains, puddles of blood, and felt bad for the man who was driving as I stood staring.

My brother and sister screamed as it happened and then burst into sobs. The man parked, exited his car and I watched my parents emerge from the house. They consoled my brother and sister and then my dad calmed the driver. While ushering me inside, I turned to my mom and, blurry with tears, cried, "Can we get another dog?"

. . .

Sunday, June 23, 2002

Dear Bradshaw,

First of all, what's a mistake? Is it a mistake when a three-year-old reaches out to touch a hot stove? Is it a mistake when a couple in love marries, but divorces twenty years later? Is it a mistake when I buy a book and don't enjoy reading it? If you make a mistake and learn your lesson, it's not a mistake.

Don't be bitter. Once you start pointing the finger of blame there's no end to the number of culprits you can indicate. Be stoic, suffer silently, and remember that you're responsible for your own actions.

It's up to you to decide if you made a mistake or not. We're our own judges.

. . .

Substitute teacher report

Mrs. Goosh,

Do you realize you have a student named Perfecto in period two? What is this country coming to? Next thing you know parents will call their kids Stupendous, Awesome or Radical. Imagine me: Sensational Scott.

I fear the future where people name their children Firecracker and Hallelujah or Amen, Kangaroo or Boomerang. A name should be a name. Not a grunt, not a groan and definitely not an adverb or a superlative.

What says society when it names its children with phrases or entire sentences like "Hey, Pass the Salt" or "Come On Outta There"?

I don't know what to make of it. It's ridiculous already. I hope you had a wonderful weekend. Welcome back!

Your Sub,
Scott

• • •

To: Bart Arnold
Re: Hitler was right

Right now the class is completing a worksheet about World War II. A girl said to me, "I think Hitler was right to kill the Jews because that's what they deserve for crucifying Jesus."

"Are you sure it wasn't the Romans who crucified Jesus?" I asked.

She said, "That's not what my pastor said."

. . .

Saturday, September 28, 2002

Dear Bradshaw,

What do you think about before you fall asleep? What do you do during your free time? Who, in your opinion, is the most important person who has ever lived? What is your highest aspiration? If you could travel back in time, what moments in history would you witness? What's something somebody said to you that you've never forgotten?

Before I fall asleep I think about the lovely ladies I saw that day, or flowers. I think about the mistakes I made and how I can avoid making the same ones in the future. I think about who I am, who I was, and who I will be tomorrow. I think about you sometimes, pal. During my free time I read, write, play the harmonica, listen to music, take walks and dream.

The most important person, in my opinion, is Buddha or Jesus. I love prophets. My highest aspiration is to self-perfect until there's less than the smallest amount of me. I want to transcend to a higher evolution, to achieve nirvana. If I could travel back in time, I would witness the first human being born, the earliest form of musical instrument, or else I would watch Moses part the Red Sea so I could return to tell what really happened.

"Surround yourself with nourishing people." That's something someone said to me that I've never forgotten.

Your seesaw,
Scott

. . .

To: Paul Shepard
Re: my grandma's grief

My grandpa died of prostate cancer, nine years ago. At the funeral, my grandma's grief was so severe that she dropped to the ground and lay there sobbing until others forced her to her feet and carried her on. He died three weeks after the diagnosis and it hit her hard.

My grandma lives in a convalescent home now, sharing her room with one, and sometimes two, other ladies. I visit her once a week, my mom goes every day, my dad sometimes, and my brother and sister as often as possible. She's been in bed, suffering pneumonia and grinding coughs for two years. She stares at the blurs of walls and various assortments of flowers, oblivious to everything but the inevitable. She's partially deaf so I have to scream to be heard. The place is depressing. The air sticks to me like sap and there's a constant hum of machines and echoing music mixed with her roommate's television.

Today I asked my grandma if she remembers her dreams. She was quiet for a few moments and then she looked at me and said, "There's one." I asked her to tell me about it and it seemed like she was going to, but then she laid her head back and closed her eyes.

Earlier in my visit, I was telling her about my Italian class when her phone rang. She answered it and I heard my mom's voice in the background. My grandma told her she had a visitor and my mom asked who it was. My grandma was silent, struggling to remember my name. Then she looked at me and said, "I'm sorry. What's your name?"

My grandma says funny things sometimes. Once, her eyelids were drooping and I asked if she was tired. "No," she said, "I'm not tired. Sometimes my eyelids get heavy and are hard to hold up."

Today she was talking about something that had happened sixty years ago when suddenly, her eyes popped open, her hands spread and she said, "Everything that was, isn't."

. . .

It's dark and I'm running through shadows away from a monster. I imagine a door and suddenly it's before me. I start to open it, hoping to escape, but I'm moving slower than the monster is catching up.

As I grip the knob and pull open the door, I realize I'm not going to make it. I want to see what it looks like so I turn around to behold a figure, cloaked in blackness, with beams of light shooting out from where its face should be. The instant it reaches me, we become one, and I wake up surging with excitement.

. . .

Monday, December 9, 2002

Dear Bradshaw,

Would you give up a lung for world peace? Would you lose a kidney to feed the hungry and house the homeless? If I asked you for your arms to cure cancer and your legs to give sight to the blind, would you be willing? What would you do, Bradshaw, really?

Jesus, Galileo, Gandhi, what do you think of those guys? *Do* you think of those guys? Is it possible that, perhaps, just maybe, I might be the next Albert Einstein or Charlie Chaplin or Moses? After all, how hard can it be to part the Red Sea? Let's see someone part the Pacific Ocean, or hop from here to eternity, or turn the Earth into a raccoon. Let's see someone win the lottery fifty times in a row, or memorize the Bible, backward.

Think about Euripides, Aristophanes, Socrates and Aristotle. Anyone can happen, with or without luck, but who really remembers· their names and can recite all their sentences by syllable? So many slip into the void of oblivion, volumes of names unknown. Remember Beofolus, Hippintrotter and Qullosophes? Naturally not!

· · ·

Substitute teacher report

Mr. Piedmont,

I apologize for not covering your class today. I sent a second-generation clone of myself. It is, however, an exact replica and I'm sure nobody noticed. The reason for my absence is unsatisfactory. I was too tired to get up in the morning. When my alarm rang, my head was magnetized to the pillow and, no matter how hard I tried, impossible to lift.

Luckily, I had left the clone charging all night so it was supplied with sufficient electricity. Besides, it has been programmed to plug into classroom sockets during snack, lunch and, if necessary, discreetly during passing periods. Although only three months off the assembly line, it is, I assure you, almost as efficient as I.

Please don't tell anybody about this because, as you know, they won't pay me for a day I didn't work and I need the money. Again I apologize.

Scott

• • •

I'm a lizard, resting on a rock. The sun heats me like a lover's kiss and I feel strengthened by its invigorating energy. I'm the color of a walnut shell with a scattering of hazel patterns decorating my back. My body is scaly and my tail long. I feel itchy and irritable as my skin stiffens, flakes, and then peels off completely.

I'm still a lizard but now with human hands. I etch words in the sand with my fingernail, describing this dream. Then I wake up and write it down for real.

NICOLE BRAUN

A Life of Depression and Writing

These fragments about my life are snapshots of where I have been that contrast with the way I feel today. Since writing this piece, I have spent time retreating from the world and have learned to appreciate what I never before could appreciate: a sunny day, a snow-storm, a good cup of tea...

+ + +

Age 7

I give all my toys to my sisters after my mother has gone on one of her rampages and I want to die. I don't know what is wrong with her. She is scary. I am a bad girl. I am sloppy and messy and lazy. I want to give my sisters my toys because I am either going to run away or kill myself. I imagine that I will pack a bag and disappear into the woods. I will build a little house, underground, and I will have supplies there like canned soup and my favorite pillow. All my books, too. In times like this, my stepfather forgets how much he hates me and seems lost. He follows my mother around looking sheepish. My mother goes through the house screaming, her hair pinned on top of her head. She looks ugly and her eyes are red and swollen from crying. She is pulling all the clothes out of our closets, telling us we are messy, dirty, bad girls. She throws dishes. Breaks them. Empties the linen closets. Sheets and towels are all over the floor. She screams. Then she leaves the house and the mess. I clean it up, comfort my sisters, and tell my dad she will be better tomorrow. But she never really is.

Age 9

My parents have a minister come to our house. He comes to our house to talk to me because I am worried about what happens to people when they die, and I also want to know the meaning of life. We sit in the family room. Eating Pringles. I remember the Pringles, eating all of them from the can, more than I remember the specifics about the conversation. He tells me that I think too much and I must have faith and forget reason. He wants to know if I want to be saved. I do. He saves me via Jesus. I don't feel saved.

• • •

My parents think there is something wrong with me. I overhear them in hushed voices telling the minister how I saw my biological father get shot and perhaps that is the root of my questions and angst.

Age 12

I write stories. I write stories and don't have to take regular English. I get put in gifted language arts classes. But I am not so gifted. I write dark, bleak stories about death, and about my death in particular. I write stories about the meaning of life, stories that get me all A's. I get published in several children's magazines. I write about the Holocaust and I write about the future. A future after nuclear war.

My parents don't care. They don't see reading and writing as accomplishments. They tell me I am lazy.

"Get to work. Put that book down. Stop day-dreaming," my stepfather says to me over and over again. I imagine I am Anne Frank, writing in my diary and then living in a concentration camp after hiding in an attic for many years. I read books about the Holocaust and I read about Hitler. I imagine I am Jewish. I want to be Jewish. I meet a girl who is Jewish and I love her.

Age 14

Diary entry: "Blessed is the man who endures trial for when he has stood the test, he will receive the crown of life which God has promised to those who love him." (From a Bible verse in James.)

I don't know what my problem is. But I do know that I want to die. Everything feels black and bleak. I am 14 but I feel old and tired. The years fly by. I am sad all the time. I pray to God to make me ok.

I have goals. I write in my journal: "To pray regularly, to live life deeply, to give as much as I can to people, and to learn the lessons I need to learn. Forgive me, Lord, for what I am not. There has got to be a purpose. Let me be strong. Let me forgive my parents for taking my journal and reading it. Let me forgive them for lying to me about taking it. Please Lord, forgive me, and help me. My parents think I'm crazy. Maybe I am. I'm a sinner for what I think and feel. I'm falling. I don't know what life is for. Everything is dark. I want to die. Please forgive me God for wanting to die. How can I witness if I die early?"

Age 17

I am on the road. On the road and on the run. I have run away from home. It was either that or kill myself. I swallowed 30 extra strength Tylenol before I ran away, but before I swallowed more I decided I wanted to live. I took some clothes, all the money I had from working as a waitress, and this diary. I ran from Flint, Michigan to Miami, Florida. I didn't expect to go this far. But I did.

. . .

I remember my dad saying that the way to Florida is to take I-75 South. In the car that I purchased with my waitressing money, I go. I am afraid. Please help me God. No one knows where I am. I have found a little place to live and two jobs. I lie about my age. I watch TV in my winter rental that is furnished. It has a toaster so I eat a lot of toast. As I watch TV I imagine that I will see my distraught parents on the news. I imagine they are looking for me and that they miss me. I look at the milk cartons in the store to see if my face is on the missing children's section. I go to church and pretend that I am saved. I meet a prostitute and take her to church. I pretend that I love church and religion. I pretend that I have a family at home that loves me. I fill up pages and pages of my diary and wonder if my parents miss me or if they are glad to get rid of me.

Age 19

I am in a treatment center for an eating disorder. The therapist wants me to write down the reasons I am angry. I don't want to write down my anger list today, but I do. The therapists here expect us to fill pages of paper with words, images, thoughts, and feelings that will, supposedly, give us insights into the rage that got us in the hospital in the first place. I have to cooperate, or at least give them the illusion of cooperation. I have to conform.

I am angry with blah blah blah. Some things I make up. Other things I figure I should be mad about, so I list those things, too. Like I am angry that my father was shot by the police when I was a child, in front of my eyes. And I am angry that my mother and stepfather kicked me out of the house for being bulimic instead of getting me help. I am angry with my sister for acting so perfect and for telling on me when she heard me throwing up in the bathroom. I am angry with the power-hungry men in my life who use women. I am angry because my parents didn't help me go to college.

But I don't really feel angry about any of those things. Mostly, I am angry with myself. I spiral down from there into a litany of examples, mostly about the ways I fucked up my life from the time I was born until age 19.

"You aren't supposed to go there," the therapist tells me.

The purpose of the assignment is to verbalize anger towards others, not towards oneself. Depression is, according to the experts, anger turned inward and it is not productive to spiral down into self-blame and self-hatred. Better homicidal than suicidal, was their motto.

I am not angry, and I know it, but do as I am told, anyway.

The list is not cathartic, just stupid.

• • •

We take turns the next day reading our anger lists to one another in group. But when I try to read my list, something happens. I begin to laugh. Not the sort of laugh that erupts when something is funny, like when you laugh at a good joke. This is a scary laugh, a laugh that sounds like the cry of a wounded animal trapped in a cage, or some stupid analogy like that. The other patients start to laugh as well.

The more they laugh the more I laugh. It's as if I have had laughter bottled up inside of me for 19 years and it is now just bursting out. The therapist says I must calm down, and orders the group to stop laughing. Laughter is not acceptable for something as serious as this. He instructs me to begin reading my list again.

So I begin reading again. Only I laugh again, too. Naturally. When you are told not to laugh, it is that much harder to keep it inside. So I howl. I am hysterical. Roaring. The group laughs, too.

But the truth is: nothing is really funny at all. Most of all, not me. I am not funny. I am out of control. And then I start to cry. Shake and cry. As hysterical and scary as the laughter was, crying is a lot worse.

I transform from a young woman with some depression and an eating disorder into insanity. I've crossed the line and I know it. I keep crying and laughing while everyone sits in silence. The therapist gets a medical doctor to escort me out. I am taken to an examination room. I am diagnosed for the first time as "manic-depressive" and put on lithium. I take the medicine just for something new to do.

• • •

I meet a rich older man in the hospital (he is 65). He is a patient as well. He tells me God came to him in a dream and wants him to pay for my school, my college education. I want to go to college. I am shipped off to a fancy liberal arts college in Denver, Colorado, to study theater. The man pays for it since God is on his side.

But he doesn't have pure motives. He wants sex. Sex for money. Sex in exchange for school. He wants me as his sex slave. No one does something for nothing. Since I need and want to go to school, and have no parents anymore, and no sense of self, I say what the hell and fuck him for an education. But I flunk all my classes, too busy smoking pot and hanging with the hippies to do my schoolwork. I really want to be a hippie.

Age 22

I am pregnant. I slit my wrists when I find out. What will people say when they find out I am pregnant?

I live nowhere in particular and work two jobs waitressing in Flint, Michigan. How can I have a baby? How can I expect to give birth to a healthy/normal person? My ex-boyfriend wants nothing to do with the baby. Or with me. I didn't think I could get pregnant. My mother won't speak to me. Because I am pregnant and not married…

The psychiatrist I see after slitting my wrists tells me I will never be able to handle having a baby. He says that I must give the baby up for adoption. But I want to keep the baby.

Ages 23-25

One of my friends thinks I should go back to school. To the community college in Flint. I do, even though I fear I will flunk. I always fuck everything up. But I get all A's. I transfer to the university and continue to get A's. I am chosen to be the commencement speaker at my graduation. I want what I say to be so earth-shattering that I contemplate suicide just to get out of it because I cannot bear to do anything less than the best.

My baby is growing up fast. We struggle with no money and no resources. Sometimes I feel I am going crazy. Other times, though, I am happy with my son. He gives me purpose and life.

Age 28

By a fluke, I am accepted into the Ph.D. program at Rutgers University. My friends in Flint raise the money for my son and I so we can afford the trip across country. I am frightened, and I write my feelings in my journal. I like to imagine that I will become a famous writer and will transform my earlier years into something positive. I want to give to the community. I want everything to be ok. I write pages and pages of journal entries.

Age 30

I struggle to make sense of my life in the thousands of journal entries I have written. I write to save myself, and I write to learn. When I am not writing, I am depressed. And when I am writing, I am mostly frustrated with my lack of ability and my constant focus on how I feel and on the details of my life, rather than transforming my pain into an art form. I still want to die—simply because I cannot continue to live like this. Yet, I want to write. The two desires are at war, and I'm not sure how things will turn out.

Age 35

My students tell me I think too much. That I don't appreciate life. That I am full of despair. That I care too much. I analyze too much. I am too in tune, too aware, too concerned with the world, too busy trying to save the world at the expense of myself, too saintly, too angry, too sensitive, too too too. I am tired of being told I am too this or too that. Why can't I just be whatever it is that I am—whatever it is I feel—without the critique of how I am "too"? Without people trying to capture me, cage me, label me, quantify me, box me in…

I write letters to my students—letters to the whole class, analyzing the group dynamics from a sociological perspective. I spend hours on these letters—nights, days. I put my pain and energy into my students, but never allow myself to become a guru.

I imagine I am a dangerous woman. I imagine I am dangerous because of the ideas that I present. I imagine that the depression so many of us experience is not chemical at all, but has its roots in the social structure. The personal is political. I teach the students this concept. I tell them how women, white middle class women in the 1950s, were discontent with the social roles imposed upon them…and that these women didn't initially realize that the source of their angst had more to do with the oppressive culture in which women were immersed than their individual deficiencies. I tell the students how it was not until women were able to make the links between their individual situations and the larger social structure that the next wave of the women's movement was born. I imagine that my idea about depression being tied to the larger social structure is going to shatter the world. Depression is economic, it is the inability to express oneself, it is a lack of social support. Durkheim says that people who commit suicide are less socially integrated. Marx says depression is tied to alienating jobs that lack creativity and autonomy. I imagine I come up with a new theory. Like Betty Friedan did when she wrote about the "feeling with no name." The depression we feel is a feeling with no name, and it is my personal responsibility and life purpose to name that feeling, and to show the students the way to common ground. This feels dangerous. It feels like revolution.

The more depressed students come to me. They gravitate to me. We are a secret society. Never mind age, race, gender, class, sexual orientation. Those are simply social constructs. We share pain, awareness, loss, and humanity. I am quick to say that I am not together. Quick to relate with them on their level, my level. Quick to share theories that are mere possibilities. Possibilities that will never get them any real answers, just more possibilities and more questions.

Welcome to my world, I think to myself, cynically, when my students report that their minds are spinning and they cannot find their way to truth after taking my class. Welcome to my world.

CHRISTOPHER COKINOS

One Breath, then the Next: Trihedra
(selections)

The aphorism: The spirit of poetry in a flash of prose.

The sentence is a tiny expedition.

Trihedron: the figure determined by three planes meeting in a point.

. . .

My skin so cold it only seemed wet.

Skin is more than ink can stain.

Vow enough to sweat white beads.

. . .

Sound can falsify memory into truth.

Some rooms are cages, some cages are for healing.

Many pills, one mouth.

. . .

Better to court your love than to court disaster, though not always.

A lie is a truth giving in.

We have dreams between our legs.

. . .

We each have beginner's mind, beginner's skin.

One stroke where one will do.

The tongue is miracle enough.

. . .

Is. Yes.

Need is creed enough.

Birds bow before water, giving praise with their thirst.

. . .

So "common" is strange, so "ordinary" is mystery.

My mother's last words to me: *Happiness is, is…is…o-kay.*

The wind in grasses need not whisper *samsara.*

. . .

A chair in grass. Dew & shadow. Still seeking god?

Now is immersion for the long coming-after.

There are planets in the trees, white blossoms in the sky.

. . .

Last night a game-show host told of a bird the color of Mars.

Light shines best in the dark.

The dignity of attention, quietude as sky.

. . .

To misunderstand this is to understand that.

Smiling in the mouth of paradox, sitting on its teeth?

Sorting receipts to file despair.

. . .

It's not enough to close your windows against the wind.

The magpie perched on a haz-mat drum.

What was he thinking to dress in black beneath a desert sun?

. . .

What do we call what used to be summer?

A cynic's prism: only black-and-white.

To love abstraction is to fail the lungs.

. . .

Buildings like mistaken punctuation.

Buildings with Hopper's rooms.

Buildings where vows die.

. . .

Before using, save. Before saving, love. Before loving, look.

Like glaciers, dominion can recede.

We're each a flame that lights the wood.

. . .

Better to live the possible than to obey the ordained.

Thoughts like pebbles & seeds.

Even in dying, we grasp.

. . .

Picking a scab while reading a book.

Patience is a root.

What seems weightless is held by a string.

. . .

Neglect: Sending words to the page.

Solace: Listening to the dead.

Ambition: Speaking to the yet-born.

. . .

When birds are gone, the stars remain.

Even in the usual darkness, there is chant & canyon wind.

Stars moving without wishes, & my lover's hair—a better treatise.

KATHERINE DICKSON

The Hill and Field

March 1, 1973

I don't remember exactly how the scene across the street looked when we first moved in. The hill had been so recently bulldozed that it was just a clay bank with nothing growing on it. There was no curbstone and no sewer. But I do remember the beautiful sunset the first night we moved in and the way the sky darkened in the southwest after the sunset.

March 2, 1973

That was the view from our living room window to the hill and field across the street. The field was a cornfield and to its right there was a thick stand of trees. The trees were so dense they looked like a forest. At the far end of the stand of trees was the white farmhouse.

March 3, 1973

We moved into the house on September 1, 1969. Katherine Louise was born September 21st and I remember seeing the autumn colors as the leaves on the trees gradually changed. As I held and fed her, I watched from the living room and bedroom windows. During the summer the trees were more or less the same shade of green. But as autumn came, the colors became more differentiated, some trees turning sooner than others. Each tree turned at its own pace and stood out against the background of evergreens. Burnished gold and red trees.

March 31, 1973

In April of 1970, the Butlers and Joan visited us. The rain came down in torrents the whole time they were here. We stood at the living room window and watched it come down. The hill across the street was still bare red clay and appeared to be eroding fast, just being washed away by the rain. There was still no sewer and so the rainwater had no place to go and collected there like a lake. In May we went to Nagshead, North Carolina. Before we left, I began to feel that the ocean lay on the other side of the hill. The earth seemed to undulate like the ocean. The street was still unpaved so there was very little traffic. Just the feeling of open expanse. When we returned from Nagshead, I was happy to see that the trees were still there. For some time, any time we went away, I expected the trees to be gone when we returned, and then after a while, I began to feel they would be there forever.

Finally the street was paved and a sewer and curbstone were put in. A guardrail was put up at the head of Joyceton Drive to keep cars from going into the field. Corn was no longer planted and the field was allowed to go to seed. But, imperceptibly, the most miraculous thing happened. Grass, weeds, and flowers began to grow on the bank. It changed from raw clay to soft green, and the roots held the bank together. It became beautiful to look at.

I don't remember when those changes took place, they were so gradual. I also don't remember when I first became aware of enjoying the view; that too must have been gradual. I do remember the excitement of the first spring and seeing the new leaves appear and then the dramatic color changes in the fall. What I noticed first, I think, was the contrast of the seasons. Then slowly I became aware of the beauty of each day.

It has always surprised me that so few people seem to notice the beauty. Traffic increases all the time. The people look at the houses rather than the view across the street. Several people have remarked how convenient it will be when Joyceton Drive is extended into the cornfield so that it will be easier to get to the shopping center. But when Jane and Armand stopped by in June of 1972 before they went to India, Armand commented on how beautiful the scene across the street was. And in October, while out walking, a very happy-looking couple stopped to tell me how beautiful the yellow flowers on the bank were and that the whole scene was beautiful.

Many birds fly across the field to and from the stand of trees. Especially on foggy days or after it has rained, one can see many robins and cardinals. Bill said one day that we don't realize how much life this area supports.

. . .

The first summer we lived here I used to sit at the teak table in the dining room and look out the front door. Light poured down through the leaves of the trees. The small trunks and branches of some of the trees formed a frame that looked like an entranceway. Like a symbolic entranceway into the unconscious. It was during the day in 1970 and 1971, when Katherine Louise and Thomas took naps, that I used to write in my diary. When they went to sleep, I sat down, looked out the door at the trees, and collected my thoughts. Looking at the ocean used to feel like that. Once I started writing, I found that I had to do it during the day. Watching the leaves on the trees was like watching a fire—like having a screen on which to project the images of my mind. It was around this time that I heard on a public television program that some mental patients who had been confined inside for a long time were taken into the woods. One patient who hadn't spoken a word for many years said, "This is freedom." That was only the beginning of my realization of the restorative power of nature.

April 1, 1973

Yesterday there were kids riding mini-bikes and motorcycles up and down the hill. The ground was wet from rain. In about ten minutes they had gutted out the hill's side. I think the days of the hill and field and trees are numbered. Townhouses are planned, and Joyceton Drive will probably be extended through the cornfield to the parking lot at the back of the shopping center on Central Avenue. The mini-bikes and motorcycles have already made their own changes. And another part of authentic Maryland landscape will soon be gone. Nature is destroyed so easily, and in a hundred years people might work very hard to try to recreate this landscape. When the trees and field go, the birds will too. This morning it is dark and rainy off and on, and when I opened the front door, I was amazed at the birdsongs and the sweet smell of the air. The wind is blowing the petals off the cherry tree and they look like snowflakes in the air.

April 20, 1973

The cherry blossoms have come and gone. At night, just after it gets dark, the petals look phosphorescent—like snowflakes one can see in the dark. And I discovered something new. When the blossoms are on the trees, there are no leaves. The leaves come after the blossoms have gone. I wonder why spring flowers seem so fragile and pale in color. Bill says it might have something to do with pollination. The flowering crabapple tree on the front lawn is now in bloom; pink rose-like flowers appeared just after the cherry blossoms had gone. But these flowers have leaves—leaves that at first were brown. The new leaves are visible on the trees. The stand of trees by the field has become shades of yellow and green. The movement of the leaves is fascinating to watch, and there is a feeling of depth as the light comes down through the leaves. And now the dogwood is starting to bloom. I was surprised because I thought it wouldn't bloom until the end of May. Like the cherry blossoms, they too are blossoms without leaves. Last year, when I saw the woods filled with horizontal bars of dogwood, I was reminded of Chinese scrolls where flowers float. I didn't know why, but now I do—because there are no leaves. An ethereal, mysterious quality. Today is Good Friday.

May 10, 1973

The dogwood blossoms have just about gone. The air at times has been so full of pollen and petals (cherry and dogwood blossoms, dandelions, etc.) that several times, for a few moments, I thought it was snowing. The trees are now more uniformly green. When the leaves first came out, there were so many shades of green—from yellow-green to the black-green of the evergreens. All the trees and grasses seem to be in full bloom now. There are about six new trees in the field. Except for blossoms that will come and go, the scene will look like this until the leaves begin to come down in the fall.

May 19, 1973

I have almost decided that I cannot write well enough to describe the scene across the street. It is too difficult. Some time ago I read that Edward Steichen, when in his nineties and bedridden, devised a project for himself. Every day he would photograph the same two birch trees from the same spot for one year.

May 26, 1973

I thought that I could do something in words similar to what Steichen did with the camera. But it is so difficult. I don't even know the names of the trees, flowers and birds. And I certainly have more in mind than just to say that the seasons change and this is very nice. I cannot describe the scene scientifically. And since I started out trying to do this, I've realized that nature is really a metaphor for the state of one's soul. Perhaps Emily Dickinson's poetry is a good example of this. She doesn't describe nature as much as she uses aspects of nature to describe states of being. The hill and field across the street are my solace and inspiration—being able to see this scene every day, at different times and in different seasons. It is like a vast moving screen on which to project the images from my unconscious and lets me know what I am thinking. My debt to the hill and field is that they made it possible for me to live here. But it is only recently that I began to realize this. It would have been so different if I had to look at other people's front or back doors instead of the hill and field. Gradually I have come to feel that I would really miss something if we moved and, paradoxically, I have also come to realize that perhaps —by the same process—it doesn't matter where I am. I used to think that I could only write in a Deck House but I really think that I could do as much writing here. Having had the experience of the hill and field, I can carry this feeling anywhere. The more I realize my debt to the scene across the street, the more I can happily feel that it doesn't matter where I am.

July 9, 1973

About June 1st everything was as green as it was going to be and as grown as it was going to be. Already, though, it has begun to look like fall. Last year I saw hints of fall as early as July 4th and I was pleased and surprised that I saw these signs. But this year, to my greater surprise, I have seen the signs even earlier—perhaps mid-to-late June. One change is that the light looks more golden and the shadows are longer. The other big difference is that the green growth on the hill and in the field is gradually becoming different shades of yellow and brown. The honeysuckle has come and gone. Now there are daisies and Queen Anne's Lace. I try to remember how the hill gradually changed to the way it is now. I think it used to have more wildflowers and more flowering weeds. Also, there seem to be more wildflowers in the fall than in the spring. I love to watch them move in the breeze. The other day Bill said, "Aren't nature's weeds wonderful!" I look forward to the fall—to those long, golden afternoons when it doesn't rain but is warm and time moves slowly. A time of stillness and ripeness and the excitement of things to come. As I grow older and time passes more quickly, nature's show across the street is even more dramatic, the contrasts sharper. The sun sets so late now—about 8:30 and it isn't really dark until after 9:00. The woods are filled with fireflies. Once I started this diary, I realized how impossible it is to describe the natural changes on the hill and field. Bill has taken some slides because the bulldozer may start work any time. But once I realized it would be impossible to describe the scene with any accuracy, I felt that if I kept this diary it wouldn't be to record the changes in nature but to help me to see. There is no inner life without nature. Nature helps me to dream, to know my fantasy life. We have lived in this house for almost four years. My life here feels enchanted and dream-like. This is where my inner development began. I already knew how to live in the world, and here is where I began to live inside myself. And the hill and field helped me to do this.

September 30, 1973

This is my favorite time of year—from now until Christmas. I keep pushing the season. As early as July, I was looking for autumn leaves. There is something deadening about the still, heavy heat of summer. In the cooler fall weather, everything seems to come alive. Daisies cover the bank across the street. Everywhere yellow daisies. Once in a while someone picks a bunch of them. The colors on the bank have gradually changed from solid green to varied shades of green, yellow, russet, and white. The growth is thick and it gently moves in the wind. The leaves are beginning to turn. I could sit for hours and look at the scene from my living room window, but sometimes whole days go by when it seems I barely have a chance to glance across the street. What used to be the cornfield is now completely bulldozed. The field looks like several pyramids in the desert. I wish I could remember what the scene looked like those first few years we lived here. Bill said, "It's a house that makes you feel you'd like to read in it." Maybe this is a house for dreaming. I almost resent being away. Especially since the days of the hill and field are numbered. This wildness is my solace and inspiration. The leaves rustle now when the wind blows. In the cold weather, the trees (especially the evergreens) moan in the wind. Suddenly I am aware of the golden light in autumn; it comes into the kitchen and dining room windows in much longer slants. The change seems sudden but I know it is gradual. The sunsets behind the hill are beautiful. The position of the sun changes, but I am not sure how. At some time of the year it is closer to the farmhouse. If I was watching time-lapse photography I could see the way the light and colors change.

November 16, 1973

As the leaves fall they twirl and flutter. I watch them fall and blow along the ground. After the daisies go, the colors on the bank change to red, green, and orange. There is a tan wildflower that looks like the strawflowers from the Design Store. The growth on the bank is thick. Perhaps that is the most striking change since we moved here—the bank has gone from bare red clay to thicker and thicker growth. I never thought nature would be so interesting to watch, or so difficult to write about.

November 29, 1973

One or two windy days, and now the branches on the trees are bare. The hill is the color of fallen leaves. All of autumn's bright colors have gradually faded to brown. It feels unusual to look out and see bare black lines of trees in the distance. It is a winter landscape now. Besides snow, I can't imagine what other changes could appear before spring. The farmhouse is much more visible now. The sunsets are thick gray-black puffs of clouds against a pink-purple background.

January 5, 1974

The trees are dark outlines against the sky and the hill is crowned by a lacy mesh of leaves. Everything looks linear and calligraphic. There is much less motion in the winter landscape and one can see many more birds. Nature looks peaceful, perfect, but is anything but that. All landscape is symbolic. Nature is a large, receptive screen on which I throw images from my psyche in much the same way that we throw images from our minds into the dancing flames of a fire.

January 31, 1974

I didn't think I would like the winter/early spring landscape as much as I do. An earth-brown mulch of leaves covers the hill where motorcycles have not been. If one watches closely, one can see many birds hopping around or moving from one low branch to another. There is more sky to see now, and more sunsets. The trees have a spare beauty. Just this side of the farmhouse is a birch tree in two parts, a Y forked birch. The bark is white and gorgeous in the morning sun. The other day the children and I walked towards the farmhouse through the bulldozed cornfield. All the topsoil was gone. It was flat and looked like a desert. I didn't know that the earth beneath the topsoil looked like this. Maybe many desert-like areas once had trees and other greenery. Bill said that only about two feet of topsoil covers the earth and supports life and that the amount of topsoil in the world is shrinking. From the ex-cornfield I can see the open landscape of undulating hills and fields. The rolling earth is like the restful motion of the sea.

March 1, 1974

There is so much more sky visible that I find myself noticing the cloud formations and the light on the tree trunks and branches. This light seems whiter, brighter, more intense than the light in the fall. Everything still looks spare and hard, everything seems to be roots, seeds, filaments, vines, lines, wires, networks. The hill and field embody creation and destruction.

March 9, 1974

I keep waiting for changes to show that spring is coming. I feel that a great dramatic change is about to take place but as yet everything seems fixed, the same. The changes going on are not visible yet. Because we are on daylight savings time already (rather than April 30th), it seems we are closer to spring. It doesn't get dark until about 7:00. One year ago I began this diary. I no longer think of it as an objective record of nature's changes. When I can sit for a while and look into the trees, I can sometimes make difficult choices and see solutions to problems. It is as though I could find out what I really want to do. If I had more factual information about flowers, weeds, trees, birds, and other forms of wildlife, I would be watching nature objectively. But because I have so little intellectual knowledge of what I am looking at, I believe that the scene holds my conscious mind at bay while my unconscious is then allowed to project images onto nature which I can then sometimes understand. Looking into the trees, everything seems hopeful. Solutions will come forth like spring flowers. This sounds exaggerated, but it is similar to the process of sleeping on something to get a solution. From looking at the trees I have discovered how I experience my life. I know about the cyclic quality of nature now, and the cyclic quality of my own nature. I have become aware of how much I project the qualities of my subjectivity upon what I see. I have learned that the secret is balance. Balance between creation and destruction, between cleaning the house and writing. Between doing and being. On a daily basis, changes in nature are almost imperceptible and yet dramatic. Because nature is constant process, it always seems the same from minute-to-minute. The hill and the trees have made me conscious of the feminine principle of life—creation, destruction, matter, process, the circle. And to think that only two feet of topsoil supports all life on earth. They say one's unlived life becomes one's fantasy life. My fantasy is to be able to sit for hours, undisturbed, and look at a view like the hill and field—to look into woods, or watch snow, or look at the ocean. Do my fantasies reflect a desire for peace and quiet or do they reflect a need to experience nature?

June 28, 1974

The second field behind the hill has been bulldozed and is now being graded for townhouses. Every now and then, through the trees, I catch sight of the corner of a piece of heavy, yellow equipment. The first field, which I can clearly see, is thickly covered with green. It looks like grass but it is probably moss. Bill says nature tries to repair the damage. Just behind the black and white fence is a pool of stagnant water that had tadpoles in it one day. All around the pool now there are cat o'nine tails that wave in the breeze. It already looks like fall—the golden light, the shadows, the Queen Anne's Lace. The hill and field might be completely gone by fall. When he heard that grading for townhouses was being done, Bill said maybe we would at least get the summer out of it. I asked him if he could photograph the scene framed by our front door. "No," he said. "A photo wouldn't do justice to what you see." The more I try to write about the hill and field, the more I realize this is true. The lesson I have learned is that what I see is symbolic of my deepest self. Metaphors of growth, creation, and destruction.

LESLIE WOOLF HEDLEY

Aphorisms: The Last Gasp
(selections)

Aphorisms never know their mother or father.

. . .

Speech is an obsession to prove one is alive.

. . .

The subject and the object become the same thing only in death.

. . .

Some people are famous just for being famous.

. . .

Philosophy can be a delicious poison that slowly drips into a glass of fine wine.

. . .

Sadists are never satisfied.

• • •

Art is serious, life is a joke.

• • •

Death comes when no one remembers you.

• • •

Art is to believe in the impossible.

• • •

Tomorrow is the postponement of a promise.

• • •

Imagination isn't hallucination.

• • •

Memory is like an archeological expedition digging up graves and mummies.

• • •

One law too many is like one bullet too many.

• • •

Art is like writing a letter to people from whom you'll never get a reply.

• • •

Successful evil has no memory.

. . .

An artist working for the state is like a prostitute married to a priest.

. . .

Every new wave contains debris.

. . .

No one is more polite than an executioner.

. . .

Lying is a game without rules so everyone can play.

. . .

Fiction without hell is merely journalism.

. . .

Innocence is the refusal to be curious.

. . .

The prime function of the artist is to create miracles.

. . .

No one on earth will ever forgive you for telling the truth.

ROY ARENELLA

O Postcards!

(For Martine)

If things were otherwise you would be reading these words on a postcard, handwritten in ink & addressed directly to you.

On the picture side of the card would be a photo I took, developed & printed on photographic paper. The photo would be related in some way to you, to my words on the back of it & to me. The card as a whole, both recto & verso, photo & words, is what I call a photo/card. It's the best form I've found for personal expression & communication—it's my "letter to the world" & to you.

But the words you are reading now are printed on pages & bound in a book—the whole process is mechanical. I love books & realize that to have them abundantly available I must give up the home-made, singular quality. Nevertheless, it's necessary to acknowledge straightaway that you are holding & reading a substitute, a stand-in for some other, more direct, personal & unique form of communication.

The hand-written intimacy—the errors & the aura—of words on a postcard are lost in the pages of a book. But I have attempted here to keep the direct address & informal style typical of cards. Because this book page is comparatively spacious I am able to be more discursive, to loosen the characteristic pithiness of postcards. But I have tried to keep clear of frills. The writing will be in individual segments, usually short, reflecting the snapshot & fragmentary nature of post-cards. But most of all I hope I can keep the card's ability to carry *sociability across distance.*

· · ·

This essay is in 3 separate & distinct parts. The first is a personal meditation on what postcards mean to me—specifically, the photographic postcard of the homemade variety. The second is an account in snapshot-like vignettes of someone (this writer) who finds sustenance in the activity of making & mailing out such cards daily. The last section contains quotes as notes that support or underlie the text, some footnoted to the text, others free-floating.

- 1 -

Definition

The terms *postcard* & *photo/card* will be used often & sometimes inter-changeably. But it is the latter, the *photographic* picture post-card (a subspecies of the postcard) that I want to focus on.

I define the photo/card as a small, self-made photograph, developed in the home darkroom & printed on photographic paper of about 4 x 6 inches in size. The verso is blank, to be used for a handwritten message. The card is sent thru the mails to another person as a way of communicating &/or expressing. A response is anticipated, expected—even courted.

The 3 essential characteristics of the photo/card are: 1. The photographic image & the words of the card itself. 2. The person who

makes/sends it & the recipient at the other end. 3. The distance between the two that the card travels in the mails. The card is a cipher in an economy of personal exchange.

Vernacular, accommodating & democratic

From its inception the postcard was a vernacular form. Made of heavy paper with space for an address on one side & a brief message on the other, it was invented as a "postal instrument" for business use (advertising) & for the general populace as a convenient form of contact. From their beginning, cards were universally welcomed by the majority. They met a need, were simple to use & struck a chord. In Austria (where invented in 1869), in England & in the United States, postcard sales & usage within the first weeks of issuance were phenomenal. A few years later, with the birth of the *picture* postcard, collecting cards (apart from mailing them) became a craze. It remains a major hobby in many countries, at all levels of society. Postcards have both a human usefulness & an appeal as objects in themselves.

. . .

The postcard continues to be a popular form, still used by a wide spectrum of the public.

People who otherwise never hold a pen (except to jot down phone numbers or make shopping lists) will sit in motel rooms while on vacation, writing card after card to family & friends back home, broadcasting the news of where they are & how they are doing there.

At the other extreme, a professor on sabbatical might judiciously select an image from a postcard rack & carefully craft a short message on the verso for a colleague back at the university in order to instigate a subtle agenda. The postcard has no vested interest at either end of this spectrum. It is not exclusive but democratic & inclusive.

Public & Private

The postcard in form & content is open & vulnerable. Everything about it is uncovered & clearly visible, traveling the route from sender to receiver. Yet at the same time it shelters a personal & private side. The Society of Arts in England fought the introduction of the postal card on the grounds that privacy in the mails would be violated. Others were concerned that devious people could commit public libel under the guise of sending a private mailing card. Elitists suspected that the preciseness & preciousness of personal communication would be jeopardized by the constricted space allowed for writing & by its unconcealed manner.

This public vs. private "contradiction" is part of the mystery & appeal of the postcard.

Homemade, handmade

Even at the most superficial level of postcard communication—the "Wish you were here" tourist card—intimacy is implied: "...here *with me.*"

The personal, homemade postcard can be even more private, direct & definite in intent when the picture-side of the card is made by the sender. Personally made photographs allow for the image as well as the words to be tailored for a specific recipient. Private or mutually shared images can home in more closely & allow stronger connections & deeper intimacy.

This intimacy will seem more intensified—paradoxically—because the photo/card travels publicly thru the postal system. (And unlike a letter in an envelope, a card exposes its *essential* self at all times.) The photograph & message, though coded for only one person, are available for all to see. "Wish you were here" means different things to the different eyes reading the card along its route from sender to receiver.

. . .

Maybe the card can survive the scrutiny of strangers because its public part is but a very small fragment of a larger & less visible on-going agenda. Postcards are more like an unannounced but neighborly drop-in visit at the side door rather than a formal visitation at the front entrance.

Letters are usually more formal wholes, with greetings at the beginning, full-bodied middles & cordial endings. There is room for rambling, for meaningful asides, purposeful false starts & all the maneuvers available to writing intended for the standard 8½ x 11 page. Postcard writers usually jump head-first & full speed into the message proper. It is not only a question of the card's limited space. When you choose to send a card rather than a letter, your mind & hand are already set to think tight, write small: be pithy.

Big

The most striking characteristic of the picture postcard for me is the realization that it is twice as big as it looks.

Turning a card over from the recto to the verso side offers entry into 2 worlds: a *picture* world & a *word* world. And to skillful practitioners of postcarding, a third world opens up. There, images & words can work together generating possibilities beyond those of a simple merger. This is the world of *"pictures as enriched language."* (See **Quotes/Notes** #13.)

A further enhancement occurs if the writer of the card is also the photographer who makes the picture on the front. Under these conditions expressive possibilities multiply.

With a homemade card, the traditional spaces for "Address" & "This Side for Message" can be rearranged. Room can be made for drawings, cartoons, rubber-stamped images & idiosyncratic or calligraphic writing. Postcards offer a natural surface for these varieties of mark-making. When personal photography—yet another mark-making process—is added, the card as format or form is capable of carrying so much more than its real size seems to indicate. It permits—in careful hands—a wide, deep & subtle means of expression & communication.

Performance

I like to imagine the recipient of one of my cards turning it around in her or his hand, not only from back to front, but from near to far, to look closely at a tiny detail in the picture, or read a word written smaller than the others, or a phrase written upside down or tilted diagonally. The card involves the recipient *actively*. This underlines the physical character of the card, its function as an object. To have a postcard read to you (as a letter is read to a blind person) is to miss half of what that card offers. The postcard in this sense is part performance.

No waste

I began sending photo/cards about 30 years ago. The first were regular photographs (my prints have always been small) that had some printing flaw, some mistake in the darkroom. Rather than discarding them I recycled these errors as cards to mail out. Or sometimes I would trim away a part of a larger picture & use that part as a card. The pictures proved useful as contacts, carrying messages to friends & family and, at the same time, showing them what I was up to in my photography.

Me

Gradually I began printing negatives as both regular photographs & also as photo/cards. The photographs stayed home, stored in boxes; the cards went out into the world.

Now, the bulk of what I print is cards. And when I take photos I often have in mind first their use as cards, sometimes made for a certain person for a particular occasion. I've gradually shifted the bulk of my need for contact, for exchange & for sociability to the cards. They've become the way I stay in touch, give my news, & keep connected.

Caviar or bread

I sent a photo/card to a photographer friend. He praised the picture but scolded me: "Why send the picture in the mail like that? If you want to mail it, at least put it in an envelope—protect it." My response at the time (via another photo/card!) was partial; here's a fuller one:

As a practicing photographer, only a few of the regular pictures I make get published; some few others are exhibited in galleries or museums. But most are stored away in boxes, seen by no one. These stored-away pictures probably want to think of themselves as precious, as biding time in boxes until their day comes to play the exalted role of either a document in a magazine or a fine art print, framed on a gallery wall. But most of my photos will never see that day, will never function in the world beyond being *potentially* useful.

I risk using the mails because I want my pictures to have some use, to have a fair chance of realizing their potential by being seen.

Bonus

I think of the "caviar," fine art pictures as prima donnas or elitists, as wanting to rise above the hubbub of the real world. They want to exist in the more rarefied air of "art."

On the other hand, photo/card pictures perform a real job in far away places beyond my home, out in that hubbub where most of the world lives. In my eye it is thanks to their travels thru the mails that photo/cards seem richer, deeper & more interesting than those pictures that stay at home, ex- & re-clusively.

Two identical photographs—one on a postcard, the other on a larger sheet of photo paper—are really two different "beings" for me. Among my own photographs, the photo/cards almost always seem the more mature. They will be marked & mellowed by the world of hands, machines, distances & contingencies. And like everything else, they will be exposed to *chance*.

Chance

Chance has its catastrophic side, & postcards—more so than other first class mail—are more likely to be lost or totally ruined. But I find that chance usually enhances a photo/card—if it doesn't actually destroy it, or totally cripple it (or lose it completely). Chance can be a gift in the mails as it can be anywhere else.

I might be persuaded to change my Zen-ish attitude about this in the face of strong evidence to the contrary. But I'd rather focus now on a more exemplary "chance disaster" that happened to one of my cards sent out recently. Ten days ago a friend in Wisconsin returned a card in an envelope. With it was a note that read: "Knowing your feelings about your cards and the importance of the history they accrue as they travel thru the mails, I thought you might like this one back. It appears it got damaged in Madison, but someone here at the post office thought enough of it to take the time to do some extensive repairs with "magic tape." And on the verso of the taped-up card—in the only blank space I left on that side—appears a 3-line, rubberstamped message that reads: "Damaged in handling in ??? (not readable) / Postal service at Madison WI 53707 / Please accept our apology." I accept, gladly. I love such en route chance additions to my cards.

Philosophy 101

If you are speculatively minded you might want to dwell on the list of the double-sided aspects of the picture postcard that have already been mentioned:

recto	verso
image	word
pictures	writing
public	private

361

If you are philosophically inclined you can expand (stretch?) this list to include:

mechanical	manual
(camera)	(pen)
outside	inside
objective	subjective
world	self

One-directional & Occasional

Though considered by a few as a legitimate literary &/or visual form (see **Quotes/Notes** #4), for many reasons the postcard resists Fine Art aesthetics. Some have already been mentioned or are obvious: postcards are ubiquitous, cheap, easily accessible, & ephemeral. Traveling thru the mails they are often bruised, marked, creased, torn, or otherwise devalued & "ruined."

Cards are addressed to one other person & usually are motivated by a specific & relatively circumscribed occasion (see **Quotes/Notes** #5). For the traditional aesthete these characteristics soil the cards because, for them, Art's proper appeal should be towards a more universal audience & broader, more timeless occasions. Postcards—at least as they are initially put in play—are directed towards other ends. They are not aimed at a Fine Art audience.

Non-Art

The first intention in making and sending a photo/card is not an aesthetic one. Even though the maker might be an acknowledged artist, his or her postcards are considered marginalia & of much less value (economic & otherwise) than more serious work in established formats. (Of course there are exceptions. The painter Franz Marc's series of postcards to Prince Jussuf is a good example. See **Quotes/ Notes** #3.)

Even photographic postcards made by well-known & successful photographers have very little status in the world of serious photography. Lee Witkin, founder of an early & prestigious NYC photo gallery, said of these cards: "...on the whole, while postcards are fun, I think it's a very minor thing. They're either good to send to friends, or if you collect them, they fall into the range of bottle caps."

Amateur, not professional status

The perceived shortcomings of cards as investments give them marginal status as a serious art form. This neglect, however, allows them to pass with discretion thru the mails as documents—sometimes of extraordinary human expression & communication. For the serious maker & mailer of photo/cards, this non-art status is a gift that permits a freedom of approach that professional artists don't have with work made to sell—the freedom to respond unguardedly & spontaneously to any incident (whether "art-worthy" or not) and to work with little regard for art-critical standards. If any standards do apply, they are those of the amateur (in the root sense of "lover of") & not the professional.

. . .

The fine arts establishment has nothing to fear from the lowly postcard. Cards will never threaten work made to be sold at substantial prices. As a form it has little or no place on the agenda of the collector, the curator or the critic. A once-a-year gallery exhibition of postcards may be used to raise money for one cause or another, but the small size of the cards won't pay the regular monthly gallery rent. The Fine Arts world ranks the postcard as a form of charity, or a pauper's form.

O Postcards!

It is these non-art characteristics of the postcard & especially the photo/card that I want to praise here. When pushed too hard the postcard protectively hides its strengths & presents itself as a slight form with a humble function. When burdened to carry "art" it does not make a good impression. It does not need an audience, but asks only for a sender, a recipient & some mutual reason to be sent between the two. Postcards do not gracefully support the idea of a virtuoso tour de force, pretension or an overbearing ego. Postcards will not support a "career" in art. It is difficult to imagine such an exalted concept as a single "Masterpiece of Postcard Art."

"French postcards"

I wonder if the Kinsey Report could tell us what percentage of young men got their first glimpse of pornography from "French postcards."

Some of the salacious atmosphere still lingering around postcards might be leftover from the era when they gladly carried pornography all over the world (though certainly hidden inside of envelopes). The aura of tainted fantasy is still detectable to many of us of a certain age when we think about the word "postcard."

The Ideal Postcard Rack

If a random sampling of every picture postcard ever produced was placed in an Ideal (imaginary) Postcard Rack, the resulting composite picture would depict a world more fantastic than real. In the great bulk of commercially produced cards, from the erotic, French postcards in warm, sepia tones to the "picture perfect" tourist card with pure blue skies, the world of fantasy triumphs.

Homemade, personal photo/cards can of course join this bulk by adding to it the actual fantasies of real individuals. On the other hand, the photo/card can be an antidote to commercially engendered fantasy by focusing on the world as it actually appears to one person thru the lens of a camera. If the latter case were to prevail, the sum of cards in the Ideal Rack would begin to equal reality.

"Poor man's copyright"

The mails are under government auspices & postmarked dates can have the weight & awe of authority about them. Rules of a mail-away contest on the radio often stated that "entries must be postmarked no later than...." And the most dreaded postmark in this country for people prone to lateness is the April 15th income tax deadline. But there are other, less known examples of the authority & power of postmarks.

As teenagers, my friends & I believed that if we invented a device it could be "patented" by detailing the invention in a letter that we mailed to ourselves. If we didn't open the letter when it arrived, its postmark date would be proof, if contested, that our invention was the earliest.

None of us ever had any need of this quick copyright (& I know now that it is ineffective & has never prevailed in court: one could *steal* an invention & mail it to oneself). But the idea that the passage thru the mails verifies or authenticates an activity still remains with me.

Sometimes when I find an interesting visual form for an "idea" I'll put it on the verso of a regular postcard & mail it to myself. It's not a question of protecting my new discovery, but a way of dating it more officially than with my own hand. A chronological file of cards dated in this way feels official & establishes them with a greater authority in the eyes of the outside world.

The Paris "Pneu" & V-Mail

Throughout its history the postcard has been involved in many schemes to get the mails around quicker, cheaper & more efficiently. The famous Paris Pneumatic—the network of underground tubes carrying first cards, then letters—is one such scheme. V-Mail, used by Americans during WWII, is another.

Though considered "advanced" at the time, neither process used what we would now call high technology. These systems were able to preserve the "hands-on," "from-my-hand-to-yours" nature of the mails that our current electronic communication does not have.

In terms of personal communication, the basic idea of the pneumatic mails was not radical. The sender bought a pre-printed card, wrote a message on it & brought it to a local station. Here it was put into a tube by a postal worker and then vacuumed-sucked speedily across Paris, underground. This same card was eventually delivered into the hands of & read by the intended recipient. Not a hard *copy*, not a *fax-simile*—the thing itself traveled the distance & was handled by both sender & receiver.

How important it must have been in that city of lovers—this aura of touch! And knowing that a message traveled *underground* thru dark tunnels surely added yet another level of romance to contact by mail.

V-Mail, used in WWII between soldiers & home, was less tactile. A message was written on a single sheet that was then folded along pre-made guidelines into the shape of an envelope & mailed to a central location. There it was microfilmed. The recipient didn't receive the actual sheet the letter was written on but—the next best thing!—a picture of it on photographic paper.

"sticky-backed pictures"

One recent Bloomsday (June 16), while listening to a marathon reading of James Joyce's *Ulysses* on the radio, I heard the phrase: "Stamps, sticky-backed pictures." With these words the affinity that I had long felt existed between photography & the mails received outside endorsement from an important writer. It helped confirm my sense that the mail & photography were kin.

. . .

Is there a congenial connection between photography as a means of communication & the mails as a ready-made route established for that same communicative impulse?

In my eye there is an aesthetic rightness about the format of a post-card. This comes from the graphics of its writing & cancellation marks; the form & color of its stamps; the design of its layout; & the addition—by chance—of unofficial markings. It is a vernacular aesthetic with a modern feel that is similar, I think, to snapshot photography.

The guidelines for appreciating this aesthetic are not classical but pragmatic. The playing field for it is wide & open, not pinched & elitist. And most importantly, the aesthetic of the mailed postcard—like snapshot photography—accepts the intrusion of daily contingencies & makes the most of them.

...

For a short period of time during the early 20th century, the French government permitted the postage stamp to be placed on the picture side of picture postcards. I have a small collection of these cards. They are rich with visual meanings & insinuations & are often more beautiful to me than much "fine" art hanging on the walls of galleries. They are naive & unpretentious. I am reminded of a similar feeling the French poet Blaise Cendrars had about postage stamps compared to museum art: "I know more than 120,000 different postage stamps and they give more pleasure than Number This and Number That in the Louvre."

1839 & 1840

There is not only an esthetic fit but also an historical linkage between mail & photography. It is interesting that most people would probably date the introduction of the first postage stamp to well before the invention of photography. But the historical fact is that the English Black Penny stamp (the first stamp to be sold separately to be affixed to an envelope, facilitating common mailing) was available in 1840, just one year *after* the invention of photography. These 2 birthdays for me are close enough to affirm the family resemblance I find between them.

Distance

"Distance" appears as the last of the 3 essentials in my definition of the photo/card. In our wired age, distance—as the physical space between 2 places—has been lost sight of. The word seems to be contracting itself into non-existence.

Distance is the surface space across which communication travels—*must* travel. In other times, Romantics in the arts saw distance as the enemy. Communication from "soul to soul" or between "Man & Nature" needed to traverse this dreaded distance in order to achieve the longed for unity. In more modern times, distance came to be identified with the psychological concept of alienation.

Currently, distance is only a word, something "covered" without cost by using "free, frequent-flyer miles." Or a closer-to-home example might be: a young husband a few steps away from his front door tells his wife via cell phone that he is "on his way home"; he's "almost there!" I see the word "there" as "t/here," where "non-distance" is represented visually in the contraction of the 2 words.

These 2 situations are indicative of how distance is overlooked or underplayed in our electronic age. When you're wired to everything else and anyplace else, distance as a word has no weight or force. (And a zero "romantic factor"!)

But the mailed postcard *knows* distance—true miles—intimately. Unlike e-mail, telephones, television or other electronic-based means of communication, postcards are subject to gravity. They inhabit the same air as our bodies, are subject to the forces that we are subject to. Doesn't this elemental connection endear us to them on some level—a level that electronic communication cannot touch?

Communication seeks to collapse distance. But for participants using electronic means, physical distance is not actually experienced as part of the process. For practical purposes, the space between things is ignored. With no real distance for a spark to jump across, the stored-up energy to communicate leaks away, losing its charge. For me electronic forms of communication are soft & enervating.

On the other hand, the mails carry visible markings as evidence of the distance they've covered. These marks are reminders of what actually separates us. And the mails operate in real time, in *felt* time. For me a letter or postcard in my mailbox reaffirms distance while gratifying the desire to bridge it. This is a handy metaphor for our situation as desiring communicants.

Fragmentary?

Why the question mark? Because I've been asked to consider whether or not the postcard should be included in a book about *fragmentary writing*. I'd like to think out an answer here, on the page.

The postcard itself is complete in itself; in that sense it is not a fragment. But its small size, few words, & episodic occurrence make it feel fragmentary.

Yet I do, in practice, consider my photo/cards as fragments. Hopefully they are part of something larger & ongoing. Each card is an addition to what will become a series of cards to another individual. Each will add a small particle to a larger & more detailed picture that is being created by the exchange between us.

In an ideal exchange, one part of this picture is being created by me & another by the response of the recipient. If the exchange is a true one (a dialog not monolog) each response (sender's & receiver's) will depend to some extent on the previous one. Neither sender nor recipient controls the complete picture. (There is no complete picture.) Each mailing becomes part of an aggregate & each card exchanged is a fragment in that formation.

I like to think that the words I write on a card add to the dialog of an ongoing story. And the photographs on the cards will become part of a giant mosaic, a picture forming on the wall in the room of my correspondent. The effect of the sendings—words, pictures & their combinations—are in this way cumulative.

Furthermore, each dialog between one recipient & myself is only part of a larger web of such connections (& hopefully the same is true for the recipient). Nowhere is there a complete whole, but only a sustained connection of fragments.

- 2 -

First postcards; too young to read

When I was a pre-school child, two picture postcards arrived at our house on two consecutive Decembers with messages to me from my uncle. During WWII he was a foot soldier in the American Army in North Africa & Italy. One card had a photograph of a theater on a street in a foreign city (probably in Algeria). Along the bottom edge of the card was a nicked-out space where the name of that city had been clipped away by Army censors. The second card was a reproduction of a watercolor showing a small boy in short pants holding a teddy bear & peering into a bird's nest. Printed under the picture were a few words in Italian. On the back the Army censor had scribbled over the name of the town in Italy where my uncle had written it. I still have both of these cards—from 21 December 1943 & 12 December 1944. They are the first 2 of several thousand I have saved.

Box tops

In the 1950s, writing a letter & mailing it was one of the few ways that I (as youngster) could actually engage the wider world beyond family, home, & school without being stigmatized as "only a kid." Though an adult had to drive to the village post office to buy stamps for me, I was able to do the rest on my own: to write the letter, put it (unseen by adults) into an envelope & post it at the corner mailbox.

On radio & TV shows, the commercial world took advantage of the child's desire to behave like an adult by offering toys & gadgets which could be ordered thru the mail. All that was needed was the box top from the cereal advertised & a quarter taped to it. Here the joy for the youngster was not so much in *sending* something out into the adult world but in *waiting* for that world to respond by sending something back—by reciprocating. The anticipation & final joy never diminished, no matter how many things were "sent away for."

Stamps

The only Boy Scout Merit Badge I earned was for stamp collecting. I never went on to be a true collector, but an interest in stamps continues into my adult life. When writing to a friend I would try to find a good stamp for the envelope, one that—if my friend should notice it—might show that friendship extended even to the care of choosing a stamp.

Paying attention to stamps shifted to include also the envelopes that held them, to their cancellations & extraneous markings (from handling in the mails). The envelope itself as a "chart" interested me more than did its basic function as carrier & protector of what was inside. The often strange writing on the envelope—names, addresses, numbers—was engaging & exciting.

In grammar school the idea of having a "pen pal" in a foreign country (though it never happened for me) was as exciting to think about as what I would be when I grew up.

Maximaphily

This is a branch of stamp collecting that involves a postcard, a postage stamp & the stamp's cancellation. When a new stamp is to be issued, collectors of maximum cards try to find a standard size postcard with an image that matches as close as possible the image on the new stamp. They affix the stamp to the front (image side) of the postcard. The third part of the maxi card trinity is having the stamp cancelled with a postmark relevant to the stamp's image (& therefore also to the postcard image). This is usually a special First Day of Issue postmark applied by the city issuing the stamp—a city chosen because of its relation to the stamp's subject. The idea of maximaphily is to try for the strongest conjunction—the maximum—among the 3 parts: stamp, cancellation & postcard image.

After learning about maximaphily & the maximum card, I began using this format in a more personal & direct way, imaginatively adopting its rules for use with my own photo/cards. This offered possibilities for participation beyond the level of mere collecting.

Village post office

The interior of the post office in my childhood hometown had an ambiance 50 years ago that is vivid in my mind today. I was browsing thru an art book a few years ago & stopped at a painting of a winter scene set in a small town. Immediately I recognized it as a reproduction of the mural in the lobby of our post office. Painted as part of the WPA project by William Gropper, it pictures a compressed composite of views of the town where I grew up. A central figure is the mail carrier leaning into a strong wind, in deep snow, making his way past the church (I once attended) & heading "across the tracks." The scene was painted 3 years before I was born & 10 years before we moved to that village, which was by then a suburb. The village has today reached the population of a small city.

. . .

The postal clerk at the counter of our post office was a man who lived directly across the street from our house. Going to the post office to mail packages was also paying a neighborly visit to him in his "second home."

Eventually that neighbor became a colleague when I worked at the post office for 2 full summers in the mid-1950s to earn college tuition. Since summer time is vacation time, there were always tourist's postcards in my mail sack. And there was always time to look at & read them, between houses as I walked.

By the end of the second summer I had delivered mail to each of the houses in the suburban village where I grew up. The map of the town was learned on foot.

Job in the City

After college I worked in The City as a social service worker. I had a colleague whose hobby was sending postcards to the "Letters to the Editor" columns of newspapers. He would write his personal reaction to a wide variety of news stories onto standard size postcards bought in batches at the post office & mail these to New York City's major newspapers *every day*. Occasionally he would show me one before sending it. And sometimes he clipped out one that had been published to show me, proudly.

What I realize now is that my colleague no doubt worked hard to compress his ideas clearly & concisely onto the cards. It was more than a leisure-time hobby. He was a large, awkward man, a bachelor who had few friends at work. I imagine that writing these cards was what he looked forward to most after a day at work. I think he enjoyed being thought of as "the man who wrote postcards."

Bank

Remembering again the post office in my hometown brings me to think also of the bank. (In old, aerial view postcards of small towns, you can often pick out [under the perfect blue sky] the trinity of Church, Bank & Post Office.) But I remember nothing specific about the bank's interior. From the outside the building was tall, one of the tallest in town. It was near the railroad station.

I mention the bank because I see how strongly I've come (now) to contrast it with the post office. Freud's observation that money is not part of the child's universe of desire & therefore does not touch the adult in an elemental way seems relevant here. Maybe an allegiance (in a simple-hearted sense) either to bank or to post office defines (or at least marks) one's adult character. If so, count me among the post office people.

Disclaimer

These little stories are obviously selectively chosen to make a specific point. I've been trying to find a way to make a portrait (or at least an *outline* of a portrait) of someone who finds the mails to be a more friendly way of being in the world. A way to be more (as the French say) "comfortable in your skin." I've searched my memory of childhood & youth for those incidents that might identify the kind of person who finds sustenance in the idea that mail both confirms & diminishes the distance between people. I make no claims at defining a type, but only of trying to picture one individual.

Misdirected letter

For a number of years I worked in a large office building near Union Square in Manhattan. It contained the staff of a municipal agency & included hundreds of workers in many offices on 12 floors.

One day I found a letter on the desk in my cubicle. I did not recognize the hand-written return address; the letter was probably personal.

Looking more closely, I could not find my name anywhere on the envelope. Furthermore, though the building number was correct, the street number was wrong by a few digits.

What astonished me was that the letter was addressed to a very well known photographer, Duane Michals, whom I knew lived in the neighborhood. He was at the time one of my favorite photographers.

How did the letter get to me? Or more exactly: *why* did it come to *me?* As a misdirected letter with a wrong street number & an addressee not part of our agency, it could have been dropped on any of 100 desks in the building; why mine?

Was it a co-worker's little joke? Probably not. I could think of none of my colleagues who had enough of the necessary information & who also had access to delivering the mail. I investigated & got blank stares & sincere-sounding denials (both of which I believed). I concluded that the letter came to me by pure chance.

Instinctively I decided to do the right thing: to call the error to the attention of the mail carrier. I wrote on the envelope, "Delivered in error to *16th St.*"

Only later, when telling this story to friends, did I discover a new slant to the incident. They asked: "Why didn't you take the letter to the photographer yourself? You could have gotten to meet him, maybe talk to him. Show him your work!" I had no ready answer. At the time, personal contact didn't feel right; a letter seemed the better way.

Though I'd since seen this photographer on the street several times, on the subway, & in a museum, I never approached him about getting his mail in error.

But a few years later (when my wife bought me one of his photographs) I did have my chance to write him a letter. He never answered. The mail route often finishes in a dead end.

New York 10012 – Paris 75018

An old college friend from New York (living then in Paris) invited me to visit him for an extended stay in his adopted city. The invitation was his effort to rescue me from the turmoil of a divorce that had driven me to what he called a "point mort" (dead end). He had recently survived a divorce himself & was trying to be helpful.

Arrangements were made for my stay. At the last minute he wrote to say that he wouldn't be available on the day of my arrival. He was a professor at the University of Paris & had asked a former student of his (who was now a friend) to welcome me. She became my guide to Paris for a few days. Two years later she became my wife.

Martine was earning a Master's Degree (in concrete poetry). Her summer vacations were long & we spent several of them together in France & in New York getting to know each other. The rest of the year we corresponded on a regular basis.

Phone calls were expensive & had to be carefully timed because of our different time zones & personal schedules. Trans-Atlantic phone contact was often poor (static, delays, echoing, etc). So we wrote constantly, exchanging letters, postcards, packages & objects.

The postal service was more lenient then & very odd objects (with attached address labels) managed to get thru. Our mailboxes were like Cracker Jacks boxes: anything could be inside. This was not only fun, it also allowed us to share more than merely words.

For 2 years the mail between Paris & New York carried our developing relationship—until we married & lived in New York.

· · ·

What we wrote, or made or found to send to each other, wasn't art or an exercise in aesthetics. We were involved in an exchange & a communication that had different stakes than art does. We tried to make our relationship—though separated by an ocean—as full &

satisfying as possible. We had to trust that the mails could do this—could carry all that was shared (minus physical proximity) between two lovers living in the same city. And the mails did that.

PS:

It delights me, in writing the last section above, to notice—& for the first time—that my wife's Paris Zip Code of 30 years ago, 75018, is exactly the same as the first 5 of the 6-digit numbers of my current post office box. And my last digit now is the same as her first then: the lucky number 7!

- 3 -

Quotes/Notes

1. "Above all [Daguerre, the inventor of photography] admired the postcard as the supreme expression of art. This was why he was attracted to the new invention." —Manuel J. Borja-Villel, *Brassai: From Surrealist to Art Informel* (1993)

2. "By 1902, Eastman Kodak Co. took advantage of the postcard boom by issuing a postcard-size photographic paper.... Thus did every amateur photographer have the potential of being a postcard maker." —Charles Reynolds, "Wish You Were Here" (*Popular Photography*, June 1983)

3. "The postcards are a crowning achievement of [Franz] Marc's work. They encapsulate all his experience of pictorial form... They also gave pictorial expression to a whole series of statements on life and the world." —*Franz Marc: Postcard to Prince Jussuf,* Introduction by Peter-Klaus Schuster

4. "The postcard is a great neglected literary form about fifty words in length." —Garrison Keillor, quoted in *The Man from Lake Wobegon* by Michael Fedo

5. "The poem is at last between two persons instead of two pages. In all modesty, I confess that it may be the death of literature as we know it." —Frank O'Hara, "Personism," *The Selected Poems of Frank O'Hara*

6.   "It is not easy writing
     someone a postcard.
     The size and shape
     of the card cut you
     down to size..."

     —Ron Padgett, "Postcard," *Triangles in the Afternoon*

7. "Picture postcards really excite me." —Henry Miller, *My Life and Times*

8. "Everything in the world exists to end up as a postcard. (Mallarme

adopted.)" —Tom Phillips, "The Postcard Vision," from *Works.*
Texts. To 1974

9. "Blizzard in the suburbs
        —the mailman
    And the poet walking."

    —Jack Kerouac, *Book of Haikus*

10. "Every human being has a different way of achieving closeness
and separation." —Anais Nin

11. "When I am alone
    How close my friends are;
    When I am with them
    How distant they are!"

    —Antonio Machado, *Times Alone*

12. "I had not realized how little alone one is in a postoffice. Before
I had merely posted the letters and wondered." —Jack Spicer,
"Letters To James Alexander," *A Caterpillar Anthology*

13. "I submit that the end-product of intuitive, personal photography is not a picture at all but the offspring of pictures as enriched language." —Paul Vanderbilt, "A Few Alternatives" (*The Massachusetts Review*, Winter 1978)

14. "I often wish there was some way in which a photograph could go directly to its intended target. Like a welcome letter or a telephone call, directly to a specific person at the precise moment that the recipient is ready for it." —Paul Vanderbilt, "Reflections," *Barbara Crane: Photographs 1948–1980*

15. "Send me things in the mail. Wherever you go, I don't care where you go, just send me something in the mail from where you are." —Wallace Berman, as quoted in *Wallace Berman: Support the Revolution* by Tosh Berman et al

ABOUT THE CONTRIBUTORS

JASON ANTHONY lives in Maine. He is currently seeking a publisher for "Albedo."

ROY ARENELLA is a self-taught photographer. He holds a BA in comparative literature from Columbia College, and for over 30 years he was a social service worker in various neighborhoods of New York City. His photos have appeared in a variety of publications, including *The New York Times, Popular Photography, The Sun, The Village Voice, City Talk* (a book of poems by children), and in small press literary magazines that offered him the opportunity to develop his interest in visual writing—combining word and image and working in the space between them. His work has been exhibited in galleries in the U.S. and Europe, including the Whitney Museum and the Bibliotheque Nationale in Paris. The photo/card continues to be Roy's preferred format for expression and communication. He is married, has one son, and lives in upstate New York.

ELLIS AVERY has been writing and exchanging daily haiku with anthropologist Melissa Demian since 1999. She is the author of *The Smoke Week*, an award-winning personal account of life in New York after September 11th, 2001. She lives with her partner, Sharon Marcus, and teaches creative writing at Columbia University. Please visit her online at ellisavery.com.

JUDITH AZRAEL has taught writing workshops at art centers and colleges and held a three-year position as Visiting Writer at Western Washington University. Her poetry, fiction, and lyrical essays have appeared in many magazines and anthologies. Four books of her poetry have been published, and her prose collection, *Wherever I Wander*, was published by Impassio Press in 2004. She travels to Greece whenever she can and is now working on a book set in the Greek islands. She lives on an island in Puget Sound.

MARY AZRAEL is a poet, teacher, and editor. She is the author of *Victorians* (Red Dust), *Riddles for a Naked Sailor* (Stonevale), and *Black Windows*, a hand-made book created for the Smith College Rare Book Collection. Her poems have appeared in *Prairie Schooner, Calyx, Chelsea, Harpers, Chattahoochee Review, Kansas Quarterly, Poetry Daily*, and elsewhere. She has written the libretto for *Lost Childhood*, an opera based on the life of Holocaust survivor Yehuda Nir. She lives in Baltimore, where she teaches creative writing at Johns Hopkins University School of Continuing Studies, and co-edits *Passager*, a national literary journal featuring the work of older writers.

AUDREY BORENSTEIN has been writing in a variety of literary genres since the 1960s, and her fiction and essays have appeared in many literary journals and anthologies. Her awards include Fellowships from the NEA and the Rockefeller Foundation, and her published books include *One Journal's Life: A Meditation on Journal-Keeping* (Impassio Press), *Chimes of Change and Hours: Views of Older Women in Twentieth-Century America* (Fairleigh Dickinson University Press), and *Redeeming the Sin: Social Science and Literature* (Columbia University Press). In 2004 she co-founded the Life Writing Connection and currently serves as consultant. She lives in New Paltz, New York.

NICOLE BRAUN has a BA in Sociology and Women's Studies from the University of Michigan and an MA in Labor and Industrial Relations from Rutgers University. She has taught sociology at various universities, and currently is finishing another graduate degree in holistic studies and counseling while contemplating who she is and what she wants from life. She has a wonderful partner, a struggling teen son, one dog, one cat, and lives in a growing mid-west city that has too much snow in the winter but is paradise the rest of the year.

MATT CARDIN is a writer and musician living in southwest Missouri. He is the author of the short story collection *Divinations of the Deep* and the novella *The God of Foulness*, and is seeking a publisher for "There Is No Grand Scheme." His stories, essays, and reviews have appeared in various print and electronic publications, including *The Children of Cthulhu*, *The Thomas Ligotti Reader*, *Studies in Weird Fiction*, *The HWA Presents: Dark Arts*, *Penny Dreadful*, and *Strange Horizons*. He has a master's degree in religious studies and a bachelor's degree in communication, and has worked professionally as a teacher, video producer, mortgage broker, and piano and keyboard salesman. He resides on an 800-acre farm with his wife, stepson, and in-laws.

STACY CARLSON grew up next to a graveyard in Seattle, Washington. Her three book-length manuscripts won the 2003 Dana Portfolio Award, and she was a finalist for the 2004 Writers at Work Fellowship and the 2003 Pirate's Alley Creative Writing Competition. After finishing her MFA in fiction at Sarah Lawrence College, she received a fellowship for the Gerlach Writing Retreat in Nevada. Stacy is working on a novel, "Among the Wonderful," which chronicles the rise and fall of PT Barnum's American Museum.

CHRISTOPHER COKINOS is the author of a poetry collection, *Killing Seasons* (Woodley, 1993), and a work of creative nonfiction, *Hope Is the Thing with Feathers: A Personal Chronicle of Vanished Birds* (Tarcher/Putnam, 2000; Warner, 2001), which won the 2001 Sigurd F. Olson Nature Writing Award. In 2002 he was named recipient of the Glasgow Prize for an Emerging Writer, and in 2003 he won a Whiting Writers Award. His poems, essays, and reviews have appeared in a wide range of publications, including *Poetry*, *The Iowa Review*, and *Science*. A native of Indianapolis, he now lives in Northern Utah and teaches at Utah State University, where he edits *Isotope: A Journal of Literary Nature & Science Writing*.

KATHERINE DICKSON was born and raised in Boston where she graduated from Simmons College. Her first diary at age 15 began her lifelong fascination with journals. Behind graduate school, a career in professional librarianship, marriage, birthing and raising three children, the journal has been a constant in her life. In 2005 she published her memoir/diary, *Conscious Motherhood: One Woman's Journey*. She lives in Maryland with her husband, William Dickson.

OLIVIA DRESHER is a publisher, anthologist, and aphorist. Her poetry, essays, and notebook fragments have appeared in a wide variety of magazines and anthologies. She is co-editor of *Darkness and Light: Private Writing as Art*—an anthology of contemporary journals, diaries, and notebooks—and is co-founder and director of the Life Writing Connection (www.lifewriting.org). She is actively involved in historic preservation and lives in Seattle in an award-winning 1918 bungalow.

CATHERINE EDNIE lives with son Blair and boyfriend Sam Di Bella in Stamford, Connecticut. With city arts funding, she published a poetry anthology and a website for local writers. She spends a lot of time online, an environment naturally suited to writing practice, illustration, collaboration, and other colorful experiments.

JENNA EVANS was born in 1969 and was raised in New York and Los Angeles. She became a Buddhist at fourteen, dropped out of high school at fifteen, and left home at sixteen. She has been a truck dispatcher, housepainter, masseuse, soda jerk, commission artist, fortuneteller, and farmhand. For two years she snuck into the San Francisco Art Institute to study writing with postmodernist author Kathy Acker. Currently she is a freelance editor and, with partner Rachel Jones, is half of the food-criticism duo Dish & Spoone. She lives in Lincolnville, Maine, and is seeking a publisher for "Diary."

GUY GAUTHIER was born in Winnipeg, Manitoba. He moved to New York in 1969 and began keeping a journal in 1971. His plays have been performed in New York, Canada and overseas, and his poetry has appeared in U.S., Canadian and European publications. He has published one book of poetry, *North of the Temperate Zone* (Midnight Sun Press), and two books of journal writing, *Water & Earth: A Journal* (Impassio Press) and *Journal 5.1* (Les Editions du Ble). He is committed to non-fiction in all its forms: journal, autobiography, travel writing, poetry and criticism.

GILES GOODLAND is a UK-based poet who has also lived in America and Australia. He has had several long poems and sequences published, most recently *A Spy in the House of Years* (Leviathan, 2001). He currently works as an editor of the Oxford English Dictionary.

RICHARD GOODMAN is the author of *French Dirt: The Story of a Garden in the South of France*. He has written on a variety of subjects for many national publications, including *The New York Times*, *Creative Nonfiction*, and *Vanity Fair*. He wrote the introduction to *Travelers' Tales Provence*, and his essay about Paris appears in the collection *The Best Travelers' Tales 2004*. He wrote and narrated a six-part series about New York City for Public Radio in Virginia. He has taught creative writing in New York City, where he also works as a landscape gardener, and currently teaches creative nonfiction at Spalding University's Brief Residency MFA program in Louisville, Kentucky. His web site can be found at www.richardgoodman. homestead.com.

LESLIE WOOLF HEDLEY has published stories and poetry in nearly 100 publications in the United States and abroad, and 14 of his books have been published by various presses. He is the recipient of the Poor Richards Award (USA), the Ampersand Poetry Prize (Canada), and the Prix de Satire (Holland). Some of his work has been set to music, including his *Holocaust Memorial Cantata* that was conducted by Yehudi Menuhin on PolyGram Records. He lectures in the U.S. and England, and has served two civilian tours in Iraq. He lives in California.

THOMAS R. HEISLER has an MFA in writing from the School of the Art Institute of Chicago.

ESTHER ALTSHUL HELFGOTT is a diarist and poet with a doctorate in history from the University of Washington. She edits the online literary anthology *The Psychoanalytic Experience: Analysands Speak* and is writing a biography of the Viennese-born Seattle child psychoanalyst, Edith Buxbaum (1902–1982). Esther teaches writing privately, facilitates women's writing groups for United Way agencies, and is currently at work editing her mother's diaries (Anna Helfgott, 1899–1996) and her own.

MATT HETHERINGTON is a musician and writer based in Melbourne, Australia. He writes for www.cordite.org.au, and his first poetry & haiku collection, *Surface*, was published by Precious Press in 2004. More of his writing, and an extended Bio, can be found at www.innersense.com.au/salonim/projects/2003/matt.html.

ARTHUR WINFIELD KNIGHT has published more than 2,000 poems and short stories and, with his wife Kit, has edited eight volumes dealing with the Beat Generation, including *Kerouac and the Beats* (Paragon House). He is the author of *The Darkness Starts Up Where You Stand* (Depth Charge Books), *The Secret Life of Jesse James* (Burnhill Wolf Books), and *Johnnie D: The Story of John Dillinger* and *Blue Skies Falling* (both from Forge Books). He has photographed many famous writers, and has over 200 book jackets to his credit. He is the film critic for the *Anderson Valley Advertiser*, a literary newspaper, and has taught at the University of San Francisco and the University of California-Davis.

PHYLLIS KOESTENBAUM has had eight books published by small presses, and her poems have appeared in two volumes of *The Best American Poetry*. She has received grants from the California Arts Council and the National Endowment for the Arts, and is a senior scholar at Stanford University's Institute for Research on Women and Gender. She lives in Sunnyvale, California.

KAREN AN-HWEI LEE lives and teaches on the West Coast. Her book-length poem, *In Medias Res*, won the Kathryn A. Morton Prize from Sarabande Books, selected by Heather McHugh. Her chapbook of prose poems, *God's One Hundred Promises*, received the Swan Scythe Press Prize awarded by Sandra McPherson. A regular contributor to literary journals, she has completed several novellas and poetry collections. Her work has also won fellowships from the Yoshiko Uchida Foundation and the National Endowment for the Arts. She holds an MFA in creative writing and a PhD in literature.

BIANCO LUNO is a recluse living in the Pacific Northwest. His philosophical writings, edited by Victor Muñoz, can be found online at www.aporia.net.

AMY S.F. LUTZ's poetry and prose has appeared in many journals, including *The Mid-American Review, Puerto del Sol, The Greensboro Review, Another Chicago Magazine* and *The Prose Poem: An International Journal.* She lives in Pennsylvania with her husband and their three children.

ANDREW T. MCCARTER's online notebook, *Entries and Exits*, the purpose of which "is to grow, to spread, to pursue an existence as meaningless as any other organism's," can be found at www.entriesandexits.com. He has also written a children's book manuscript, "My Big Blue Blanket," which is currently being reviewed by publishers. Professionally, McCarter writes and develops questions for national and state exams. He has a beautiful life in northern California with his love, Danielle.

DARBY McDEVITT was born in Spokane, Washington. He has lived in Bellingham and Dublin, and is currently living in Seattle. He recently finished writing his first book, "Volume Void," a self-contained collection of interrelated narrative fragments.

CARLOS V. REYES lives in Berkeley, California, where he divides his time between writing and teaching modern and contemporary literature. He has degrees in math and English from the University of California, where he wrote a thesis on ethics in Spinoza, Proust, and Joyce. He has been piecing together fragmentary writing for ten years. His blogs can be found at: alifeinhabits.blogspot.com and mazemapping.blogspot.com.

YANNIS RITSOS was born in 1909 in Monemvasia in the Greek Peloponnese, and at his death in Athens in 1990 left an enormous body of work: lyrics and epic meditations, plays, novels, and translations. Frequently imprisoned for long periods for his anti-fascist beliefs, he was and remains Greece's most popular poet. Paul Merchant, the translator of Ritsos' monochords, lives in Oregon where he is director of the William Stafford archives. One of his collections of poetry, *Bone from a Stag's Heart*, was a 1988 (British) Poetry Book Society Recommendation.

WILLIAM PITT ROOT is the author of seven collections of poetry, and his work has been translated into twenty languages. He has been published in hundreds of literary magazines and in over 100 anthologies. He has received three Pushcart Prizes, and has been nominated for the Pulitzer Prize and National Book Award. He teaches creative writing and lives with his wife, poet Pamela Uschuk, in Colorado.

HELEN RUGGIERI teaches in the writing program at the University of Pittsburgh, Bradford campus. Her poetry has been published widely in national and regional magazines, and she is the author of *The Character for Woman* (Foothills Publishing) and *The Poetess* (Allegany Mountain Press). She is a life-long journal keeper.

KIM STAFFORD is the author of a dozen books of poetry and prose, and the founding director of the Northwest Writing Institute at Lewis & Clark College, where he has taught since 1979. He holds a PhD in medieval literature from the University of Oregon, and has worked as a printer, photographer, oral historian, editor, and visiting writer at a host of colleges and schools. He is the literary executor for the estate of William Stafford, and lives in Portland, Oregon, with his wife and children.

WILLIAM STAFFORD (1914–1993), one of America's most celebrated poets, was consultant in poetry to the Library of Congress and Oregon's poet laureate. Among many honors, his first major collection, *Traveling Through the Dark*, won the National Book Award. He was a lifelong pacifist, and a respected teacher and literary mentor who was in demand for poetry readings and workshops in every region of the country. A famed proponent of daily writing, he was the author of more than sixty volumes of prose and poetry.

SCOTT SUSSMAN has a BA in creative writing from California State University, Long Beach, and is a teacher and former stand-up comedian. He has been published in *The Chiron Review*, *Dreams International Quarterly*, and *Lucid Moon*. Currently he lives in Rome, Italy.

EBERLE UMBACH lives in Adams County, Idaho. Her stories have been published in the *Whole Earth Review, Northwest Review, Timbuktu,* and in the anthology *High Sky Over All* (Idaho State University Press). She received an MA in fiction writing from John Hopkins University, and in 1988 was awarded the position of Idaho Writer in Residence. In 2003 she received a grant from the NEA to co-write a play based on Letters to the Editor that have appeared in local newspapers over the past hundred years. She works as a reporter for the *Adams County Record.*

FELICIA WAYNESBORO was raised by a war-widowed mother in Baltimore, Maryland. She received a BFA from Carnegie-Mellon University. She has worked as a feature correspondent for the *Times Leader* newspaper of Wilkes-Barre, Pennsylvania, and was editor and chief writer of the newsletter for New York City's Cultural Council Foundation. She is a former instructor of Speech & Oral Interpretation of Literature at the American Academy of Dramatic Arts, the nation's oldest drama school. Her essays have appeared in *Victoria Magazine* and in an anthology. She lives with her husband in a country house on four wooded acres in Pennsylvania.

PERMISSIONS ACKNOWLEDGMENTS

Heisler, Thomas R. Excerpts from unpublished manuscript, "Insider Artist." Copyright © 2002 by Thomas R. Heisler. Printed by permission of the author.

Helfgott, Esther Altshul. "Anna's Last January." Copyright © 1996, 2004 by Esther Altshul Helfgott. A portion of this piece, "Guarding Mother," was first published in *Spindrift* (1996). Reprinted by permission of the author.

Hetherington, Matt. "Fragments from Notebooks, 1990–1999." Copyright © 2003 by Matt Hetherington. Printed by permission of the author.

Knight, Arthur Winfield. Excerpts from unpublished manuscript, "Swimming in Sand: The Imaginary Autobiography of James Dean." Copyright © 2002 by Arthur Winfield Knight. Portions of the manuscript previously published as *James Dean's Diaries* (24th Street Irregular Press, 2002). Excerpts have also appeared in the following publications: *Clackamus Literary Review, Drought, Entropy Magazine, Planet: The Welsh Internationalist,* and *Skyline Literary Magazine.* Reprinted by permission of the author.

Koestenbaum, Phyllis. Excerpts from *oh I can't she says* (Christopher's Books, 1980). Reprinted by permission of the author.

Lee, Karen An-hwei. Excerpts from unpublished manuscript, "Anthropomorphism." Copyright © 2004 by Karen An-hwei Lee. Printed by permission of the author.

Luno, Bianco. Excerpts from online writings, *The Philosophical Notebooks of Bianco Luno* edited by Victor Muñoz (www.aporia.net). Copyright © 1998–2000 by Bianco Luno and Victor Muñoz. Reprinted by permission of Victor Muñoz.

Sussman, Scott. Excerpts from unpublished manuscript, "The Clever Antics of Lizard." Copyright © 2003 by Scott Sussman. Printed by permission of the author.

Umbach, Eberle. Excerpts from unpublished manuscript, "Weiser River Valley Pillow Book." Copyright © 2002 by Eberle Umbach. Printed by permission of the author.

Waynesboro, Felicia. Excerpts from unpublished manuscript, "Pulled from the Fire." Copyright © 2002 by Felicia Waynesboro. Printed by permission of the author.

OTHER IMPASSIO PRESS TITLES

One Journal's Life:
A Meditation on Journal-Keeping
by Audrey Borenstein
ISBN: 0-9711583-0-4

This Is How I Speak:
The Diary of a Young Woman
by Sandi Sonnenfeld
ISBN: 0-9711583-1-2

Water & Earth:
A Journal
by Guy Gauthier
ISBN: 0-9711583-2-0

Traveling Light:
A Photographer's Journey
by Deborah DeWit Marchant
ISBN: 0-9711583-3-9

Wherever I Wander
by Judith Azrael
ISBN: 0-9711583-4-7

These books can be ordered at your local bookstore, at major
on-line bookstores, or directly from the publisher.
For more information, visit www.impassio.com.